Taming the Automobile

Selected Other Works by Kerry Segrave and from McFarland

Women and Bicycles in America, 1868–1900 (2020)

The Electric Car in America, 1890–1922: A Social History (2019)

Parking Cars in America, 1910–1945: A History (2012)

Drive-in Theaters: A History from Their Inception in 1933 (1992; paperback 2006)

Masking America, 1918–1919: Efforts to Control the Great Influenza Pandemic (2024)

Tarring and Feathering in America: A History, 1865–1920 (2024)

Dying for Chocolate: Cordelia Botkin and the 1898 Poisoned Candy Murders (Exposit, 2021)

The National Security League, 1914–1922: Wall Street and the War Machine (2020)

"Masquerading in Male Attire": Women Passing as Men in America, 1844–1920 (2018)

The Women Who Got America Talking: Early Telephone Operators, 1878–1922 (2017)

The Hatpin Menace: American Women Armed and Fashionable, 1887–1920 (2016)

Police Violence in America, 1869–1920: 256 Incidents Involving Death or Injury (2016)

Chewing Gum in America, 1850–1920: The Rise of an Industry (2015)

Policewomen: A History, 2d ed. (2014)

Beware the Masher: Sexual Harassment in American Public Places, 1880–1930 (2014)

Wiretapping and Electronic Surveillance in America, 1862–1920 (2014)

American Television Abroad: Hollywood's Attempt to Dominate World Television (1998; paperback 2013)

Payola in the Music Industry: A History, 1880–1991 (1994; paperback 2013)

The Sexual Harassment of Women in the Workplace, 1600 to 1993 (1994; paperback 2013)

Women Serial and Mass Murderers: Profiles of 85 Killers Worldwide, 1580–1990 (1992; paperback 2013)

Extras of Early Hollywood: A History of the Crowd, 1 913–1945 (2013)

Vision Aids in America: A Social History of Eyewear and Sight Correction Since 1900 (2011)

Begging in America, 1850–1940: The Needy, the Frauds, the Charities and the Law (2011)

America Brushes Up: The Use and Marketing of Toothpaste and Toothbrushes in the Twentieth Century (2010)

Lynchings of Women in the United States: The Recorded Cases, 1851–1946 (2010)

Taming the Automobile

Early Regulation of Motor Vehicles in America, 1895–1903

Kerry Segrave

McFarland & Company, Inc., Publishers
Jefferson, North Carolina

ISBN (print) 978-1-4766-9491-7
ISBN (ebook) 978-1-4766-5219-1

LIBRARY OF CONGRESS AND BRITISH LIBRARY
CATALOGUING DATA ARE AVAILABLE

Library of Congress Control Number 2024021040

Front cover image: "Privileged sport," Udo Keppler, artist, *Puck* illustration (Library of Congress).

Printed in the United States of America

McFarland & Company, Inc., Publishers
Box 611, Jefferson, North Carolina 28640
www.mcfarlandpub.com

Table of Contents

Preface

As automobiles began to appear on American roads, rules to govern them quickly sprang up. Regulations including the control of speed, the issuance of driver's licenses, and the imposition of license plates were implemented. This book recounts the earliest attempts to control how automobiles were used and the contentions that arose in the process. I chose the period 1895 to 1903 because the earliest attempts to regulate the car began almost as soon as the machine had any presence at all. The lobbying organizations were set up by the trade beginning in 1895. By 1903 the lobby had fully established itself and was pressing for its views to prevail. It preferred no legislation at all, but if legislation had to be imposed, then the auto lobby wanted to control it. It was at that early date already writing the legislation that was adopted in some jurisdictions.

Local and regional lawmakers were a little slow in adopting any legislation regarding the automobile. However, by 1903 most, if not all, jurisdictions accepted the premise that the automobile had to be regulated, although some still had not done so. By 1903 legislation was an accepted fact but the auto lobby generally managed to prevail. While the lobby could not prevent legislation from being implemented it could work to neuter and weaken any such laws and regulations. The issue of speed also was resolved by 1902–1903. Initially the industry promoted speed and road races enthusiastically. The general public often protested about being endangered by the speeders (mostly rich people) dashing about on the roads. Their protests had little effect. The auto lobbying groups and organizations sponsored road races all over America. Mostly these races were held on city streets and more rural roadways, often without permission from any local authorities. Editorial cartoons featured the rich speeders driving too fast and leaving the bodies of the general public in their wake. But to no avail.

Then in 1902–1903 a series of disasters occurred. There was the Staten Island road race which saw a contestant run out of control into the crowd, killing and injuring spectators. There was the death of Charles Fair and his wife in a single-car accident near Paris, France. Speed was the cause. The Fair deaths generated a lot of media coverage as did the Staten Island disaster. Other prominent people died in single-car crashes in that period. Fair and his wife were part of the Vanderbilt extended clan. They were very rich. A brother-in-law of Charles was William K. Vanderbilt, Jr., a notorious speeder himself. Dramatically he announced he was finished with racing and speeding, a vow from which he would later stray. Suddenly the auto organizations abandoned their enthusiastic support of road races and the sport was quickly removed from unsupervised events on city streets onto specifically built racing tracks. So, by 1903 the unbridled and always-supported desire for more and more speed was curbed and limited, to some degree. But because the auto lobby groups controlled the industry by then, those curbs were limited. The death toll of Americans in sacrifice to the automobile gave mute testimony to just how efficient the auto lobby was in controlling such curbs and legislation.

Since most of the early automobilists were from the wealthy class there rose up in opposition to regulations a strong lobbying effort on the part of the owners and the manufacturers to stop all regulations. If those rules could not be stopped, then the lobbyists wanted them to be as blunt and as weak and as limited as they could manage. By 1903 the major lobbying groups were set up and well-funded. The major groups were the American Motor League, the Automobile Club of America, the Automobile Association of America, and the National Association of Automobile Manufacturers. Also, by 1903 the industry had established and held major automobile shows in many of the major cities of America.

The battle from the beginning of the industry until 1903 consisted of a small group of wealthy men going up against the general public and the politicians and civil servants who supposedly represented them. Despite their small number they usually got their way. For the decades to come after 1903, the forces of the automobile grew rapidly as the percentage of car owners steadily increased. The battle against the car quickly and quietly ended.

Research for this book was done using online databases. Among those databases were the Library of Congress' "Chronicling America," newspaperarchive.com, and newspapers.com.

Introduction

When the automobile arrived in America in the 1890s it did so from the top down. It was only the wealthy that could afford to own cars in that first decade or so of the industry's development. It was sometimes referred to as a "plaything of the rich." The media brought up that point on occasion but it was largely ignored. It had an impact on the regulations imposed on the automobile as the wealthy had ample money to lobby and buy politicians. When they battled proposed rules they usually got their way.

One of the first orders of business for the new automobilists was to get rid of the horse. Lobbyists were not content with just pointing out what they saw as the vast advantages the car had over the horse. Autoists felt compelled to attack the horse as an irrational beast prone to be afraid of everything, including his own shadow. The commercial horse was a dangerous maniacal animal putting his driver and others in the immediate area in constant and life-threatening danger. The drivers of horse wagons were also often portrayed in a negative light, compared to the motor vehicle driver. With horses gone and cars in command of the streets, everyone would be a whole lot safer. There would be no more congestion.

Entering the parks of the cities of America was the first major battle for the auto lobby. These parks were about the only amenity provided by the state for the lower classes to enjoy, for free, in the little time the capitalist class allowed the workers to call their own. There were holdouts here and there but the battle was quickly lost as the cars took over the city parks quickly.

Organizations were quickly set up to lobby state and local governments not to pass regulations against the automobile, and when that strategy failed, they sought to blunt and neuter any rules that were imposed. When the reckless driving of the rich produced a growing protest and demands for greater controls on cars, the auto lobby tried to write any actual rules.

Speed was an integral part of the early years of the industry. Articles appeared about the millionaire autoists, constantly risking their lives in this new sport. Around 1900 a car cost $600 to $800 at the low end of a given manufacturer's model range. The rich were then paying $10,000 and up for the fastest racers available. Those low-priced models were not capable of fast speeds but the racers were. When a famous American couple, members of the plutocracy, died in a single-car accident in France, speed was the cause. They were traveling at 60 miles an hour in a car capable of 72 miles an hour. Accidents, injuries, and deaths mounted quickly in this period. Most people killed that way in the early days were pedestrians of the working class. As the millionaires quickly spent increasing sums for a car that went a little faster, the plutocracy began to become the victims, often in single-car crashes.

Opposition mounted, especially to races held on city streets, often without any local authority permit. Auto clubs and lobby organizations suddenly came out against such races and promoted no races except in purpose-built tracks. They came to condemn speeders in general, at least in their rhetoric.

Rules for driver's licenses and license plates began to be imposed. An initial idea supported by the lobbying pro-automobile groups was that license plates only needed to have the owner's initials on the plate. Somehow it seemed like a good idea to the auto lobby that all John Smith needed for a license plate was "JS" on the plate.

Police were hampered in those early days in their attempts to deal with speeders. Police officers were on horses, or bicycles and had no chance to stop a speeding car. Also with no license plates, or only one saying "JS," they had little chance to identify the driver. By 1903 the situation had changed considerably. Most people who wanted to drive needed a license and license plates, bearing real numbers issued by the state. Most cities had speed limits in place but enforcement was erratic. Races on the streets were rapidly vanishing to tracks built for that purpose. Gone was the day a ten-year-old kid could jump into his father's car and ride around town without a license or any identifying markers, with impunity.

Did the regulations imposed on the automobile through 1903 and continuing to the present succeed? See Appendix C, Motor Vehicle Deaths in the U.S. by Year. In 1903 there were 117 deaths. In 1918 the deaths numbered 10,390 and never again dropped below 10,000. In 1925 the number of deaths topped 20,000 and have never dropped below that level. A peak was reached in the 1966–1973 period with deaths greater than 50,000 every year. For the last two years that statistics are available, 2021 and 2022, the numbers of deaths were, respectively, 42,939 and 42,795.

Chapter 1

A Class Arrival

The magazine that was to become the main trade journal of the automotive industry was *The Horseless Age*. The editor and proprietor was E.P. Ingersoll. It began as a monthly publication and its inaugural issue was November 1895. It has been published continuously ever since. After undergoing some name changes it is currently published as *Automotive Industries*. In his inaugural edition Ingersoll wrote, "the new civilization that is rolling in with the horseless carriage will be a higher civilization than the one we now enjoy." Ingersoll informed his early readers that the first race for motor vehicles, from Paris to Rouen, France, had taken place in June 1894. It had been well publicized and covered heavily by the media. The 750 miles of the race were covered in 48 hours and 33 minutes. And the automobile age had commenced.

Around September 1, 1895, there were on file at the United States Patent Office in Washington, D.C., over 500 applications on motor vehicles alone. In the United States between July 1 and November 1, 1895, no fewer than 300 different types of motor vehicles were available. Ingersoll waxed eloquent in contemplating "this array of horseless vehicles. From the gradual displacement of the horse in business and in pleasure will come economy of time and practical money-saving. In cities and towns, the noise and clatter of the streets will be reduced, a priceless boon to the tired nerves of this overwrought generation."

And there would be more benefits. One was the humanitarian aspect of the vehicle. To spare the "obedient beast, that since the dawn of history has been man's drudge, from further service at the industrial treadmill, will be a downright mercy." Then there was the benefit on sanitary grounds resulting from the banishing of horses from city streets. Streets free of manure would be a blessing. And, Ingersoll glowingly concluded, "Streets will be cleaner, jams and blockages less likely to occur, and accidents less frequent, for the horse is not so manageable as a mechanical vehicle."[1]

Some were more practical with their view of the just-arriving automobile age. An article originally published in a New York publication and reprinted in Kansas City began by saying, "Are the days of the bicycle supremacy numbered and the poor horse threatened with extinction?" Even though the original was published in New York City, the editor declared, "Many people have heard of the real horseless carriages but few have seen them." He thought their increase would be a "wonderful sight. To the clang of the trolley and jingle of the bicycle will be added the fire alarm bells and whistles of the horseless carriage." He did predict that in the days to come when autos outnumbered all other styles of vehicles on the streets "the present laws of the road must be radically revised. A rule of keeping to the right and turning out to the left would be a necessity. All streets and boulevards will be divided into two sharply defined sections, which will be indicated by a line of posts or a narrow strip of parking." He believed that another thing that could be looked forward to at a coming session of the legislature was "the passage of laws regulating the maximum speed at which horseless carriages will be allowed to run."[2]

Some inventions start from the lower classes and percolate upward to soon envelop the population as a whole. One example was the motion picture industry. It began in the same general period as the automobile age. Movies were a lower-class item with attendance often held in sawdust-on-the-floor nickelodeons. The upper classes had live theater performances. They were expensive, movies were not. Live theater held a snob appeal, movies did not. But the glitter of Hollywood soon swept all strata of society. The auto industry was the opposite. It began in the wealthy classes and, eventually, filtered down to the masses through such developments as Henry Ford's Model T. But in the beginning, it was an upper-class invention. It was that class of people who shaped the laws, rules, and regulations of the early auto industry. When the wealthy classes lobby the politicians, they often get their way.

A brief editorial in an Oklahoma newspaper observed that "So far, the automobile is a rich man's fad. When they begin to carry passengers for a nickel, all of us can go automobiling." Another equally brief editorial in an Illinois newspaper remarked that it had been reported that $15,000 was the price paid for an automobile by a wealthy New York gentleman of "fashionable tastes."[3]

The link between wealthy car owners and auto racing was also established early. A New York newspaper reported in the fall of 1900 that automobile racing, the new sport America had introduced that year from France, Austria, and Germany, "promises to be the proper sport for rich men next season." A racing auto cost in the neighborhood of $10,000, according to the article. "It is a rich man's sport, at least until the prices come down, but they regard it as worth the money."[4]

In one of the local police station houses in Washington, D.C., an incident took place in March 1902: a member of the United States House of Representatives whose red auto was conspicuous on the streets of Washington "not alone for its color but for its uniformly high speed, was arrested by a policeman" for speeding. The police lieutenant heard testimony and finally discharged the accused representative, ignoring the policeman's assertion that the speed indicator proved a violation of the law. The politician involved was Oliver Belmont.

An editorial in a local paper commented, "There can be no doubt that had

Oliver Belmont (date unknown).

the accused person been an obscure citizen collateral would have been demanded and, failing its production, he would have been held behind bars until morning for a court hearing." He also believed the police officer making the arrest "has since been made very uncomfortable by the reflection that he had offended gravely against the proprieties." The editor wondered, rhetorically, "Are the ordinary processes of law to be ignored in the case and for the benefit of a person of wealth and position, and applied strictly in the case of the unimportant offender?" Was the patrolman to be given flexible rules so that "the patrolman will hereafter use his judgment as to the character of the offenders he arrests? If this is done, it is easy to see, the streets will be made safe for pedestrians and other vehicle users only when the automobiles of the wealthy congressman or other high and mighty personages are not abroad." The public hope that the wealthy, argued the editor, "will not be permitted by the police to imagine that indifference to the rules of public safety is one of the prerogatives of political success or wealth or personal prestige."[5]

The Reverend Dr. George C. Lorimer denounced reckless auto owners in his annual sermon to the American Tract Society delivered in New York City. "Every life that is sacrificed by reckless rich men in fast automobiles ought to be paid for in the electric chair." Lorimer added, "The men who ride down persons in an automobile are generally wealthy. They are likely to be persons of cultivation and personally, their feelings toward the poor are doubtless amiable enough. But when it is a matter of interfering with their amusements, the life of a poor man counts for nothing with them."[6]

An Atlanta, Georgia, newspaper printed a short and sarcastic editorial on the topic. "Now that the automobiles of the rich have taken to killing the occupants instead of pedestrians, it is announced that 'scorching' [speeding] may be discontinued."[7]

The craze displayed by the rich for speed was commented upon early in the development of the auto industry. And, declared an editor, "Men on whose safety depends the investments of thousands pay constantly increasing prices for machines." The millionaires were said to pay tens of thousands of dollars for machines that would best by a fraction of a second those of their neighbors and friends. The sport of auto racing "is not confined to the moderately wealthy, but its greatest devotees are among the men with many millions." The more millions the faster they demand that their machines shall be driven.[8]

When a New Jersey court verdict was announced it was greeted with applause by some. The $12,000 in damages were awarded in favor of a man who was injured in a runaway, caused by his horse being scared by an automobile. That verdict, thought a newsman "will let the rich 'scorchers' understand what is in store for them.... The man who was responsible for the reckless movement of the automobile was a rich banker...."[9]

The main mouthpiece speaking in favor of the auto industry, the *Horseless Age,* admitted to the class aspects of the beginnings of the industry. In a piece published on September 10, 1902, the editor said, "It was certainly a happy idea that in the Labor Day parade in New York City, the labor leaders took part in automobiles. There has been altogether too much talk recently about the automobile being only a plaything of the rich, a fad that will soon pass away. The circulation of such notions, together with the uncivil behavior of many automobilists owning fast machines, has created prejudice and antagonism toward the automobile in the lower and middle classes, to the existence of which the touring automobilists gives ample testimony." He argued it was easy to show all such prejudice was unfounded and that all classes would in the end be benefited from the automobile movement.

George C. Lorimer, sketch, 1893.

The editor continued, "So far, of course, the automobile has been confined to the wealthy classes, to a certain extent, but the fact that these classes have taken up the automobile with such enthusiasm is in itself very fortunate." He thought that fact had made possible "rapid progress in construction and reduction in price for equal value, thereby hastening the day when the automobile will be within the reach of a very much larger class of the population." Also, he argued the auto had passed the point of being a pleasure vehicle only, and was used commercially. He cited physicians, with hundreds of them using cars in their medical practices, a fact that "directly disproves that they are only 'the plaything of the rich.'"

He pointed out that 10,000 workmen were employed in the manufacture, care, repair, and so on, of cars, and "if then, the laboring classes have so far been unable to enjoy the advantages of automobile travel they have indirectly profited by the movement and have therefore, in reality, every reason to be kindly disposed toward it." Concluding his piece the editor asserted, "Unfortunately, many of the newspapers circulating chiefly among the working classes try to make capital out of class hatred and lose no opportunity to hold up the automobile as a means of oppression of the poor by the wealthy."[10]

According to a later article, abuses were spreading among the chauffeurs of "wealthy automobiles" who had charge of employers' cars and were extorting commissions from garages on all bills charged to owners. The matter had been called to the attention of the Automobile Club of America, which was wondering what to do about the situation. It was noted, "As there are few employers of chauffeurs in New York City who are not members of the club," therefore the organization should have clout.[11]

Henri de Rothschild (1872–1946).

A report published in September 1903 announced that the richest man in Paris had been sentenced to jail. He was Baron Henri de Rothschild. He remained in jail for just one day. His offense was for speeding. It was the fourth time he had been arrested for the same infraction. On the three previous occasions when he had been arrested his case was pardoned each time. As well, he had been warned by the police about his speeding "times without number." In every case Rothschild had haughtily refused to obey the law, treating the police officers with contempt. When he was arrested for the fourth time he was accompanied by his rich friends in a procession to the jail, and on his release from jail. Some of his wealthy friends applied for permission to stay with him in prison to cheer him up. Permission to do so was denied. The reporter who wrote the article then stated, about the U.S. privileged classes, "They make no display of opposition to the law such as the friends of Rothschild make. They secure priority of benefits, not by opposing the law, but by means of the law. They get immunity, their prerogative, by special legislation—a safer method."[12]

From the beginning of the auto industry, wealthy car owners tried to assert their will over politicians and bureaucrats. They usually prevailed. According to a story from New Jersey, "Backed up by many wealthy automobilists of this state, a movement has been inaugurated looking towards the purchase from the county of the old Bellevue Turnpike, across the Kearny meadows, for use principally as an automobile driveway." In the event the group failed to buy the property, it hoped to persuade the New Jersey State Road Commission and the Hudson Freeholders to alter existing plans for the area to improve the road in the area. Negotiations for the group were carried out by the Automobile Club of America and the American Automobile Association. Advocates of the scheme were mostly residents of Newark, Montclair, Bloomfield, and their suburbs. They wanted better access to New York City for their automobiles. The idea also was to deny permission to use the road, if their purchase plans were successful, to streetcars and heavy-weight traffic they felt would soon destroy the Macadam road "necessary for the enjoyment of automobiling."[13]

A furious editorial from a New York newspaper was picked up and published in Washington, D.C. The editor asked rhetorically, "Is it possible that the men in this city who can afford to own automobiles are as a class so stupid that they do not see that the laws should be obeyed...." He compared the rich automobilists to the gang members of the slums who ignore the police. Each one of those thugs had "no use" for the police since he owned nothing, had no stake in the system, and felt capable of protecting himself. "Yet his rule of conduct does not differ from that of the automobilists who run their costly machines to suit themselves and when they see a policeman in uniform put on speed and defy him."

It was when the two classes of offenders reached the police court that a "radical difference" was seen. The hoodlum could not as a rule get bail and was sent to jail to await trial, the newsman explained. "The man rich enough to own an automobile is also rich enough to secure bail. Also, he is rich enough to pay without feeling the fine that, so far, is the derisory penalty affixed to his offense." The disgrace of what happened to the rich should have worked to modify their behavior, but it did not. "In reality the trouble with them is that they cannot be punished as they deserve." The article concluded, "If there is any sense of self-respect in the automobilist class, extreme measures will not be needed. Surely they ought not to be. Men with some property, with some education, with an interest in the maintenance of order and the secure and stable working of free society cannot desire continually to set an example of lawlessness and defiance of the rights of others." And, "if the safety and comfort of the men of the community shall continue to be sacrificed to the despicable selfishness of a lot of wealthy featherheads, some radical remedy will be applied."[14]

Two more short and sarcastic editorials emerged. One observed, "The foolish virgin expendeth her wealth on an automobile coat, the wise virgin weddeth the man who can afford the machine." In the other piece, it was said that Edison was about to put on the market a charging machine that would enable anyone of "ordinary means" to own and run an automobile. "Hitherto it has been a godsend to the poor that they could not own an automobile. Only the rich were killed or maimed. Now it seems as if discrimination will no longer be made and the opportunity for self-destruction is to be open to all."[15]

In a statement made in Harlem, New York Police Court Magistrate Crane denounced the wealthy for their cold indifference to and disregard of poor people. He made that statement in imposing $200

Illustration shows a wealthy old man as a passenger in an automobile driven by his chauffeur. Racing through the countryside during a cross-country auto race, they have struck several pedestrians who are not used to encountering automobiles on country roads. 1902. The caption at the bottom has the owner saying to the driver, "Don't stop! It only costs about ten dollars apiece to run them down. I must break the record even if it costs a hundred."

One of the manifestations of the speed craze was this 1904 ad in a Richmond, Virginia, newspaper. A Cadillac dealership in the area challenged the readers to an automobile race through the streets of Richmond. Nothing indicated the dealership had any permission from local officials to tear through the streets at high speeds.

bail for Jackson Gourand on a charge of speeding. Crane declared, "The power of wealth is becoming one of the greatest evils in this country. Men, when they get rich, have no kindness toward others as a general proposition, and especially where they are in automobiles.... The state of things is becoming terrible when rich people can ride over poor people in the streets and escape without punishment. Rich people don't care for anybody."[16]

A small display ad placed by Foster Automobile Company in Richmond Virginia issued a challenge for a road race. Foster was a Cadillac dealer and the firm issued an open challenge to any auto owner in Richmond to a run of 50 to 100 miles over any road leading out of Richmond. The route was to be selected by the parties accepting the challenger. The losing contestants in the event had to "entertain" the entire party on completion of the run.[17]

An article that appeared originally in a Brooklyn publication was reprinted in a paper in the nation's capital. It declared "we are assured by the observant that the enmity of the slum populace for people who ride in horseless carriages is founded on nothing deeper than superfluous vitality. It is a hate of the rich, which is encouraged by the yellow papers, that are owned by the rich, but edited for circulation among the poor, whose pennies make the rich still richer." That hatred was supposedly manifested in attacks by the poor on automobiles, mostly in the form of throwing stones and rocks at the vehicles. One car owner reported that in a single ride of a few miles, he was attacked no fewer than 25 times by such people, although no details were provided. The reader was led to believe that throwing stones at cars was a popular pastime.[18]

Another tiny editorial appeared in a Seattle, Washington, newspaper. This editor was completely off the mark as he forecast the auto was a fad that would be replaced by something else in a few years. Meanwhile, "The auto is a rich man's plaything, and until the fad wears out will be popular among those who can afford to own it."[19]

A hymn to the middle class appeared at this time. Its theme was the hardships endured by that class. It was a tragedy, because "We are being buried alive. We are submerged under the rival masses of rich and poor." The article was written by Julius Muller, who declared, "In suburbs and in town, the middle class sees its tax rate go up steadily to pay for lovely sanitary tenements for the poor and playgrounds for the poor and parks for the poor and bands of music for the poor and art galleries for the poor and asphalt and macadam for the automobiles of the rich."[20]

Chapter 2

Removing the Horse

A prescient article that appeared in August 1895 discussed the issue of the horse versus the horseless carriage. Pointed out was the financial advantages of the automobile. The author argued that "before many years have passed a horse in New York City, will be almost a rarity." One big difference that would accrue from the passing of the horse "will be a vast increase in the cleanliness of the streets." That would be followed by a lessening of infectious diseases. The system in place in the last few years of the 1890s concerning the movement of goods from distributor to retailer to the home was horse-oriented. For the motor vehicle to usurp the horse and take over the animal's role in society it was necessary to quickly banish the horse from the field of commercial activity. This was especially true as the motor vehicle was seen, in the period of 1895 to 1900, as a plaything of the rich and even seen by some as a fad.

People with ordinary and low incomes relied upon the horse for their daily needs, or the rental of a horse and buggy on occasion if they lacked the space or the money to own an animal outright. Livery stables had to be banished and replaced by garages. Delivery services that featured horse-drawn vehicles had to give way to motor trucks. The first order of business was to get rid of the horse. Attacks on the animal centered on its unhygienic aspects. Sometimes the automobile was praised, in comparison to the animal, and its overall superiority in efficiency was stressed. But the horse as a working animal was a decided drag against the rise of the auto nation and it had to be eliminated.[1]

Answering applications from the omnibus company and the Compagnie des Voitures of Paris, France, the Prefect of Police in Paris decided to allow automobiles to take the place of horse carriages and tram cars in the streets of the city. Other firms in control of various means of public conveyance had turned their attention to the subject of automobiles and were preparing for the "revolution in traffic," a revolution from which they would derive considerable benefit. Automobiles privately owned and driven were then a common sight on Paris streets and would soon frequently be used as a public means of transportation. Among the benefits of changing the mode of transportation was said to be protection from the uncertainties of expenditure caused by the mortality of horses and by the great fluctuation in the price of fodder. Another point in favor of the change was

Cartoon showing weeping horse in automobile with procession of other animals riding in automobiles and on bicycles; sign by road reads "To the Museum of Natural History." 1909.

made by M.P. Leroy-Beaulieu, a writer on economic topics. On the substitution of cars for horses the company would have little to fear from a strike. At present, in case of a strike the company could not hold out long because its horses were consuming food all the time. Automobiles, on the other hand, would cost nothing when they were out of work and idle.[2]

A society known as the Society for the Prevention of Noise was organized in New York City in 1897 with the express purpose of mitigating noise. An editor with the trade publication *Horseless Age* called that work "a most commendable one, worthy of the co-operation of all good citizens." He noted that harm was done to humans, possibly, by discordant noises. Noises, he believed, could be divided into two categories, "useful and pernicious." Under the first category came various warning signals that were necessary for the protection of life and so forth. And, he continued, "Of the pernicious noises the horse and the rough pavements provided for him are a most prolific source. The impact of horses' hoofs and the clash and clang of iron tires made up a large part of the disagreeable noises of a great city. Smooth pavements and motor vehicles running upon them will reduce this class of street noises to a minimum." Such an argument was designed to make the acceptance of cars easier and the removal of horses quicker. The noisiest vehicles of the time were automobiles. They were inherently noisy at the time regardless of the condition of the pavement.[3]

A different editor wrote that the street car and the bicycle had affected the value and the use of the horse, causing a lessening of both. But the coming of the automobile threatened to relegate the animal still further and eliminate him. This editor lamented the predicted passing of the horse. Streetcars had begun to proliferate in American cities of all sizes in the late 1880s and into the 1890s. That made it easier for city dwellers of lower incomes to get around the city and not have any need for a horse, which was difficult to stable in a city by anyone without a relatively high income. The bicycle, thanks to the invention of the safety bicycle, also experienced a boom in growth and use, especially in the 1890s. That also led to decreasing use of the working horse.[4]

In Washington, D.C., the Federal Commissioners refused the application of a local firm, in the summer of 1897, that wanted to run a motorized delivery wagon in the streets of the nation's capital "on the ground that it would frighten horses and thus endanger life and property." A pro-automobile journalist moaned that such "official fossilism" at the very center of American legislation, in a city of wealth and culture "will excite amazement among Europeans who have been told of the progressiveness and alertness of the American people." As far as he was concerned the issue had already been grappled with in Europe and settled in favor of the motor vehicle. "Locomotives and bicycles often frighten horses and so destroy life and property, but no lawmakers would undertake to sweep them from the face of the earth on that account," he asserted. In conclusion, he declared, "The march of events will soon compel them to reconsider their action, but the earlier they do this the more graceful will the recantation be."[5]

Another attack on the horse came in July 1897 and was authored by J. Frank Duryea. The average horse carriage driver, said Duryea, "is constantly lifting his hand and signaling the motor vehicle to stop until he can get his horse under control, which in reality means until the horse himself decides to go ahead." Reinforcing that view was E.P. Ingersoll, editor of the *Horseless Age*: "This is too true. The horse is a willful, unreliable brute. The ever-recurring accidents due to horses which are daily set forth in the papers prove that the horse is a dangerous motor and not the docile pet of the poet. The mechanical motor is his superior in many respects, and when its superiority had become better known his inferiority will be more apparent." One thing Ingersoll failed to mention was that many of the accidents and runaways involving working horses were due to the tremendous noises and smoke and steam generated by the automobile that often frightened the animals and caused them to shy or to run away. Also not mentioned was who Duryea was and that he had a vested interest in eliminating the working animal. James Duryea and his brother Charles invented the first gasoline-powered automobile in America[6] and began commercially manufacturing cars in 1895.

A bleak assessment of the horse and his future as a working beast came from the editor of a Barton, Vermont, newspaper. He remarked that the "passing of the horse, by the way, is very generally deplored." He added the horse was "the victim

Top: **Man changing tire, as others watch, with two oxen alongside;** ***Bottom:*** **Couple on horse, with auto broken down behind them. 1907.**

ever of man's ignorance and until later years the victim of his unchecked brutality, ... the horse has led a life of ghastly tragedy." He concluded by observing, "but the common lot of the horse has been the tortured fate of any sensitive creature at the mercy of that most cruel of created things—mankind."[7]

The trade journal *Horseless Age* was relentless in its attack on the working horse. In an April 1898 article, the publication cited a large owner and user of workhorses in New York City who stated that the average life of the best stock they could get was not more than four or five years. "At the end of this period, if they survive, they are unfit for service," he insisted. Ingersoll then added that the Anti-Noise Society "ought to espouse the case of the motor vehicle and good roads. Horses and the cobblestone pavements they require for a foothold are two of the most prolific sources of noise in the metropolis."[8]

A worrisome article in July 1898 observed that the question of liability of car owners had repeatedly been raised in the United Kingdom and was about to be considered in America. A journalist remarked, "The opinion seems to find credence that an owner of a motor vehicle is responsible for all damage done by a horse which may take fright at his vehicle and run away." He argued that such was not the case. His opinion was that cars and horse-drawn vehicles had equal rights on the road but "inasmuch as the motor vehicle is an innovation and horses are as yet unaccustomed to it, the law and common prudence dictate that the driver of a motor vehicle shall use extreme care to prevent an accident."

Upon the appearance of a frightened horse, the car driver should slow down or stop his vehicle altogether, or seek the far side of the road beyond the animal's range of vision. Such was the view that the French and the British had reportedly taken "and such is the view that the American courts must take of it, as it is the only reasonable ground." Thus, no one needed to hesitate to purchase a car for fear that he would be subject to undue damages. "If ordinary precautions are observed accidents will be few, and of those that do happen the majority will be chargeable to the owners of horses, whose care it must be not to bring upon the highway unruly animals that are a menace to the public safety."[9]

The price of horses reportedly fell "greatly" in the five years up to 1898. According to a reporter, "The use of electricity as motive power for street cars and the ubiquitous bicycle are the chief reason for the lessened value of horses." Concerning the role of the automobile in that decline he declared, "The horseless carriage is still so expensive that it has cut a small figure in this competition, but in it the horse may soon find a hurtful rival."[10]

In an issue of a publication on the carriage trade, advice was given to its readers to cooperate with horse shows and horse-loving people and thus further their interests. A writer in the publication of the auto industry *Horseless Age* sneered at that thought. To the carriage builders, he thundered, "the motor vehicle is no more a fad.... Its horizon does not end with the few pleasure carriages that will be added to the stables of the aristocracy." Concerning the idea that some of the elite were returning to horses, he gibed, "It does not seem to have occurred to the defender of the horse that the reason why these upper circles are resuming carriage and horseback riding may be because motor carriages are not yet to be had here in sufficient numbers to supply them."[11]

An editor with a Kansas newspaper was somewhat optimistic about the future of the horse, although most writers then agreed that the automobile was here to stay and to expand dramatically. The Kansas newsman noted that more horses were used in the United States in 1897 than in any previous year. "When a steep declivity, a few inches of snow, and a muddy road will not stop the cycles and automobiles it will be time enough to lament the passing of the horse. Until then it is advisable to keep him in the stable for use when the cycle and automobile are out of order or inoperative." (In the United States in 1897 there were 15,623,000 horses.) "A few thousand automobiles are not enough to make the number decline appreciably. The cycle did not do it, and until the automobile is perfected it will not do it."[12]

Another attack on the horse appeared in the pages of *Horseless Age* in May 1899 wherein Charles Duryea (brother of James) and Ingersoll took turns bashing the animal. The dateline was Peoria, Illinois, on May 1. The piece appeared as a full-page letter to the editor—Duryea to Ingersoll. This article tried to shift the blame onto the horse driver for most of the horse accidents "now so common." According to the article, "It seems to the writer that the stupidity of drivers is responsible for more trouble from the horse than the horse's own lack of sense." Duryea argued, "most of them are reasonably tractable, and lack of intelligence reflects upon their masters. Most horse accidents, now so common, would not occur if reasonable care or diligence were exercised by the drivers."

If horse drivers were stupid, careless, and so forth, would car drivers not be the same? An anecdotal example Duryea cited was of a horse-driven wagon greatly overloaded and manipulated by a "sleepy" junk dealer. Inevitably, the frightened (by a car) horse increased its pace and the load overturned the wagon, throwing out the driver. Another "example" Duryea gave was of a "small, nearly blind boy" driving with his mother beside him. The boy did not see the motor vehicle approaching; the mother was not paying attention. The horse was "so sleepy and sedate" that before it had time to think the motor vehicle was upon it. The result was a sudden bolt sideways by the horse that dumped the wagon over, throwing the passengers out of the carriage. However, little or no damage was done and no one was hurt.

Duryea declared, "It is a very common experience to find drivers who do not have their horses under control and make no effort to guard against possible danger until the damage has been done." After a few more equally ludicrous examples, Duryea fumed, "If the public knew these facts they would realize the safety of the motor vehicle and favor it instead of condemning, as they often do."[13]

One example of the many legal cases involving horse and automobile accidents concerned J.B. West, the Rochester New York inventor, who was sued by Mason Brothers, laundrymen of the same city. The brothers sued West for $49 damages for alleged negligence in driving a steam car through the streets and frightening the plaintiff's horse. West lost his case in the municipal court but promised to launch an appeal.[14]

Some months later Jonathan West obtained a reversal of the judgment rendered against him in the municipal court. The appeal was argued before County Judge Sutherland. In his decision, the judge stated, "Bicycles used to frighten horses, but no right of action accrued. Electric street cars have caused many runaways." Sutherland added, "The temporary inconvenience and dangers incident to the introduction of these modern and practical modes of travel upon the highway must be subordinate to the larger and permanent benefits to the general public resulting from the adoption of the improvements which science and inventive skill have perfected."[15]

"The horse as a machine, has his drawbacks. One is that he wears out too soon. Another is his general unreliability and his tendency to spavin and heaves when overworked. His fuel is comparatively expensive, and whether he is working or standing idle it must be supplied to him," declared a journalist. He admitted the horse could still be seen trudging up and down the streets in American cities "but now that the automobile has passed out of the experimental stage of its existence and is firmly established in popular favor it is simply a matter of time till the merchant and the millionaire, the drayman and the doctor" will all use automobiles.

Echoing the thoughts of many others, the newsman continued, "The automobile is clean, economical, and convenient. It never eats its head off. It never balks or shies into a ditch. It does not get distemper and have to be shot. It does not leave dirty streets behind it, and it can wriggle through a crowded thoroughfare quicker than an equine Stradivarius can flick off a fly with his tail." The horse, he believed, may not pass away for the next few years, but the time would certainly come when he "will be forbidden on the carefully kept streets of our twentieth century cities..." At the end of 1899 a car cost about $600 to $800 at the bottom of a manufacturer's range.[16]

Near the end of 1899, the *Horseless Age* again attacked the working horse and the handler. It declared, "The motor vehicle is rendering good public service in exposing the carelessness of drivers of horses. Contributors to our 'Lessons of the Road' columns have repeatedly shown that a large proportion of the accidents ascribed to the motor vehicle are due to the stupidity of drivers who habitually drive with loose reins, so that quick control of their horses is impossible or are themselves more frightened than their horses at the appearance of a horseless vehicle." No details were provided, no statistics were offered and no anecdotal reports were echoed. All that was presented were blanket statements such as stating the majority of runaway horse mishaps were the fault of the horsemen. "A little while later, when the inferiority of the horse as compared with the motor is generally admitted, the horse will be quietly and quickly dropped until the responsibility as between horse and motor will be clearly fixed where it has always belonged—on the owner of the untamable brute which marches cowed and beaten into partial subjection, but which in revenge bursts his bonds occasionally, carrying ruin and death through our streets," concluded the essay.[17]

In a damage suit then underway in Providence, Rhode Island, the owner of a steam car was being sued by parties who were driving a horse carriage in front of the steamer. The horse became frightened and ran off with the carriage. That led to the passengers in the carriage being thrown from the vehicle and injured. No mention was made of excessive speed or negligence. Nonetheless, a newspaper editor confidently predicted, "The truth is, we are just beginning to realize what a fractious, unreliable animal the horse is ... the animal is treacherous and dangerous, and his gradual elimination from the centers of civilization is not only much to be desired, but is coming to be recognized as a necessity."[18]

John C. Higdon of Saint Louis wrote a letter to the editor of a pro-auto journal to state he was being sued by people who claimed his automobile frightened their horse, and that led to their injuries. Higdon claimed the account of the incident that appeared in the press was inaccurate. He then stated, "In conclusion, I suggest that you hand this letter to the attorney of the Motor League, so that he may co-operate with me in the defense of this suit." Three different people had launched suits against Higdon for various injuries. In the suit, it was alleged that Higdon, who was driving the auto, could not control the vehicle properly and it ran dangerously close to the horse, causing it to shy. As a result, two women were thrown from the vehicle. One of them died nine days later from her injuries. Reportedly, driver Higdon did not stop at the time of the accident, but a passerby (in a horse and buggy) followed him to his home and thus learned his identity.[19]

A couple of weeks later editor Ingersoll penned an editorial about Higdon in which he urged that people with similar experiences should contact him. Ingersoll declared, "Mr. Higdon should receive the support of the entire motor vehicle fraternity in his fight for equal rights upon the road." Later, in June 1900 one of the suits against Higdon, filed by Katherine Anselm, was dismissed.[20]

A 1908 image of a four-in-hand team of horses becoming flustered and shying as an automobile passes.

A "prominent" member of the Automobile Club of America came up with a plan for educating the horses of his fellow townsmen to the auto by advertising in the local newspapers his willingness to bring to the stable of those who wished their horses broken and, upon request, taking his machine himself to the neighbor's stable and putting the horses through a "course of education." *Horseless Age* liked the idea and, after thinking about it for a week, decided it raised the issue of the legal responsibility of one who pursued such a policy. An editor with the journal argued both car and working horse had a right to the road but common courtesy rules—unwritten—dictated the motorist should exercise all reasonable caution to avoid accidents. But, he argued, since the motor vehicle was a fact—"a necessary concomitant of our advancing civilization," an equal responsibility rested upon the horse owner to take all reasonable precautions to avoid accidents. Consequently, he argued, we believe that in places where such training was offered "the burden of responsibility for accidents caused by horses taking fright at these machines is shifted to the owners of the horse, unless it can be shown that the motorist was guilty of misconduct. The horse owner who fails to take advantage of this opportunity to safeguard himself and his fellow citizens is guilty of contributory negligence."

Just one more effort by this trade publication to shift the blame and responsibility for all accidents involving the car and the working horse onto the horse. The "prominent" citizen who offered that training was not identified by name or even by the city of residence. He was only described as living in the suburbs.[21]

The idea of training horses was evident in other places. In England, steps had been taken to protect Queen Victoria from dangers while driving around in horse-drawn vehicles with automobiles in the area. All the horses in the royal

Novel Device for Stopping a Runaway Horse.

Designed by Ed. Richenbach, Orrville, Ohio.

An 1892 sketch of a device to prevent horses becoming runaways after a fright. The idea never seemed to have captured the public's heart.

stable had been drilled in the presence of an automobile. The horses in the three stable yards at Windsor were first led and then driven around a stationary car. Then the car was driven around the horses. Finally, the car was moved between the horses in a "dangerous way" as they stood near each other. "The automobilist finally made the car as objectionable as possible."[22]

George M. Bennett, sales manager of the Rambler Automobile Works, had concluded that the horses of Kenosha, Wisconsin, were badly in need of education. To that end, he decided to start a school for the education of horses. A report noted, "Any one desiring to enter their horses in this unique class can receive full information at the Rambler plant."[23]

A St. Paul, Minnesota, newspaper published the story of a young woman, never identified, who found herself in a quiet country town one summer. When she arrived in town she was shocked to see, in less than one week, every farmer's horse within miles had run away once and every village horse, half a dozen times. All due to being frightened by cars. She decided to open a small business teaching the horses of her friends and neighbors to become accustomed to automobiles. Not only was the woman not named but the city was also not identified, leaving the astute reader with the impression the story was false and planted, for some reason.[24]

An article in the summer of 1900 supposedly looked at the cost of a horse versus a car. All sources more or less agreed the horse was more costly than the car. This piece declared, "Vehicles can be operated at a cost of only two cents a mile." An officer of one of the car manufacturers told a reporter, "The horse is a thing of the past for certain kinds of work. We know that automobiles are at least one-third cheaper than horses, depending on the size of the plant." Then the reporter gave a detailed cost comparison although he gave no details about who supplied the figures. The first cost for horse wagons comprised a wagon for $380; two horses at $125 each ($250) and a harness for $75. The total was $705. For an electric wagon, the cost for an electric wagon complete was $2,250. Then there was the maintenance cost per year. For the horse wagon there was interest on investment at five percent a year ($35.25); stabling two horses at $36.50 per month for both ($438); shoeing two horses ($30); harness repairs for two horses ($20). The total was $535.25. For an electric wagon, there was interest on investment at five percent ($112.50); the cost of electric current at ordinary central station rates for 12,000 miles ($300); for a total of $412.50. Or, for an electric wagon, interest ($112.50); current, if generated at a private plant ($21.30); for a total of $133.80.

It was also argued that a gasoline wagon could easily cover 50 to 60 miles, a distance that would tire any team of horses. The article did present a lone voice in favor of the horse. James Heffernan, general manager of the New York Cab Company, said there was "no possibility whatever of the company retiring the horse in favor of the automobile." The horse was cheaper and gave more satisfaction than the automobile. Heffernan said carriage horses were scarcer and brought higher prices then than they did five years earlier. The Spanish and South African wars took a great many horses out of the country and the bicycle riders grew so numerous that the farmers stopped breeding horses. But, he added, breeding had been resumed. One department store that used six autos had two of them in the repair shop most of the time. Electricians had to be employed for repairs and they were expensive.[25]

The new fire chief of Washington, D.C., R.W. Dutton, decided to use automobiles instead of horses for himself and his men to get back and forth to fire call-outs. The cost of using horses for each fire official was about $1,000. Two wagons were necessary with one being held in reserve. Two horses were assigned to each assistant and the fire chief. An automobile could be bought for that sum and it was estimated that the expense of operation and maintenance would not come anywhere near the cost of horses. It was proposed to make the switch in every branch of the fire department. A reporter observed, "The fact that the price of good horses has gone up considerably of late is having its influence on the matter."[26]

Lawsuits resulting from automobile and working horse accidents increased as cars became more numerous. At a trial in Hackensack, New Jersey, John L. Guyre of Walwick sued Dr. William Vroom of Ridgewood for damages for the loss of his wife. She was thrown from her buggy after the physician's automobile frightened her horse. That horse bolted and threw the woman out of her buggy.[27]

The case of Walter S. Williams and his wife against Alonzo T. Cross in which the plaintiffs, residents of Providence, Rhode Island, sued for $5,000 in damages, came to court in October 1900. It was alleged the plaintiffs suffered injuries as a result of a runaway caused by the steamer driven by Cross. The pleas division of the Supreme Court of Rhode Island awarded $1,400 to Mr. Williams and $200 to Mrs. Williams.[28]

When the *Horseless Age* addressed the question of noisy automobiles, its editorial on the subject began by saying there were no acceptable standards of noise, nor were there any accepted methods of comparing noises. Despite the latter part of that statement the editor then went on to directly compare noises. He admitted it was often argued against autos, particularly against gasoline-powered cars, that they were too noisy. They were much noisier than the horse and the horse vehicle and that defect had to be remedied. However, the editor argued, since no standards existed "it would be impossible to either support or deny this assertion of any positive and exact statements." He then argued, "It is a matter of fact that some of our American gasoline carriages have advanced so far in reducing noise that it is absolutely useless, and even objectionable, to proceed any further in this direction." He made the far-fetched argument that cars might be made so quiet that pedestrians would be unable to hear them and then would be suddenly startled to hear a car horn. Lastly, he mentioned the "objectionable" noises of some gasoline vehicles such as the grinding of gears, the clatter of valves and so forth. Those noises, he claimed, "are due to faulty construction of these parts, and can be avoided by paying more attention to such details."[29]

In the spring of 1910, a case was settled by Judge William J. Gaynor in the Supreme Court of Nassau County (Brooklyn). Charles W. Knight sued James F.D. Lanier for damages alleged to have been caused by his horse running away at the sight of the defendant's car. In dismissing the case Gaynor reiterated that automobiles had as much right to be in the street as did the horse.[30]

Meanwhile, the case of Jonathan West remained alive in the courts although West had died. The plaintiffs were the Mason brothers, who were laundrymen in Rochester, New York. They sued for damages of $41, alleged to have been sustained by a runaway of their horse that had been caused by the steam automobile owned and driven by West. That steamer, asserted the Mason brothers, was a noisy terror to horses.

The plaintiffs secured a victory but the case was appealed and the decision of the lower court was overturned by Judge Sutherland. Another appeal was taken to the Appellate Division with the result that Sutherland's decision was overturned. That decision held West was negligent in running a machine through the streets that emitted steam in such quantities. And, "Automobiles must be quietly conducted to establish their right upon the highway." Another appeal was expected in the case.[31]

Plaintiff Charles H. Mason had the help of an early lobbying group for the automotive industry in the form of the Automobile Club of America. Its law committee had decided to take an appeal to the Court of Appeals on behalf of Mason. It was reported that the law committee believed "the principles involved in the decision are vital to the whole automobile industry...."[32]

A case that began in the Supreme Court of New York State was *Collard v. Beach*. The case had its origins in Bridgeport, Connecticut, in the spring of 1898. Frederick Beach (one of the proprietors of the publication *Scientific American*) was driving in his electric car when he passed the plaintiff Collard. Dr. George Collard was making his rounds in his horse and buggy. The horse took fright and ran off, dragging the doctor some distance on the ground. Collard claimed he was permanently disabled and sued Beach for $50,000 in damages.[33] Just before Christmas in 1901 a decision was reached in the case. After a short deliberation the jury decided in favor of Beach and no damages were awarded. Justice Charles F. McLean reinforced, from the bench, the idea of all vehicles having equal rights to be on the roads and highways. He remarked that if both sides were at fault, then the verdict must be for the defendant.[34]

In another incident, frightened by the sound of an automobile, a horse attached to a buggy broke loose from its harness and threw the two occupants of the buggy to the ground, injuring both. The accident took place in New York City at Fifth Avenue and 54th Street. After breaking loose the horse rushed down

Fifth Avenue injuring at least four more people on the way. No mention was made of the automobile driver except to say that he "whizzed by."[35]

An editor with a major New York City newspaper remarked that if the automobile was here to stay then it seemed likely the horse would have to go. He then outlined some of the major incidents from the previous couple of days. One day earlier a Hackensack horse, terrified by an auto, trampled his owner Richard Henche to death while seriously injuring John Krieger (see below). A day before that, plutocrat J.J. Astor paid a $300 indemnity for a horse his automobile had frighted to death. In Washington, D.C., a fractious cab horse, backing in fear from an approaching car, caused the vehicle's wheels to pass over the toes of Chaplain Miller, crushing them. In light of such incidents, the editor declared, "Some remedy must be devised." He then suggested, "Why not put the horses through a course of schooling in familiarizing them with the sight of the machine and issue to each graduate a certificate of fitness to appear upon public streets?"[36]

Two weeks later an inquest was held into the death of Richard Henche. The car was owned by the Blum Brothers, millionaire silk dyers of Lodi. The jury returned a verdict to the effect that Henche met his death by being knocked down by a horse that was startled by an automobile occupied by Henry C. Blum, Frederick A. Blum, and Christopher Anderson, their chauffeur. Also determined by the jury was "that their automobile was traveling at an excessive rate of speed at the time." The jury recommended that the Legislature of New Jersey pass laws to meet "the automobile situation." It also recommended that the ordinance then in effect in Hackensack, New Jersey, that allowed a speed of 12 miles per hour be revised to limit speed to seven miles per hour. Anderson and the Blum brothers were all held under $4,000 bail each on a charge of manslaughter.[37]

The estate of Richard Henche then brought a civil suit against Henry Blum. It was settled with Blum paying the estate $2,000. Blum and the chauffeur Anderson were both indicted by the grand jury of Bergen County, New Jersey, for "maintaining a nuisance." On the latter charge millionaire Henry Blum was fined $500. He paid his fine and left the court room. He had been speeding at about 40 miles per hour at the time of the accident. It was then over for the two Blum boys.[38]

Another horse-bashing article appeared in *Horseless Age* in the summer of 1902. It referenced a piece that appeared in another publication. Supposedly it was notable because it came from a state prominent for horses and which then had no automobile industry. The state was not named but it was used to observe that the correspondent on the original piece had no ax to grind against horses and no bias in favor of automobiles. All of which made him a "neutral observer." The unnamed correspondent supposedly had spent a long life in the observation of horses, although no details were given. He had reared horses, broken them, raised them, ridden them, and driven them in every form from the plow to the four-in-hand. He summed up all that experience in two sentences, "I believe the horse to be part maniac and part idiot. Every horse at some time in his life develops into a homicidal maniac." He thought that any man who trusted himself and his family to a horse was "lacking in common sense and wholly devoid of ordinary prudence." He added, "No amount of observation can tell when the brute will break out.... If anyone can tell me of one good reason why man should trust a horse, I shall be glad to know."[39]

When the trade publication *Horseless Age* looked at the issue of speed limits, the editor argued, "In automobile speed cases the defense is sometimes made that the speed regulations are unconstitutional because they discriminate against automobiles. We do not believe this defense has ever been successful and fail to see any sense in the pleas." Declaring automobiles and horse vehicles to be entirely different, the editor stated that if speed regulations were to be of any practical value they had to be made specifically for each class of vehicles, "with a view to the characteristics of their class. In most places where regulations regarding the speed of vehicles are in force the limit is so low that automobiles are at a disadvantage." The editor wanted speed limits to be unrelated for the car versus the horse and buggy because he was convinced it would be easier to raise the speed limit for automobiles if was not tied to the speed limit for the horse and buggy.[40]

J. O. Sanford was the Vermont Road Commissioner to the State Legislature. He issued a report late in 1902 that covered the state of the roads in Vermont over two years. A part of that report stated, "With improved roads we have the motor bicycle and the automobile; the latter, especially, a menace to people who travel by [horse] team. The rapidly moving automobile is a terror to most horses upon the highways. One instance was brought to our notice of a heavy automobile, containing four men, running eleven miles between two Vermont villages in 24 minutes [27.5 miles per hour]. Of the runaways along the route only two proved serious, statute law regulating the speed of horseless carriages upon highways would seem prudent."[41]

A legal case the *Horseless Age* described as having great interest was partially tried and then settled out of court at New City, Rockland County, New York, in November 1902. Sarah T. Lovatt was the plaintiff against Edward Copeland Wallace. The case was tried before Justice Samuel T. Maddox in the Supreme Court sitting in New City. Testimony for the plaintiff was underway for a few days but during a recess, the defense decided to settle the case out of court. Wallace paid Lovatt $8,750 in damages and the suit was discontinued. On May 29, 1902, Wallace, an iron merchant of New York City, and his 14-year-old son started, by car, from New York City to Tuxedo Park. Their auto was gasoline-powered, had seven horsepower, and could attain a speed of 17–19 miles an hour. Wallace got as far as Nyack but while going down a steep hill on the outskirts of the community he met a horse and buggy driven by Mr. and Mrs. Edward T. Lovatt.

Mr. Lovatt was a New York City lawyer. The Lovatt horse became frightened, dashed off, and threw the couple out of the vehicle. Lovatt testified that when he saw the auto coming he raised his hand as a signal to stop because he knew of his horse's fear of the machines. It was also alleged the car was moving beyond the speed limit. On the other hand, Wallace and his son both claimed that when the signal was given the car was immediately stopped and that the car was traveling at a speed of eight miles an hour, a legal speed.[42]

Thinking the accident was not serious, Wallace continued on his way but was stopped at Spring Valley by John Lovatt, son of the lawyer. Young Lovatt barricaded the road as a result of the telephone instructions received from his father. Wallace was arrested while his son was allowed to proceed on to Tuxedo Park in the car—note that he was only 14 years old. Wallace was tried before Justice of the Peace Fisher in Nyack, charged with violating a section of the law that required him to stop his car upon a signal from a person driving a house. He was also charged with speeding at the time. After a "bitterly fought" trial Wallace was found guilty and fined $10. As a result of the accident, Mrs. Lovatt was severely injured. She sustained a broken arm while her husband suffered only minor injuries. She began an action for damages against Wallace for $20,000. At the trial, it was revealed that the son had been driving all the time although his father echoed the view of the son that the boy was a competent driver. Wallace had bought the car for his son about six months before the accident.[43]

A journalist pointed out that one of the most annoying features of automobiles was the "cut-out" appliance that caused the loud noises that attracted so much attention but allowed the driver to go faster. He said, "The 'cut-out' has been the prolific source of so many runaways, the sound having more to do with frightening horses than the appearance of the vehicle, that manufacturers have wisely provided automobiles with mufflers, which make the puffing noise almost inaudible."[44]

When the town council of Suffolk, Virginia, held a meeting in May 1903 it adopted an ordinance "which virtually prohibits the use of automobiles on Suffolk's streets." One part of the law read, "No automobile, bicycle or other vehicle, using gasoline, electricity or steam as a motive power which makes or produces any sound or noise liable to frighten horses shall be propelled on or through the streets of Suffolk." There was a penalty of a fine of from $10 to $20 for each offense. The ordinance reportedly came about as a result of cases of damaged property as a result of horses being frightened by automobiles. That law was a rare victory for the horse in his legal encounters with the automobile. But by then it was too late, as the horse as a working animal was well on the road to extinction.[45]

An editor with a New York City newspaper remarked, "The horse survived the bicycle, but if the automobile is to stay, as it is, it seems likely that man's trusty steed will have to go. When puffing gasoline juggernauts pass they frighten him. It is to his discredit that he is so timid, but nerves are nerves in horses as in men...."[46]

William A. Clark was a United States senator from Montana. He was best known for bribing members of the Montana Legislative for their votes to make him senator. That was in 1899 at a time when only state legislators voted for the people who would be their U.S. senators, before the franchise was given to all the voters in a state for that office. Addressing the issue of horse versus car he spoke like a typical politician trying to please both sides by saying nothing. Said Clark, "As a time saver I have adopted the automobile, although I still retain my stable and always expect to stick to the horse when I want to ride for genuine pleasure. In time the automobile will to a great extent take the place of horses in industrial pursuits, but I do not think it will ever supplant the horse for pleasure riding.… As a time saver the automobile is bound to be almost universally adopted."[47]

William A. Clark, U.S. Senator from Montana, 1900. Besides making bland and meaningless political statements he was best known as a corrupt politician. In a 1907 essay Mark Twain wrote, of Clark, "He is as rotten a human being as can be found anywhere under the flag; he is a shame to the American nation."

A tongue-in-cheek editorial appeared in a New York City newspaper which mocked the constant stream of articles that appeared making the horse out to be some sort of crazy, violent, unmanageable, and uncontrollable creature. Those articles regularly appeared in the *Horseless Age* and were mostly irrational. The editor of this piece said, "There seems to be an epidemic of unmanageability among automobiles. It has become the daily plea of lawbreaking scorchers." He then cited excuses made by speeders such as the brakes didn't work, the machine was out of order, and could not be controlled. One man was pulled over for speeding at 20 miles an hour. He explained that his machine would not go any slower and he was taking it to the repair shop the very minute he was pulled out. The arresting officer let him go. He started up and pulled away at eight miles an hour, the speed limit.

The article's editor remarked, "Yet we seem to remember having heard something about the vast advantage of automobiles over horses, in that they never shied, never ran away, never became unmanageable ... for who knows but that this plague of unmanageability is contagious, like glanders [infectious disease mainly in horses], so that all automobiles may catch it?"[48]

Unfortunately for horses, most articles took a position of being against the horse, but with less extreme lunacy than displayed by the automotive industry's primary trade publication. A letter to the editor from Horace C. Chandler took exception to his Washington, D.C., newspaper's continuing its determination to have heavy fines imposed on "dangerous" autos. Chandler wondered why the paper did not go after the horse. "A far greater percentage of people are injured by horses than by autos," he stated, although he cited no evidence. He then went on to give some "examples" of runaway horses that had inflicted various forms of damage on people and property. According to Chandler, those animals were not runaways because of being frightened by cars, but because their owners had left the animals unhitched.[49]

Chapter 3

Entering the Parks

One of the obvious examples of class conflict concerning the automobile came with the successful attempts to quickly introduce the automobile into the public parks of cities and towns across America. The public park was perhaps the only place where the average working person and family could go for relaxation and to enjoy nature, in the few hours of leisure that the capitalist system afforded them. It was a place for a family to go for a picnic—a family that was perhaps confined to a small living space in a crowded tenement in some city slum area. The family had a chance to see wildlife, at least beyond the ubiquitous rat that was such a feature of urban America in the period around 1900. Perhaps the family could fish in a lake or a stream within the park. And, most importantly the park was a free service provided to the community. Virtually none of these people had automobiles in that first decade when the car was introduced, became entrenched, and moved on to dominate all phases of life. All those early car owners and drivers were of the upper class. They insisted on driving their machines, noisy and disruptive, into every corner of every park. When it came to a battle between the upper classes and the working class, the outcome was never in doubt.

As a result of a serious accident to a woman who was driving a horse that became frighted and ran away, the Boston Park Commissioners decided, in March 1899, to ban all motor vehicles from the city parks between 10:30 a.m. and 9:00 p.m. and added a clause that compelled the production of a certificate of qualification before anyone was allowed to operate a motor vehicle in the street. The enacted law read, "No person shall run or operate a motor vehicle of any kind on the public parks or boulevards until he shall have been examined and certified as competent by the inspection of the park department and a permit issued on such certificate of approval issued by the inspector of the park department, and a license for the operation or use of such vehicle has been granted. No person shall run or operate a motor vehicle in the public parks between 10:30 a. m. and 9 p. m."[1]

In an interview with the media, the park board chairman said, "We have licensed a few of these horseless vehicles before, but I do not think they numbered more than three or four. We are not opposed to horseless vehicles, but until they come into more general use, and the people and horses become more accustomed to them, we believe that the park system is not the best place to experiment with them, at least during the hours when large numbers of the citizens drive there." He added, "The matter was brought before us very emphatically by a petition signed by several of our very best citizens. Then a very serious accident resulted from one of these horseless carriages. The question, therefore, became a somewhat serious one, and we believed that some actions had to be taken. There are only a few people who use these carriages, while the great body of people desire to drive through the park system from time to time. In the interest of the many, therefore, we desired to exclude the horseless carriages, except during certain hours and with a motorman who held a license showing his capacity to manage them."

Some people, he explained, complained that "the restrictions ought to be greater, and that up to 10:30 in the forenoon is too late an hour to permit these carriage to drive through the parkway.... Most of those who go to drive [horses] through the park system do so for the purpose of soothing their nerves, instead of having them excited, and being in a condition of suppressed fear while they are there." Reiterating his position the chairman said, "Until the people and horses, therefore, become accustomed to them, we believe it only proper to make the rule we have made."[2]

When asked if the probability of frightened horses and people would not be greater if the motor vehicles were confined to downtown streets than if they were allowed in the parkway, Park Commission Chairman Stratton said there was so much bustle and excitement downtown usually that a little more or less would not make a great difference. Commonwealth Avenue, being like a public street, was not included in the order banning motor vehicles and those cars were at liberty to use that street at all times, subject only to the provision of having competent people to handle them, after securing a license from the Park Commission. Subsequently, the commissioners stated their intention that the prohibition was to be only temporary, lasting while horses and drivers of cars were becoming accustomed to the new vehicles.[3]

To demonstrate to the commissioners the ease with which a motor carriage could be controlled, Colonel Albert A. Pope took them out riding in one of his electric carriages. Pope was a pioneer in bicycle development and then in early automobile manufacturing. Following the law compelling operators of motor vehicles to obtain a license to drive in the park, an inspector, Thomas McDermott, was appointed to examine the applicants and grant licenses to those competent to handle motor vehicles. The first licenses were granted to Col. Pope and R.H. White. The latter was a dry goods merchant whose firm operated an electric delivery wagon.[4]

Not surprisingly, the Boston park rules infuriated the *Horseless Age* trade publication. Not long after the rules were imposed, the editor of the magazine fumed, "In excluding motor carriages from the parks of Boston during the usual

The steam-powered Toledo car owned by Oliver Lippincott was the first car to reach the Grand Canyon, on February 5, 1902. The driver seen is identified as either Lippincott or Al Doyle, a mountain guide who accompanied Lippincott.

driving hours of the day the Park Commissioners have taken a long step backward, and one which they will probably retrace so hurriedly as to sacrifice not a little of their dignity. These solicitous guardians of the public parks would prohibit the motor from entering their domains, forsooth! Because a horse became frightened at one of them and ran away."[5]

He dismissed the case where a woman was driving a horse wagon. The animal became frightened and ran, seriously injuring her. In the first place, he did not even mention that it was an automobile that frightened the animal. "This subject has been so thoroughly canvassed in the Old World, and the legal status of the motor vehicle has been so clearly defined that even in the United States of America stupid antagonism like this is unpardonable at this late day." Continuing his tirade the editor barked, "This decision is foolish, reactionary and worthy of a Dogberry [a foolish constable, a character in Shakespeare's *Much Ado about Nothing*]. It cannot stand for one moment before a court that knows a grain of law or common sense.... In time these wild brutes (the few that are left in parks and cities) will become so accustomed to the horseless vehicle that they will be compelled to run away from some other cause."[6]

"So far as the licensing of motor vehicle operators is concerned, no special objection can be taken to it when the newness of the art is considered, but it is pertinent to inquire why drivers of horses should not be licensed too? Every city is full of incompetent drivers, who endanger and destroy life by their recklessness or inexperience. Yet no attention is paid to it by the authorities." He concluded by writing, "The public of Boson is not with the Park Commissioners. Even they begin to realize by this time that the horseless age must invade even the sacred parks of conservative Boston."[7]

Over a year later the Boston Park Commission added a new rule to their automobile code. It was similar to a rule adopted by the Philadelphia Park Commission and required all automobile users to display conspicuously on the rear of each vehicle its license number in figures not less than one inch in height. The Boston Park Board chairman ruled the requirement would be met if the numbers were displayed only while the vehicle was in the park. The plate would not have to be a permanent fixture of the auto carriage. The driver could produce a small, movable plate to display or remove when the vehicle was not in the park.[8]

Experiments in the use of runabout automobiles for police work in the parks led the Boston police department to add several more of the cars to the department's equipment for the use of mounted police in Back Bay. However, those automobiles, added in 1903, were not intended to replace the patrolmen on horseback.[9]

In June 1899 the *Horseless Age* exploded against the nerve of the Chicago parks system. The journal editorialized that the attitude of the South Park Board of Chicago in excluding all motor vehicles from the park driveways and boulevards on the ground that they were dangerous to horses "has excited the wonder of the conservative East, where, if anywhere, such adverse action might have been expected." Continuing, the editor raged, "That Chicago with its boasted progressiveness should be guilty of such reactionary legislation proves how deep-rooted a prejudice still exists against the new mode of locomotion in great centers of civilization."

The board's action, the editor insisted, "has naturally aroused strong resentment in the western metropolis. Local manufacturers of motor vehicles are offering to users of such vehicles the services of their attorneys, free of charge, in case of arrest for violation of the law, and it is stated that if the board persists in enforcing the obnoxious measure, the very promising motor plants which had been established in the western metropolis will be compelled to move to less hostile fields. Owners of motor carriages began to openly defy the board by driving their vehicles on the interdicted ground, but no arrests were made, the explanation from the authorities being that action would be deferred until Monday."[10]

According to this article, the other park board of Chicago freely criticized the South Park Board, as did the mayor of the city "and other prominent citizens." The cause for the ban, the notion that motor vehicles frighten horses, "is generally ridiculed as flimsy and weak, comparable with the foolish objections offered against the bicycle fifteen or twenty years ago, and hardly equal force against the

Toledo, Ohio, Riverside Park, 1900–1910.

locomotive, the trolley car and other necessities of modern civilization." The editor then proclaimed, "Of course, these modern Dogberrys will soon be forced to reconsider their hasty decision and will no doubt ere long be riding in the prohibited vehicles themselves on these very same boulevards."[11]

The expected clash in Chicago took place on the following Monday when the South Park Commissioners enforced the law. C.E. Woods, general manager of the Fischer Equipment Company along with George T. Marchant and A.H. Smith, superintendent and treasurer of the same firm, appeared on the park boulevard in a car. The Fischer company was part of the early auto industry. Marchant was driving the vehicle. He was arrested but quickly released on bail. It was reported that "the matter will be immediately brought into court by the manufacturers and owners of motor vehicles in Chicago."[12]

Pressure in Chicago seemed to have worked. A reporter observed in June, "Virtually the ban on automobiles is a dead letter." Reportedly, three of the five members of the South Park Commission declared themselves opposed to any ordinance barring horseless carriages from the parks. It was also noted that the ban on autos in the parks would be raised at the next meeting of the South Park Commissioners. Rumor had it that a fourth member of the board had indicated he might also become opposed to the ban.[13]

When the case of G.F. Marchant, representing the Fischer Equipment company, came to court the judge held that "the prisoner" when he rode "peacefully" along Michigan Boulevard "had not created, aided, countenanced or assisted any riot, disturbance or other disorderly conduct" as charged by the policeman who arrested him, "and that the electric vehicles may be propelled along Chicago streets forever unless new laws are passed on the subject." The case was dismissed.[14]

Whether the South Park Commissioners had authority under the law to prohibit motor vehicles from running on the boulevards under their control was the subject of a judicial inquiry in connection with the hearing of the writ of habeas corpus petitioned for in the case of H.G. Osborn, engineer of the American Electric Vehicle Company, who was arrested while operating an electric car on Jackson Boulevard. That petition set up that Osborn was wrongly deprived of his liberty for an alleged breach of the peace in violation of the South Park Boulevard ordinance. The petition declared the running of a motor carriage on the boulevard was not a breach of the peace nor a disorderly act and declared that the act of the Commissioners prohibiting the running of horseless carriages upon the boulevards "is an unwarranted exercise of the police powers of the Commissioners."[15]

On July 5, 1899, Judge Gibbons delivered an opinion in the case of the South Park ordinance prohibiting the use of automobiles on the South Side boulevard. Gibbons declared the ordinance void: "It is a matter of common knowledge that there is less danger in the automobile than in the horse and buggy."[16]

When Gibbons gave his decision on the South Park law, the court discharged Harry G. Osborn, who had been arrested under that ordinance several weeks earlier. In his decision, Gibbons observed that the Park Commissioners "have almost plenary power over the parks, but have no right to prohibit any vehicle used for recreation or pleasure so long as it does not endanger the safety of the public." Gibbons added, "It has no right to prohibit the automobile by name any more than the bicycle or the tricycle or the dog cart, but it has the right and it is its imperative duty to prohibit any vehicle, whether bicycle horse carriage or automobile within the parks to run at a higher rate of speed than four or five miles an hour." The judge also declared, "The board has the power to set aside certain drives or places where it may prohibit vehicles from going or may designate what part of a boulevard be used by bicycles, and may prohibit other kinds of vehicles encroaching on that territory. But where there is but one north and south boulevard the board has not the power to prevent the fortunate owner of an automobile using the boulevard for his pleasure."

Thus Gibbons declared the ordinance void. He remarked that the auto had come to stay and "The time is not far distant when no horse car, trolley car or cable will be permitted to occupy any of our business streets. They have served their purpose. They should be either above or below the surface of our streets." That pronouncement forecast the coming end of the streetcar, a move favored by the automobile industry lobby. As a final comment Gibbons declared, "as a matter of common observation and scientific knowledge there is less danger in propelling an automobile than there is in driving a horse and buggy."[17]

That South Park ordinance had only been in force for a few days, at which point Osborne was arrested. The lobby immediately stepped forward to take over the defense of Osborne in court. From that time onward the Park Commissioners refrained from enforcing the ordinance until a court decision was rendered.[18]

So content was the *Horseless Age* with the Gibbons decision that they printed the judicial decision in full in their journal. The decision started in a reasonable fashion, seeming to argue that the "poor" should be permitted a monopoly of the parks. "The parks are there, they have become the birthright of the poor.... The parks and boulevards are the sacred places of the common people, and the man who would destroy their usefulness as the pleasure places of the poor should receive summary condign [suitable] punishment," went the decision. "The parks and boulevards are the sacred places of the common people, and they must not be desecrated by the mammon in iniquity." Then Gibbons went on to do just that.[19]

Other sources also celebrated the Gibbons court decision. The editor of a San Francisco newspaper declared, "the first step has been taken toward opening a clear way for the new vehicle, despite the antagonism which has been manifest in some quarters." He added, "By that decision the automobile is made available for general use in Chicago as any other vehicle. The employment of it for pleasure or for business is to be regulated as is that of other vehicles, but is not to be prohibited.... A vehicle which saves so much of labor and of time is bound to make its way. Judge Gibbons in the Chicago case has simply given a legal authority to that which is inevitable."[20]

A different California paper also recapped the decision. "What other decision could have been expected? The courts keep pace with public sentiment, and so does the law they interpret. If the city could lawfully say that a vehicle propelled by an electric motor should not roll upon the boulevard it would have the right to say that a vehicle propelled by horses or mules should not be used, and that would be the exercise of power the local government does not possess ... the decision was a common sense one." Going further, the editor asserted, "The automobile has come to stay. Of that we can entertain no sort of doubt whatever. In a dozen cities it is now in use by those who can afford to use it." However, this editor did admit there must be applied "wholesome regulations but these need not be oppressive; nor will they be." He also grudgingly agreed the working horse would not fully disappear, at least for a time. Because the automobile "is a costly machine, somewhat noisy.... But it demands nearly perfect roads and streets, and such this generation will not see." Thus the working horse would remain around for some small period.[21]

The *Horseless Age* declared the opposition of park commissioners in New York City and Chicago to the motor carriage "is already on the wane. The overwhelming tide of criticism that rose in the press throughout the country at the action of the Commissioners in Chicago must have convinced these gentlemen that public sentiment was not with them." The trade journal also stated the New York commissioners "have also been so far influenced by the general clamor and of the

Driveway, Jackson Park, Chicago, 1900–1910.

organization of the Automobile Club of America in New York, as to listen to petitions for the admission of motor carriages to Central Park. It is the beginning of the end of opposition, and the end is not far off." The newsman asserted the history of the bicycle would not be repeated in the case of the motor vehicle. The world had advanced in its ideas of locomotion in the past 15 years, he argued. "The bicycle itself has been an educator, and the motor has been so thoroughly advertised in all Christendom that the great majority of people believe in it. The prejudice against it is certainly not at all comparable with that which the bicycle encountered in its early period.... With the exception of a few old fogies who will be swept along by the procession—the world is with the promoters of the motor vehicle."[22]

An editor with a Texas newspaper remarked that as in New York, so in Chicago, the modern automobile was having to fight for its right to be treated as a "civilized conveyance." In both cities, authorities have opposed its admission to the parks. This is simply a repetition of what bicyclists went through several years earlier in asserting and maintaining their rights. There are a few members of the New York Athletic Club who are very proud of the ownership of the scarce badges and certificates that gave them the privilege of going through Central Park somewhere between the hours of dusk and dawn, he explained. Bicyclists now swarm at all hours all year round, on all the drives. He concluded, "This flexibility with perfect control is one of the reasons why automobiles have a perfect right to enter parkways; and no one will long be able to debar them."[23]

One commentator felt the United States would do well to adopt some of the laws of France for cars operating in public parks and on public highways. Those laws provided that motor vehicles had to be so constructed as not to allow any matter to escape which might cause explosions or unpleasant smells.[24]

As a direct result of what was described as "the unfriendly attitude of the South Park Board" in Chicago, it was decided to organize an automobile club at once, "for pleasure and defense." A meeting was to be held in Chicago to organize such a lobbying group and it would "endeavor to have the obnoxious measure rescinded, or to test its constitutionality before the courts." The action of the Chicago authorities also roused the owners of motor vehicles in New York City and it was reported that concerted action would also be taken there to open the drives of Central Park to private automobiles at least. Prospect Park in Brooklyn, Riverside Drive in New York City, and other parks in the city were open to motor vehicles, but the Central Park officials had so far withheld "the right of their domains."[25]

President Clausen of the New York City Park Commissioners was reported, in July 1899, to have so far relented in his attitude toward the motor vehicle as to be willing to take a trial spin through the park with some members of the Automobile Club, to see how the horses would respond to the incursion of the newcomer.[26]

The idea that Central Park under Clausen was coming around to the idea of being more open to cars in the park suffered a jolt later that same month. It had been thought the Commissioners of Central Park were simply waiting for some member of the New York Automobile Club to petition for a permit to drive his motor carriage in Central Park. However, such a petition was refused on the grounds that it might frighten horses and would be a "disfigurement to the park." A promise was made by the reporter presenting this story that "Legal action will be taken by owners of motor carriages."[27]

In the following month, an experiment was undertaken to allow the unrestricted use of all kinds of horseless carriages in the park. Permission had been given to several "experienced" operators to run the automobiles in the park, and if they were found unobjectionable the restriction would be removed.[28]

The *Horseless Age* continued to hammer away at the Central Park authorities with the journal declaring, "The position of the president of the Board of Park Commissioners of New York is beginning to be humorous." While the publication agreed that reasonable regulations were necessary. One of those was a regulation that restricted the drive to "pleasure carriages" and excluded heavy vehicles of all kinds. "But when the Commissioners go so far as to assert that motor carriages are not pleasure carriages they violate the English language and the very law on which they base their decision."[29]

Lawyer Winslow E. Buzby of New York City was arrested near the end of October 1899 while attempting to operate an automobile in Central Park. When he appeared in Police Court the charges against him were disorderly conduct and violation of a park ordinance. He was referred to Magistrate Hogan, who was informed that Buzby had brought about his arrest to test in the courts the authority of Park Commissioner Clausen to exclude autos from Central Park. Charles M. Beattie, acting for Buzby, noted the park board had the authority to make rules and regulations for the city parks but in this case, it was discriminatory because the ban was only applied to Central Park, while cars were permitted in the parks of the boroughs of Brooklyn and the Bronx. That ordinance said that none but "pleasure carriages" could enter Central Park, and the park was maintaining the position that motor vehicles were not pleasure carriages.[30]

Buzby scored a victory before the magistrate when the charge against him was dismissed in court. Defense counsel convinced the judge the park rules had to be uniform in all boroughs of the city. At a meeting of the park board a resolution temporarily excluding motor vehicles from Central Park, except by permission from the parks board, was passed by a unanimous vote of the Commissioners.[31]

The regular meeting of the New York Park Board was held on November 2, 1899. Park Board President Clausen discussed the dispute about the admission of automobiles to Central Park. Men had been arrested one week earlier for trying to force an entrance into the park with their cars. They had asked Clausen for a permit which he had been compelled to refuse because it was against the rules. Clausen offered the following as an amendment to the rule regarding the admittance of carriages into Central Park: "No horseless carriages or motor wagons shall enter upon the drive except by permission of the department." This resolution was unanimously adopted by the board.

In referring to the arrest, Clausen declared, "It is to be regretted, however, that such a body of gentlemen as the Automobile Club should allow two members, impetuous or petulant, to put it in the position they did. They recognized the department's jurisdiction. This may be described as 'tricky,' especially taken in connection with the apparently friendly but really questionable offer to me of membership free of initiation fee." Clausen explained that the men referred to had the day they asked him for a permit to enter the park with an automobile, desired him to become a member of the club. He declined. Finally, the Park Board moved to hold a public hearing on November 9, 1899, at 11 a.m. for all persons interested in the matter. Note that a meeting in the morning of a regular work day limited the number of people of average and low income from attending such meetings as they could not usually get the time away from work, or afford it for that matter if it was available. Such timings for meetings favored to a large extent the wealthy classes.[32]

On November 9 a hearing was held in Central Park. It was open to all persons interested in the proposition to ban automobiles from that park. According to a news report about 30 people attended the meeting with an equal division of those people for and against the proposition. All but two of those opposed were against the idea for business reasons, people such as livery stablemen and hack drivers. One opponent, Mrs. E.F. Ashwin, was against cars because of the danger to horse drivers. The other opponent was ex-judge Thomas M. North, who opposed the idea on the ground it made the park less safe as a playground. One of the people in favor was George F. Chamberlin, vice president of the Automobile Club. To get around the problem of uniformity of regulations in all boroughs, the Park Board passed a resolution that allowed the Commissioner in each of the boroughs to use their judgment in issuing permits.[33]

A different article on the hearing claimed that 15 advocates for cars in Central Park were present along with 10 opponents. The opposition was described as a livery stable owner, some "private persons" who were accustomed to horse-driving in the park, and an attorney for the hackmen who worked the park. Still another article further denigrated the opponents by describing them as "a few old ladies who go pleasure riding and the hackmen who ply their trade there." There was only one female at that hearing and no mention was made in the last two articles about an ex-judge being in attendance as an opponent of cars in Central Park.[34]

President George C. Clausen, chairman of the New York Park Board had, reportedly, become a "convert" to the automobile and had given his consent to the admission of motor carriages to Central Park. His two associates on the board had all along been in favor of admitting them, according to a journalist. The reason for his conversion was said to have been his experience after he went through the park in a car supplied by "friends of the cause" and found no problem. He then announced a new rule would be adopted "granting the privilege of the Park to a limited number of automobilists until the horses are accustomed to them and the Board considers it safe to remove all disability from the motor carriage. The permits will be restricted to those who, in the judgment of the Board, are cautious and competent drivers of motor machines."

As far as the editor of a trade journal was concerned autos had every right to drive through the parks of all cities and no laws should prevent it, nor were any permits needed. "But notwithstanding that the broad principles of the law are on the side of the automobilists, it is doubtful whether it would be wise to press the issue at this time. The park authorities have made important concessions, showing that they are becoming reconciled to the automobile. Their complete conversion is only a matter of a little time." Thus, patience was called for.[35]

Another publication mentioned George C. Clausen of the Department of Parks of Manhattan Borough. It noted that less than 30 days before late November 1899 he was the "implacable opponent" of the auto and his whole staff seemed to have, "judging from their words and looks, placed the automobile in a chamber of horrors ... and invariably referred to it as a destroyer of the lives of innocent children who wanted the Park for healthful exercise. They said it would rack and destroy the nerves of people in the Park to be compelled to dodge this new fangled monster." And, it would frighten the horses. Then, on October 27 Winslow Buzby deliberately drove his auto into Central Park and was arrested. Then some of his fellow Commissioners expressed different, favorable views on the car. George Clausen began to soften.[36]

By the middle of December, the New York Park Board was reportedly issuing permits to car owners to enter the park system at the rate of two or three a week. Till then the permits had been limited to electric vehicles. Gasoline-powered automobiles were being banned on the ground of being too noisy, not only in New York City but also in Baltimore.[37]

A reporter went to the office of the New York City Park Department in May 1900 to inquire whether the use of autos in Central Park had led to any mishaps. Willis Holly, secretary of the Park Board, said there had been none. It was still true that only electric vehicles were permitted to enter Central Park because Commissioner Clausen still objected to the noise made by steamers and the odor from the gasoline-powered vehicles. Holly said, of Clausen's motivation, "Mr. Clausen was influenced largely by the very general demand of the great majority of those who ride in the park in ordinary vehicles that the autos be excluded. These people feared that their horses would be scared and their own lives jeopardized."

Automobiles of all kinds could be run without permits in Riverside, the Bronx, and other parks. In Prospect Park certain roads were open to them and others were closed to them. Fewer than 50 permits for Central Park had been signed by Clausen to that date. The form read as follows, "Permission is hereby granted to __________ to enter upon and pass over drives of the Central Park with electric pleasure carriages operated by an experienced motorman. This permission to continue [to be] revocable at any time at the pleasure of the Department, and subject to its rules and regulations. In accepting this permit the holder agrees to exercise the greatest care to avoid frightening horses on the drives and bridle paths, or causing any danger or annoyance." Added to the article was a list of 42 names and addresses of the permit holders. Three were women. One permit holder was John Jacob Astor, 23 West 26th Street.[38]

Members of the Automobile Club of America continued to fight against Clausen and the New York City Park Board over access to Central Park. When the automobile regulation bill was passed at Albany the members of the ACA ("the leading motor vehicle organization of the country") were generally happy except the Park Commissioners reserved the right to regulate the speed of cars in the public parks. Clausen issued an order that autos in parks must not be run at a greater speed than seven miles per hour and had to slow down to 3.5 miles an hour when passing a horse in the park driveways. Outside of the parks in the city streets, eight miles an hour was allowed; while on the country roads, 15 miles an hour was the permitted maximum speed. Auto club people were incensed about the 3.5 miles per hour slowdown. They argued that would effectively limit them to 3.5 miles an hour all the time in the park because there was also a lot of horse traffic.

Above: **Driveway, Belle Isle Park, 1900–1910.** ***Below:*** **A, C. Bostwick, 1900.**

Then four men in two gasoline cars decided to make a test. The men were ACA President A.R. Shattuck, Vice President A.C. Bostwick, and ACA Law Committee members J.C. Church and George F. Chamberlin. On the morning of May 4, 1901, the men went to the park determined to get arrested, to then launch a legal test of the ruling. It was decided Bostwick would be the one to disobey the law and get arrested. But the park police refused to arrest him. Twice he passed horses at speeds greater than allowed, in front of policemen. Twice he pleaded with them to arrest him. Twice the officers just laughed and moved away. One officer said to Bostwick, "I can't do it, you know." Later the officers explained they had been told not to arrest any of the ACA men unless the horses were frightened. No horse was frightened by the passing auto. The ACA party then went to police headquarters in Central Park and preferred charges against Mounted Policeman No. 320 for neglect of duty in failing to arrest them.[39]

In Philadelphia, the report of the committee of the Fairmount Park Committee, which was appointed to examine and report upon the advisability of admitting cars to the park drives, recommended that certain drives be opened to automobiles as an experiment and that other drives were to be opened several months later, if the experiment was deemed a success.[40] Before those few months passed it was reported that the petition of the automobilists of Philadelphia for the opening to automobiles of all the drives of Fairmount Park was granted by the park department commissioners.[41]

Edward J. Murphy was arrested on the afternoon of February 22, 1900, for operating an automobile in Golden Gate Park in San Francisco, contrary to the park ordinance that prohibited the use of horseless carriages "on the great reservation." It was reported, "Murphy had considerable sport with the officer but was finally captured. He became abusive and was placed under arrest. Later in the day he and his machine were released and escorted out of the park townward."[42]

The rule that excluded autos from Golden Gate Park was enacted in San Francisco around the start of 1900. However, "little attention was given it as few automobiles are used in that city." On Washington's Birthday, the driver of a locomobile belonging to a San Francisco newspaper was arrested for violation of the rule. An interview with two park Commissioners, Lloyd and Zeile, elicited the information that no deviation would be made from the rule until those carriages became common enough in the city to cease to be a cause of fright to horses. Lloyd noted, "They are not allowed in Central Park, New York, although there are 50 [cars] in use there to one here." Zeile declared, "If these automobiles are allowed in the park, they will cause many accidents." Three months later the rule was rescinded.[43]

At a regular meeting of the San Francisco Park Commissioners later that year a resolution was passed concerning admittance to the park. Under it, all those who desired to drive autos through the park had to appear before the Park Commissioner and get a permit. Those permits were to be granted regardless of the motive power of the machine. All that was to be considered was the competency of the applicants.[44] More than a year later a meeting of the Stable and Carriage Owners' Association was held. At that meeting, a resolution protesting against the toleration of automobiles on the principal driveways of Golden Gate Park was adopted. That resolution was to be presented to the city's Park Commissioners.[45]

Two years later the San Francisco park police announced they were determined to punish a class of offenders who had been taking advantage of nightfall to violate park ordinances. One arrest had already been made. The use of automobiles on park thoroughfares was not permitted on the north drive, the bridle path, or intersecting avenues. That was from an ordinance passed by the San Francisco Board of Supervisors. The south drive was allotted to automobilists and

Automobiles in front of the conservatory at Detroit's Belle Isle Park, 1900–1910.

horsemen took that road at their peril. But many violated the ordinance. Automobilists regularly spun through the north drive at a high rate of speed.[46]

The Baltimore Parks Board made a ruling excluding steam and gasoline vehicles from the parks of that city on account of their greater ability to frighten horses. Electric vehicles were allowed in the parks, as in the past. There were reported grumblings from the owners of the excluded types of vehicles and threats of lawsuits being launched.[47]

The matter of the ban in Baltimore came to a head in that city late in 1900 when several members of the Baltimore Automobile Club drove their steamers into the park to be arrested to test the regulation in court. Several were arrested and released on bond; one was Ernest J. Knabe, Jr.[48]

Automobiles had to stay off the boulevards and keep out of the public parks: that was the pronouncement of the Omaha Board of Park Commissioners. That rule went into effect in August 1902 and the police department had received instructions to enforce it. A reporter remarked, "The reason is that the Omaha horse is not educated up to the acceptance of the automobile as a fixed institution and until such education has been acquired the chauffeur must keep to thoroughfares dedicated to common traffic and to the 'dirt' roads." J.H. Evans, president of the Board of Park Commissioners, explained that most of the roads in question were very narrow and thus even more dangerous from the perspective of accidents and runaways. Evans said, "It may be that, in the course of time, when motor cars become more common and horses in consequence become accustomed to them, this rule can be abrogated. This board has no desire to be severe with the chauffeurs, I am sure, but it feels that it must take this step for the safety of the majority of the public."

The vote by the Board had passed by a three to two margin. Added Evans, "Another reason we had for excluding automobiles from parks and boulevards was that the average chauffeur is too ambitious to break speed records. He declines to conform in the speed ordinances of the city, but goes tearing along over the streets at a terrific rate, seemingly forgetful that pedestrians or people in more conventional vehicles have rights which they ought to observe."[49]

In Memphis, Tennessee, the Board of Park Commissioners adopted a set of rules to govern the operation of automobiles in their public parks. Those rules were adopted in the spring of 1903 and included a speed limit of four miles per hour. When a car encountered a restive horse the machine had to be brought to a complete stop. Those rules were said to have been strongly objected to by Memphis automobilists. A newsman commented that with a population of 125,000 "it would be well for its authorities to shake off some of the backwoods prejudice to modern methods of travel so apparent in their new rules." He described the rules as "harassing restrictions." He noted the speed limit in New York's Central Park was eight miles an hour and he thought that eight was "probably the average limit in the parks of large cities."[50]

Chapter 4

Organizations and Lobbying

The automobile age had only just gotten underway in 1895 yet even then the automobilists and the industry as a whole were already initiating organizations. Those associations would be integral for car owners, drivers, and manufacturers as they lobbied incessantly to get the kind of activity from the government they saw to be in their best interests. All of the early automobile owners were wealthy and thus could easily afford the amounts of money that were needed to successfully and repeatedly lobby governments and bureaucrats to have their way.

At a meeting held in Chicago on November 1, 1895, the organizers of the American Motor League failed to agree on the policy the organization should follow in the admission of members. Therefore a committee was appointed to study the matter. Some were in favor of admitting users of motor vehicles as well as manufacturers and scientific experts; some wanted membership limited to the latter only. The early trade publication *Horseless Age,* through its editor E.P. Ingersoll, argued for broad membership. That was necessary to bring into the organization "all users of motor vehicles in order to swell the ranks and stand shoulder to shoulder in the protective work which will undoubtedly be needed from the start.... A good representation of users will at once demonstrate the practical utility of the invention, and frustrate any claim that 'the people' are antagonistic to it."[1]

Ingersoll added, "In the aggressive period the protective feature naturally assumes great prominence, but as the necessity for protection disappears so the protective feature would quietly lapse and members who had joined solely for this object would sever their connection with the organization or become inactive." Thus, there was a need for as many members as possible. The educational value of the American Motor League "will certainly be great, if it is conducted on broad and liberal lines." Even the social features of trade organizations were not to be minimized. The association fostered common interests and broadened the minds and quickened the sympathies of their members. Ingersoll declared, "even if the American Motor League could accomplish no more than this it would have good reason to exist. But it can accomplish more. It has much and varied work to do, work in which all earnest men should be invited to join."[2]

The American Motor League never got underway after that 1895 attempt at a beginning. But then it was revived and set up formally in 1902 in Chicago. It was patterned very much after the League of American Wheelmen that had formerly controlled bicycling and was instrumental in securing good road laws in many states. It was expected the AML would take up many of the issues where the League of American Wheelmen left off and would make good roads one of its main objects.[3]

Edwin F. Browne of Chicago was chosen to be president of the AML at its 1902 founding. In many ways, it was a continuation of the League of American Wheelmen which had disbanded in 1902. Its large membership had dropped dramatically in the previous two years, largely due to the arrival of the automobile. A journalist remarked that "A strenuous fight will be made by the league in all localities for good roads."[4]

When the American Motor League held its annual meeting in New York City early in 1903, it elected Isaac B. Potter president. Automotive pioneer Charles E. Duryea was elected first vice president. Potter was the ex-president of the League of American Wheelmen. At that meeting, two resolutions were passed. One expressed disapproval of a bill in the Connecticut Legislature providing for a change in the speed limit for automobiles from 15 miles per hour down to eight miles an hour and in other ways imposing restrictions upon the use of cars. The other resolution expressed disapproval of a bill in the New Jersey Legislature providing for a licensing system for automobilists who were obliged to take out a license, undergo an examination, and pay a fee of five dollars.[5]

That year Potter was said to be managing an energetic recruiting plan for the organization of individual automobilists. The laws governing cars, which varied so much in the United States, were also receiving the attention of the group. It was aiming for uniform speed limits across America and to have a license granted in one state accepted by another.[6]

The AML came out in the guise of an opponent to road racing by autos, even when permission was obtained from local authorities. "Whereas numerous accidents resulting from the racing of automobiles on the public roads have demonstrated the extreme danger of such practice and have justified a sentiment against it on the part of all conservative users of power machines...." However, the AML gave its "hearty support" to all reasonable tests of power, endurance, and so forth, and to speed tests upon race tracks and opposed all such activities on the public roads.[7]

The campaign of the AML to extend its membership throughout the country was being conducted using largely the same plan employed by the League of American Wheelmen in its earlier days—both under the leadership of Potter. A local chapter of the AML was to be established in Savannah, Georgia, and it was hoped local autoists could use the national organization to fight the passage of laws regulating the speed of autos. Letters were being sent by the AML to each of the 160 cities in America with populations of 25,000 or more to organize local chapters. By-laws and the constitution of the American Motor League were framed to encourage the operation of local chapters in every city and town containing five or more automobilists.[8]

From statistics compiled by the AML, it was estimated the number of automobiles in use in the United States, as of July 1903, was about 51,000 and was increasing at the rate of 1,200 to 1,500 per month.[9]

The appointment of official hotels for the accommodation of automobilists was taken up successfully by the AML. All such hotels were listed in league tour books. That was a continuation of the practice started by the League of American Wheelmen. Also followed by the American Motor League was the practice of providing detailed route maps for its members.[10]

Later in 1903, the American Motor League devised a series of warning signs to be put up at points along the roadside wherever conditions were such as to call for reduced speed or some other type of caution. Each sign was to be of heavy enameled steel, black figures on a white background, and 24 inches square in size. Instructions were supplied from AML headquarters to all branches on how to make their signs, so everyone followed the same pattern and signs were uniform. No mention was made about getting permission from local authorities, consulting local authorities, or consulting anybody at all. The AML merged with the American Automobile Association (AAA) in 1904.[11]

A meeting of the National Association of Automobile Manufacturers (NAAM) was held in New York City in December 1900. It was the third meeting but at the first two, no officers were elected. At this third meeting, S.T. Davis was elected president of the new lobby group.[12]

One topic the group talked about was the advisability of making the association similar in aim to that of the League of American Wheelmen—meaning that this new group would fight for better roads in the United States.[13]

Another area of concern

The American Motor League came up with its own roadside signs to guide passing motorists in 1903. The AML thought it should be in charge of such signage—not local authorities. For example, #2 means approach to a railroad, #7, approach to a ditch, and #8, approach to a city or town.

for the NAAM was the issue of automobile shows. It was announced near the end of 1901 that the next auto show to be held in New York City would take place under the joint auspices of the Automobile Club of America (ACA) and the National Association of Automobile Manufacturers. The NAAM had obtained an option on Madison Square Garden for the show that was slated to take place in January 1903. The NAAM was then refusing to sanction the proposed shows slated for Washington, D.C., and Boston. However, the group stated it would aid the show to be held in Chicago in March of the following year.[14]

At a meeting of the NAAM, one of the topics of interest was the proposed national highway being discussed in the United States Congress. Also, a committee was appointed to report on a plan to issue competent operators certificates bearing their photographs to prevent transfer. "The idea was that these certificates should be granted by the members and bear the endorsement of the association." This was a plan to usurp local officials from granting drivers' licenses and turn the function over to this private lobby group.[15]

The opening of the annual auto show in Chicago took place on March 1, 1902. It was held under the auspices of the Chicago Automobile Club and the National Association of Automobile Manufacturers.[16]

Less than a year later the automobile show opened at Madison Square Gardens in New York City on January 17, 1903. It was held under the auspices of the Automobile Club of America, the National Association of Automobile Manufacturers, and the Madison Square Garden's company. It was the third annual auto exhibition.[17]

At that show 196 booths were rented by 143 exhibitors; 77 of those exhibitors displayed completed vehicles. Of the complete vehicles on display 68 were gasoline-driven, ten were steamers, and eight were electric cars. A number of firms made two kinds of vehicles while one concern made all three types. As no gasoline was allowed in Madison Square Gardens, the makers of gasoline cars had arranged for their demonstration cars to be located outside the building. During the week of the show, meetings were held by the AAA, the AML, and the NAAM in concert.[18]

In Albany, New York, when the New York Legislature was considering an auto regulation measure known as the Bailey Bill, three organizations went to Albany to urge New York Governor Benjamin Odell to veto the measure. Those organizations were: the NAAM, the AAA, and the New York Automobile Trade Association. The NAAM continued to be mentioned in the media into the 1920s at which point it disappeared.[19]

Governor Charles A. Busiel of New Hampshire was described as a "strong advocate" of electric railways and motor vehicles of all kinds, as a means of developing his state. "The speed you will be able to obtain and the comfort you will take in riding will be governed by the condition of highways. This will have a tendency to better roads and highways. A system of good highways will be established and maintained in first-class condition throughout the country. This must ensue as a natural result of the public demand brought about by the use of motor carriages," Busiel explained. Before motor vehicles replaced horse carriages, he said, "you will see the steam roads and present electric roads combined to secure legislation to prevent these motor carriages and bicycles making over six miles an hour, to prevent them from being competitors just the same as the steam roads to-day are using their influence to prevent the progress of electric roads. But as soon as the ownership of the new motor carriages becomes general all restrictive laws will be abolished from the statutes." Thus, Busiel explained the situation early in 1897 and, without using the terminology, laid out the course for the coming lobbying by automotive proponents.[20]

The preliminary steps to the organization of an automobile club in New York City were taken at the Waldorf-Astoria Hotel on a day in June 1899. Some 30 people interested in the motor vehicle responded to the call of Whitney Lyon and George F. Chamberlin to attend a meeting. In his opening remarks, Lyon said facetiously that an auto club was needed to protect users of motor vehicles from park boards on one hand and motor vehicle manufacturers on the other. Park boards then excluded cars from their domains and manufacturers had months-long waiting lists for would-be buyers as demand outpaced supply. Lyon said the necessity of a club was forced upon him by the difficulty he encountered in trying to find a livery stable keeper who would store and care for his motor carriage.

When stable proprietors learned the vehicle was horseless they looked upon it as an enemy to their business and the car was not to be garaged at any price. Chamberlin was elected temporary president and read a statement outlining the objects of the organization. Several sections, all innocuous enough, involved the gathering of information helpful to motormen; to exchange views and information with other motormen, to contact similar groups in other countries for the same general reasons—and to establish a depot for the proper storage and care of all forms of motor vehicles.[21]

When that preliminary meeting to organize the Automobile Club of America was held, it listed several reasons for its formation: to promote the use of the automobile as sport, to secure good roads, and to avoid arousing the antagonism of horse owners. About 40 owners of cars and manufacturers were present at the meeting. A suggestion made at the meeting that people connected with the automobile trade should be excluded from membership was not met with favor.[22]

A different source stated that 30 men attended that meeting. George F. Chamberlin was elected president. According to this article, the object of the club was to advance in every legitimate way the interests of the owners of automobiles. It was thought that much could be done to advance the use of cars by securing more favorable legislation.[23]

One example of ACA lobbying could be seen in connection with the proposed construction of a national highway from the Atlantic to the Pacific. Nelson

A group of unidentified men at one of the auto clubs' gala dinners. Such affairs were often the occasion to lobby politicians and bureaucrats to favor the new industry.

Prominent men in the Automobile Club of America, 1900. George Smith (left) and Avery Andrews flank George F. Chamberlin, president of the organization.

A. Miles was a member of the commission that had been appointed to make a preliminary report on the project. He and his colleagues from that commission were entertained at a dinner put on by the ACA. One of the main aims of the Automobile Club of America was to encourage the construction of good roads.[24]

The start of an auto race from New York to Boston. In the early years of the car industry the clubs and organizations that lobbied for the industry regulated, hyped and staged car races. Many were on city streets without permission from local authorities.

Less than a year after its June 7 formation, one reporter pronounced the organization a great success. "The growth of the club and the flocking to its membership of many of the best known men of affairs in the community have already attracted much attention." Good roads were a necessity to the auto owner because without smooth roads speed was impossible for any vehicle, he argued. The members of the ACA would furnish workers for the cause of good roads, "one element which has been lacking heretofore, namely, help from the fashionable and wealthy classes."[25]

When the ACA sponsored an auto reliability test that comprised a run from New York City to Boston and return the organization claimed it was to be in no sense a race as a speed limit of 14 miles an hour was imposed. Supposedly anyone caught speeding was to be disqualified. That "test" featured 75 vehicles starting the event. Of those vehicles, 56 were gas-powered, 18 were steamers, and one was an electric car.[26]

As speeding increased among the automobilists and accidents and deaths increased, some of the automotive lobbying groups tried to claim they were against speeding and all the damage it brought—even though it was those very groups that fought speed limit laws everywhere and encouraged road races as often as possible. And these were races on public roads that were organized by such clubs, often without any permission from local authorities. Destruction grew so much that the clubs felt, in some cases, a need to back away from such sponsorship. Also, car races came to increasingly be confined to specific tracks laid out or constructed for that purpose—not public roads.

The ACA was one of the first of the groups to encourage the sport of automobiling in America and it was said to be the first to come out earnestly in favor of a discontinuance of fast speeding on the highway. Other auto organizations, it was reported, had remained quiet on the subject. Cited in the piece were the AAA and the NAAM as having taken no action. Meanwhile accidents increased across the country, causing more injuries and deaths. With speeding on the rise, police officers were often outrun and had no way to identify vehicle ownership and driver. Membership in the organization declined during the Great Depression and in 1932 the board of directors dissolved the Automobile Club of America.[27]

Delegates from eight of the leading motor vehicle organizations completed the formation of a national body composed of auto clubs to be called the American Automobile Association, on March 4, 1902, in Chicago. The question of having individual memberships was not discussed; membership was to be limited to clubs only. Each club would have as many votes in the AAA as it had active and life members in its organization. It would pay a $10 initiation fee and $3 annually as dues for each of its members. Winthrop E. Scarritt of the ACA was chosen as president.[28]

One journalist declared the organization would make laws and protect its members only and look out only for such legislation as would interest its members. In other words, it would not consider the wishes or convenience of the average automobilist unless he happened to be a member of one of the allied clubs. Scarritt was a charter member of the ACA and one of its governors. He was also president of the Automobile Club of New Jersey.[29]

George Scarritt, president of the American Automobile Association, 1902.

The AAA did take some public measures against speeding. At a meeting, the board of directors took what were called "strenuous measures" to prevent excess speed limits in endurance runs and violation of rules generally in open motor vehicle contests of all kinds. The resolution passed unanimously and had its origins in the breaking of the legal and contest speed limits in the recent endurance run on Long Island. Such excess speed drew a lot of negative reactions from the press and the public in general. Under the resolution, any contestant disqualified or suspended for violation of the rules of any contest promoted by a member of the association would be ineligible to participate in any competitive event as long as his club refused to reinstate him.[30]

Reportedly a war was threatened between the AAA and the AML for control of auto racing in America. At the time the AAA was handling the sport. However, the American Motor League had been approaching various people in racing to get them to come under their banner. One reporter thought that to a great extent the war was a personal affair between Isaac Potter of the AML and C.H. Gilette, the secretary of the American Automobile Association. When the AAA took over the AML in 1904 the question of individual membership in the AAA was solved. The AAA had only clubs as members while the AML had individuals as members.[31]

In June 1899 some members of the Philadelphia Council who constituted the Committee on Law were given a ride in electric carriages to Germantown and back so that they might have an opportunity to study the operation of the vehicles before legislating upon them. The council then had under consideration a bill to require all motor vehicles to pay a license fee of $10 a year. The group first visited the station of the Pennsylvania Electric Company where they were shown how readily the vehicles were controlled by skilled operators. After that exhibition, the councilmen and some of the officials of the company made the run to the Manheim Club House in Germantown and returned without any mishaps, except for one tire puncture.

It was stated on behalf of the company that it was not seeking legislation but, as the subject had been introduced, "the officials thought that all that was required was some reasonable regulation as to vehicles used for hire, as the running of all vehicles is already regulated by laws forbidding immoderate speed." And, the auto proponents argued, "The idea of a license for all automobiles did not meet with much favor, and one of the legal members of the party thought such a charge would not stand the legal test, as whenever the question had been raised as regards license taxes on bicycles the courts had decided that municipalities have no power to levy them." The opinion was expressed that the Legislature would take occasion to levy "a personal property tax on such electric vehicles as are used for hire, which is the form of tax imposed on carriages used for like purposes."[32]

When the Automobile Club of America was formed in New York City it caused the *Horseless Age* to state enthusiastically, "It will be a strong deterrent to Park Boards and other short-sighted authorities who would legislate against the motor vehicle." That same month C.E. Corrigan in Chicago gloated over the victory scored by auto proponents in the Gibbons decision in Chicago. Corrigan was the general manager of the American Electric Vehicle Company. He saw the Gibbons decision as establishing a precedent for car owners in other cities "to secure the repeal of prohibitive or hostile legislation against the operation of these vehicles in parks and boulevards." Corrigan suggested a movement be started for the organization of a national association of those interested in the auto industry. Such an organization "whose time would be exclusively devoted to the best interests of the industry, would be a powerful and effective means in securing the repeal of obnoxious legislation and also in preventing hostile legislation in the future."[33]

Responding to Corrigan's letter the *Horseless Age* praised the idea that a national automotive organization would be good. "A national organization such as Mr. Corrigan suggests could be made a strong moral influence in favor of good roads and the motor vehicle in general." The editor thought, though, that aggressive lawsuits against laws would perhaps be making a mountain out of a molehill. "Public sentiment is overwhelmingly with them, and public sentiment determines the action of public officials. Makers of law or its executives, who unreasonably restrict or impede the use of the motor vehicle from this time forth will rouse such a storm of criticism that they will be glad to recede from their position in any way consistent with official dignity. Hence harsh and aggressive measures are neither necessary nor advisable in upholding the rights of the motor vehicle. Patience and prudence will accomplish much more in the end." The members of an organization of that character could best be secured by an affiliation with the several local automobile clubs which are already formed or are in the process of formation in New York City, Boston, Philadelphia, and Chicago. The New York club, as the first one chartered, might take the necessary steps, he thought, if it were deemed timely to form a national association next fall.[34]

The Automobile Club of America had completed its organization by the fall of 1899. This was the group formed at the Waldorf-Astoria back in June of that year. As a suggestion it was proposed, "Among the first matters to engage its attention should be the law forbidding the use of steam vehicles in New York State, except on conditions that are virtually prohibitory, and the ordinance excluding motor carriages from the parks of NYC." It was thought the latter stumbling block would be easy to remove but it was likely that an amendment of the former was as much as could be expected. "The red flag portion of the law is obviously unnecessary, but some supervision over steam boilers in vehicles will probably be found necessary. Just what this supervision should be … will be a good subject for the Automobile Club to discuss."[35]

The Automobile Club of America adopted a constitution as part of its organizational setup. Not all members needed to own cars. There were four classes of membership; honorary, life, active, and association. Honorary members were limited to 25 in total, active members were limited to a total of 400 and membership in the other two categories was unlimited. General management of the organization was vested in a board of nine trustees—all such officers were required to be car owners. Five committees were to be appointed (1) membership committee, 3 appointed; (2) house committee, 5; (3) exhibition, contests, runs, and tours, 3; (4) auditing, 3; (5) laws and ordinances, 3. From the constitution, "The committee on laws and ordinances shall examine and report on such laws as affect the use of automobiles and shall take action; subject to the approval of the board of governors, to maintain the rights of the automobile."[36]

As the principal trade publication of the automobile proponents, *Horseless Age* engaged in lobbying of its own regularly. It congratulated itself in January 1900 as having accomplished the preliminary work it had set out for itself. That original goal was twofold: reform and education. It felt it had succeeded in reform by working to expose charlatans and scammers and remove them from the industry. Education was used as another word for lobbying. For example, the journal regularly crusaded in print against the electric car and for the gasoline-powered automobile.[37]

At the start of 1900 opinions were said among automakers that a successful automobile exhibition could be held in May or June of that year under the auspices of the Automobile Club of America. The few opportunities the public had to see the motor vehicles at that time, "had been afforded by promoters of bicycles or electrical exhibitions." It was, said a reporter, the best that could then be expected. But now the situation was different. "We have in the Automobile Club of America an organization well fitted to undertake the work of an exhibition. As a neutral body, aloof from commercial entanglements and animated by a worthy ambition to further the interests of the new industry as a whole, its position is one of impartial dignity." And so it came to pass that the Automobile Club of America decided to hold a trade show of automobiles and accessories at Madison Square Garden, New York City, in November 1900. It was also noted that "The club will exercise supervision over all important details."[38]

Albert R. Shattuck, chairman of the Good Roads Committee of the Automobile Club of America appeared before the Ways and Means Committee of the New York Assembly in March 1900 to urge an appropriation of $1 million for the improvement of the highways of New York State, according to the provisions of the Higbee-Armstrong bill that was passed two years earlier and under which only $88,000 of the sum has been spent. According to that bill half of the expense of improving the roads was borne by the counties in which the improvements were made.[39]

The *Horseless Age* editorialized in favor of good roads and, as usual, went over the top with its hyperbole. "Civilization depends on roads. Where there are no roads there is no civilization, and just in proportion to the number and excellence of roads does it flourish and extend. Barbarians have no roads." The editor mentioned Rome and that as her empire grew, so did the roads increase and expand outwards. "The relation of good roads to the motor vehicle industry is a vital one," he argued, more to the point. He felt the prospects for good roads were brightening: "Makers and users of motor vehicles are beginning to make their influence felt in the cause of good roads. They realize the importance of them and have started an agitation which is destined to spread over the entire country. The Automobile Club of America started the new propaganda several weeks ago at a special good roads meeting at the Waldorf-Astoria, when prominent leaders of the movement delivered addresses." Those addresses were compiled by the club and issued in a pamphlet called *A Plan for Good Roads*. Chairman of the good roads committee was Albert Shattuck.[40]

In March 1900 the League of American Wheelmen decided to work independently of the ACA in the good roads movement. It had been working together with that group but chose to confine itself to the construction of side paths. The wheelmen were willing to pay for them themselves. "In the second place, the hard roads will soon be overcrowded with automobiles running at the rate of 20 to 30 miles an hour, which will make the highways unsafe for wheelmen until the road builders have learned to build much wider and better roads." An editorial in the *Horseless Age* declared, "The decision is not surprising. We have never had any faith in the attempt to affiliate old and new trades. The bicycle and the carriage trades which cannot be successfully harmonized with those of the motor vehicle trade. Efforts to accomplish this will only result in friction and loss to all interests concerned."[41]

The title of the pamphlet issued by the Auto Club was *A Plan for Good Roads in New York State*. Speakers at the meeting and those whose addresses were contained in the pamphlet included: Albert Shattuck (chairman of the Good Roads Committee of the ACA); General Roy Strong (Office of Road Inquiry, Washington, D.C.); Edward A. Bond (State Engineer of New York); H.J. Budd (State Road Commissioner of New Jersey), E.J. Harrison (Office of Road Inquiry, Washington, D.C.); J.C. Maidenhall (Massachusetts Highway Commission; and Isaac B. Potter ["prominently identified with the League of American Wheelmen]" [bicyclists]). That was a lobbying effort to get the public to pay for more and better roads for the use of the wealthy class. Shattuck "spoke of the contention made in America and nowhere else in the world that superior railway facilities rendered improved highways unnecessary" and called such ideas "absurd." Examples were cited in the article to try and shame states. It was said that New Jersey and Connecticut had spent sums ranging from $1,289,000 to $3,137,00 in road improvements while New York State had spent less than $100,000 on the same thing.

Roy Stone spoke of a new hope for the case of good roads in the rise of the "powerful" automobile interests. "The accession of your organization and all the powerful business interests behind it to the forces heretofore working for road improvements form an era in the history of the cause." That good roads movement, Stone continued, "is a growing and a widening effort all over the United States, but it has lacked the co-operation of great business organizations, and to some extent, the direction of trained business minds."[42]

The *Horseless Age* was tireless in its promotion of the roads issue. In the summer of 1900, it noted that the agitation for good roads received recognition in the form of a plank of the Republican party adopted at Philadelphia. The editor noted those interested in good roads should press the agitation into Congress. "Bad roads cost more in the wear and tear of the vehicles and horses that transverse them than would be expended in maintaining good roads, and a rational move forward cannot come too soon."[43]

By the beginning of 1901, a journalist remarked that automobile clubs were already "quite numerous in this country." He argued the formation of so many clubs had to have a very stimulating effect on the industry, "first by creating interest in automobilism among the general public, and second by favoring concerted action in the cause of good roads, in urging legislation favorable to the automobile, and in protecting the common interest of users of automobiles."[44]

The pioneer car club was the Automobile Club of America, formed on June 7, 1899, at a meeting at which nine people were present. The number of members, as of January 1901, was "not far from 300." Other clubs included the Chicago Automobile Club organized on August 3, 1900, with 40 charter members and numbering 50 members as of the beginning of 1901. The Buffalo Automobile Club was another, along with the North Jersey Automobile Club (Paterson, NJ), organized in April 1900. The Automobile Club of Bridgeport (CT) was formed on September 13, 1900, with 25 charter members. The Pennsylvania Automobile Club (Philadelphia) was organized by 20 charter members while the Automobile Club of Philadelphia was organized on April 20, 1900, and had grown to 45 members. It was said to have induced the Fairmount Park Committee to throw open the park to motor vehicles. The Quaker City Automobile Club was organized in the second week of December 1900 with 18 charter members. The Long Island Automobile Club had recently incorporated with 62 members, 40 were on the waiting list and 34 of the members owned autos. The Massachusetts Automobile Club (Boston) had 32 members. Members did not have to own a car, but officers had to be owners.

Other clubs in existence included: the New England Automobile Club (Boston); the Automobile Club of Brooklyn (40 members); the Westchester Automobile Club; the Rhode Island Automobile Club (Providence, 45 members, 20 on a waiting list); Indiana Automobile Club (Indianapolis); the Automobile Club of Southern California (Los Angeles, 18 members at inception, then 30); the Automobile Club of Baltimore; Columbia College Automobile Club; and the Automobile Club of Columbus, Ohio.[45]

At the start of 1901, it was reported that the National Association of Automobile Manufacturers had 26 "active members," all manufacturers. The organization had a second category of membership, "associate." That category was open to manufacturers of accessories, sales agents, and publishers of automotive trade journals. Active membership was a category exclusively for manufacturers. The group had 23 associate members including two publications, one of which was *Horseless Age*. Associates included tire firms and rubber companies. From the constitution and bylaws the object of the group was "to advance and protect the interests of the trade; to procure an adjustment of freight rates; to promote good roads; to procure proper legislation and the modification of recent rulings of the United States Treasury Department about transportation of gasoline vehicles on the water-ways; to deal with the question of national shows and exhibitions, and with such other matters as may properly come within the scope of such an organization."

Regarding auto shows the procedure was that when the secretary of the organization had been advised of any projected or proposed show or exhibition, he should at once forward to all members a statement of the general purpose of such show, the auspices under which it was held, and any other information valuable to the association. Upon the receipt of such information, each member was to inform the secretary of his attitude toward the proposed show, "the result of the consensus of opinion thus obtained relative to the show [is] to be forwarded by the secretary to all members to assist them in forming individual judgments in the matter of exhibition."[46]

At a meeting of the executive of the National Association of Automobile Manufacturers held February 7, 1901, it was resolved that the Boston auto show (March 4–9), under the auspices of the Massachusetts Automobile Club, was approved. The resolution said, "it will be a show in which manufacturers may find it to their advantage to exhibit, and that decision as to exhibiting be left to the individual members of the association."[47]

At a meeting of the members of the Automobile Club of California President F.A. Hyde gave details of the work of the organization's directors over the previous three months in securing the passage of ordinances favorable to automobilists by the Boards of Supervisors of the counties of San Francisco, San Mateo, Santa Clara, Contra Costa, and Sonoma. No specific details were provided in the news report except that "Copies of the ordinances passed in San Francisco and San Mateo counties are being forwarded to other boards of Supervisors throughout the State, and it is hoped that they will form the basis of similar legislation."[48]

When the Board of Governors of the Automobile Club of America met late in 1901, the standing committees of the group for 1902 were ratified and announced. Most of those committees were larger than when they were first established. The Law Committee had six members; George F. Chamberlin, James C. Church, Dave Hennen Morris, Henry Rogers Winthrop, William W. Niles, and Morris Putnam Stevens.[49]

In a review piece at the start of 1902, a journalist remarked that the automotive market had been "greatly aided" by the formation of automobile clubs, of which there were then 36 "recognized by the Automobile Club of America, while quite a few are as yet non-recognized clubs." And, the newsman added, "The legal status of the automobile has been fixed during the year by laws enacted by the legislatures of New York, Connecticut, and other states which seem well calculated to safeguard the rights of automobilists and to insure untrammeled progress of the movement." Also noted was the right of automobiles to be carried on ferries, which was "brought about by the efforts of the Automobile Club of America." Initial bans had been placed on cars due to the flammable nature of their fuel, gasoline.

"So far as the question of automobile legislation is concerned the chief desideratum now is the passing of uniform laws in all the States, and a step toward securing this end has been made by the Automobile Club of America in proposing a national league of automobile clubs, one of whose chief objects would be to secure uniform legislation," the reporter explained. "The show nuisance has received an effective check by the action of the National Association of Automobile Manufacturers." He meant that if the lobby did not approve and condone a show or exhibition then none of its members would participate and thus the show would never take place.[50]

The editor of the *Horseless Age* celebrated, celebrated, early in 1902, gloating over the success of the machines. "The growing leniency toward change has been particularly noticeable in the attitude of the public toward the automobile in the United States. Notwithstanding the sweeping nature of the changes contemplated by the new system of locomotion, comparatively little opposition has been offered to the legitimate introduction of the automobile in any part of the country." He continued, "The attitude of the public has, in fact, been so favorable to the new vehicle that promoters and manufacturers have in many cases taken advantage of it to impose upon the public with worthless stocks and imperfect vehicles [not long before the editor had argued that no manufacturer would impose imperfect vehicles on an unsuspecting public], while users, too often, have ignored the common laws of the road, to the injury of other users and the detriment of the industry as a whole." Thus, the editor concluded, it was not the opposition of the public or the special vested interests that the auto industry had the most to fear. "The worst enemies of the industry are not without. They are within," such as stock jobbers and inexperienced salesmen who sold their vehicles "indiscriminately."[51]

All was not perfect, though, among the various auto organization. It was admitted that the ACA had so far been unsuccessful in enlisting the cooperation of several Indiana automotive clubs in recognizing it "as a governing body." The local clubs had, until then, been unwilling to pay the extra dues to the ACA and to lose their "individuality." As far as the ACA was concerned the object of affiliation of local clubs to the national governing organization "is to secure co-operation in all sections in the good roads movement and to break down the prejudice which exists in some quarters against motor vehicles."[52]

Charles Duryea, president of the American Motor League, said at the start of 1902 that the time was ripe to push forward the question of a national organization for motor vehicle users, that is, the American Motor League, organized in Chicago in 1895. It had been inert since that time because of a lack of members and a lack of sufficient interest to make such a body a success. He noted that membership in auto clubs had increased greatly in the past year and he claimed that his group, the American Motor League, was then soliciting members. He urged interested people to contact the acting secretary, Harry O. Koller, in Reading, Pennsylvania.[53] One week later Duryea argued it was a well-known fact that many people of "moderate means" were afraid to buy cars because of the fear of damage suits. However, his organization would be "a league with a good attorney and a large number of members will do much to remedy this state of affairs, and for this one reason alone, if for no other, the American Motor League, with a popular membership and a large number of members, should be encouraged."[54]

Discussing the proposal from Duryea to revive the American Motor League, the editor of the *Horseless Age* noted the association had a brief period of existence in the early days of the industry. The reason given for its revival was that there was an "urgent need" for such an organization, at least that was how Duryea saw it. The editor wondered if that was true. He saw interest divided into two groups; auto users and the auto industry. Thus, the editor saw a need (or room) for two organizations, one for each group, since the requirements of the two groups did not completely overlap. He cited NAAM (the National Association of Automobile Manufacturers) and ACA (the Automobile Club of America) and declared those two organizations "represent every interest the automobile movement has." At that point, the ACA was in the process of trying to get every local and regional club to affiliate with it, and "it is most probable that a basis of affiliation will shortly be arrived at which will satisfy practically all clubs and will lead to a strong national organization." Nothing else was needed the editor argued, except that sought-after affiliation.[55]

At a meeting of the board of governors of the ACA on February 11, 1902, it was resolved to abandon the club affiliation scheme as originally proposed by the club and to suggest to the clubs which had refused the affiliation plan (the auto clubs of Chicago, Massachusetts, Long Island, Rhode Island, Philadelphia, and Worcester) that they, together with the ACA, call a convention of two delegates from each club to be held in Chicago during March for "the purpose of forming a national association of clubs."[56]

At that meeting, held on March 2, at which an attempt was to be made to form a national association of automobilists, the promoters of the plan advocated an interdependent federation of clubs to aid in the development and use of motor vehicles. That proposal envisioned all automobile clubs of "acceptable repute" being eligible for membership "on an equitable basis of representation in all deliberative matters within the purview of the association. The old affiliation collapsed on that very rock for under that system the ACA was to have been vested with the sole power to make and enforce rules of every description." One of the goals of the new organization, which it hoped to reach through club cooperation, was "enactment of liberal laws regulating the use of automobiles on public highways." When the ACA offered its plan of affiliation in the fall of 1901 there was "general opposition, particularly on the part of big clubs." When the New York club decided to abandon the plan the idea of a new organization began to take shape.[57]

Some agreements were reached at that meeting. It was agreed that individuals could not join ACA, only clubs. Individuals had to join their local clubs. That was still a preliminary deal and no final, broad agreement was reached. Also agreed was, concerning voting, each club would have the right to cast one vote for each active associate, and life member. Some local clubs remained strongly opposed to the ACA. The Massachusetts Automobile Club sent no delegates to Chicago.[58]

The third annual banquet of the ACA was held at the Waldorf-Astoria Hotel in New York City on March 7, 1902, and was attended by, reportedly, 200 "gentlemen." After-dinner speeches were devoted almost entirely to the subject of road improvements, many of them "congratulating the club upon the stand it has taken in furthering the cause of good roads." The opening address was delivered by Albert R. Shattuck, president of the ACA. He observed that the good roads committee of the group had done much to improve highways by circulating printed matter and by appearing before the committees of the legislatures.

In January 1902 Shattuck was a member of the convention in the interest of road improvement held at Albany, New York. That convention consisted of nearly 300 members of the boards of supervisors and highway commissioners, from New York counties. That club, the ACA, in connection with six of the leading clubs of the country that same week had formed the American Automobile Association (AAA) in Chicago. Jacob A. Cantor, president of the Borough of Manhattan, spoke on the highways of Manhattan. Cantor declared, "The gentlemen of the club [ACA] are to be congratulated on the fact that their committees in Albany do their work in urging the legislators to provide funds for good roads.... I am with this club on behalf of good roads."[59]

At the same time in Chicago, a meeting was held, on the 6th, to attempt to revitalize the American Motor League. In elections, Edwin F. Brown of Chicago was elected president while Charles E. Duryea was elected first vice president. A committee was appointed to revise the constitution to provide for state organizations, which would employ their attorneys to defend any cases that arose against car drivers. The objectives of this group were "to secure good legislation" in the future and the improvement of the road in every state of the union.[60]

On April 1, 1902, the first meeting of the board of directors of the American Automobile Association was held, at the ACA headquarters building. The seven members of the board included AAA president W.E. Scarritt, plus two members of the ACA, of which Shattuck was one.[61]

Scarritt sent out an invitation to all auto clubs in the United States that had not yet joined the AAA. The aims of his new organization were set out as follows: (1) the securing of national legislation; (2) the formation of proper rules governing the use of the automobile; (3) protecting the interests of automobilists against unjust discrimination; (4) maintaining their lawful rights and privileges; (5) encouraging the use of the automobile and its development; and (6) promoting the good roads movement.[62]

The *Horseless Age* editor looked at the good roads movement in the spring of 1902 and remarked on the "strong initiative being taken by the automobile clubs in the movement for the improvement of roads." He admitted that local roads, especially in the spring, impeded the growth of cars. "In the country there are at present few districts where a vehicle can be used all the year around" and that impaired the further introduction of automobiles. Also, bad roads led to greater wear and tear on cars and that led to more repairs and expenses. A major dream of the automobilists was a national highway from New York to San Francisco. The editor admitted, "the automobile is more dependent upon good roads than the horse. The better the roadway the greater is the advantage of mechanical traction over horse traction." Automobile touring would only be possible when good roads had become common. "It is hoped that the newly formed American Automobile Association will use all its influence to have this national highway built. It could serve the industry in no better way."[63]

Three members of the ACA who exceeded the New York State speed law in the Long Island Endurance Run on April 26, 1902, were called before the board of governors of the organization on May 23 for possible disciplinary action. The result was that Kenneth A. Skinner was suspended from all privileges of the club for three months while John Grant Lyman was similarly suspended from the club, but for six months. A journalist congratulated the club for its stand and declared, "Another prominent club [AAA] which adopted a resolution to punish members who were found guilty of speed excesses has often been accused of never having put this resolution into force. It has also been hinted that the A.C.A. would not actually proceed against offenders..." but this action by the board of governors was "an effective answer" to such complaints.[64]

A New York City newspaper reported, "The Automobile Club of America was the first to encourage the sport and pastime of automobiling in this country, and it is the first organization to come out earnestly in favor of fast speeding in the highways. The action of the club in this respect has been well received, but considerable surprise has been expressed at the fact that other automobile organizations have remained quiet on the subject." The fact that NAAM and AAA have taken no action "has caused surprise in some quarters." J. Baynard Backus, chairman of the Committee of Fifty, opposed increasing the legal rate of speed of vehicles in the congested streets of New York City. He stated, "You might call the Committee of Fifty, a committee of public safety. It is composed of citizens so well known that it is needless for me to say that they are actuated simply by a desire to protect the people of New York from a spirit of recklessness and lack of consideration."

Backus added that his organization was not opposed to the automobile "but it is opposed to the streets of this city being used with an utter disregard for the rights of others by some automobilists who seem to have more money than brains, and who seem to be possessed of an absolutely selfish disregard for others." As soon as the Committee of Fifty was formed, the West End Association offered it assistance and support and since then the two organizations had worked together. Backus concluded, "I have been astonished at the evidence which has been brought to my attention as chairman of this committee as to how intensely the mass of the people feel on this subject. I trust the automobilists, for their own interests, may realize this feeling of indignation and call a halt."[65]

On October 1, 1902, *Horseless Age* published a list of automobile clubs both in the United States and in Europe. The American listings totaled 56 organizations including NAAM, AAA, ACA, and the American Motor League. Many of the listings gave a contact name, many did not.[66]

When the *Horseless Age* published its summary of the automobile industry in America for 1902 it remarked the year was most prominent as the year of the organization of the American Automobile Association. "Automobile clubs had been in existence for some years, but the multiplication of automobile competitions and their consequent disputes, as well as the increase of seemingly unjust legal persecution of automobile users and of tyrannical regulations, made the formation of a strong national body most desirable...." Also noted was that accidents had been "alarmingly numerous and a hostile feeling toward the automobile, or rather to the abuse of the automobile, has developed strongly in some localities."[67]

At its annual meeting in January 1903, the AAA sent a circular to all automobile clubs in the nation. "For self protection, therefore, the automobilists of the country should have some organizations representative of the entire body that could look after, protect and defend the interests of automobilists wherever seriously menaced. In union there is strength, and the strength of one should be the strength of all. How can this desirable result be better accomplished than in a well organized, clean-cut, compact, businesslike national organization?" The circular took care to point out it was not intended that the national organization should by any means undertake to defend the case of every automobilist who might be arrested for violation of the law "but the national organization should be prepared to interest itself in cases where flagrant injustice was clearly manifest and seek to have reversed any judicial decisions which were clearly wrong." The American Automobile Association also made an appeal to any automotive club in the nation that was not yet a member to join the AAA.[68]

The Automobile Club of Cincinnati was, reportedly, "taking steps" to have an ordinance passed regulating the use of cars in Cincinnati. Max Fleischman, acting for the club, handed to Cincinnati's vice mayor Christie copies of ordinances that had been passed by other cities. "The best parts of these will be taken and incorporated in an ordinance which will be handed to the board of legislation, with a request from the club for its passage." One part of the proposed bill had the automobile owner compelled to register with the city. That entailed giving his name and the number of automobiles he owned. A license would then be issued. The city "will issue an ornamental tag, of some kind, probably one with the initials of the owner of the car. There will also be a regulation as to speed, but just what limit will be asked by the club has not yet been decided."

Automobiling had become so popular with over 100 devotees in Cincinnati "that the club has come to the conclusion the city should take a hand in the regulation of their use." In conclusion the journalist noted that as the city would have doubtless regulated the automobile as soon as "the club decided if they could secure the passage of an ordinance drawn up under their supervision it would be far less likely to be detrimental to the use of automobiles than if left to some ignorant legislator to draft and to bring before the board for passage."[69]

The Cincinnati auto ordinance "which was drawn up at the instance of the Cincinnati Automobile Club" was introduced at the March 2, 1903, meeting of the City Board of Legislation. It required a car owner to register with the city and pay $3 a year for a license tag with numbers four inches tall. The speed limit was set at a maximum of seven miles an hour in an area bounded by Broadway, Water, Court, and John streets, and a maximum of 15 miles an hour everywhere else. L.S. Coulter of the Cincinnati Automobile Club said of the proposed law, "In view of the fact that the rather liberal rate of speed of 15 miles per hour is permitted in by far the larger part of the city, the automobile club members feel that they should not object to the very low speed of 7 miles per hour in the congested portion of the city ... and which bound a distance of nine blocks north and south and nine blocks east and west. In this part of the city the street traffic is so heavy that users of automobiles would scarcely be able to make with safety better time than 7 miles an hour, even if permitted."[70]

A compromise was reportedly effected in the proposed law regulating the licensing of autos in New Jersey. Assemblyman Scovel, who introduced the pending measure, held a conference with Karl G. Roebling and John S. Broughton, who represented the New Jersey Automobile Club. The result was "practically an agreement to have the committee which now has the custody of the Scovel bill report a substitute which will afford complete protection to the users of the public highways and not work hardships to the automobilists." The new bill is expected to go through the Legislature without opposition or amendment.[71]

The compromise measure in New Jersey provided speeds of 10 and 20 miles per hour with physicians and surgeons exempted "while actually going to or returning from professional calls" except of an emergency. Every New Jersey resident automobile owner and non-resident owner whose auto was driven in New Jersey was compelled to file a statement that included name and address and a brief description of the machine, and pay a $1 fee for each vehicle. An owner had to have the initials of his name and the number of his license on the back or side of each vehicle, plainly visible, with numbers to be at least three in total and not less than two inches tall. Lights had to be turned on one hour after sundown and remain on until one hour before sunrise. Automobiles had to have brakes and a horn or bell. Automobilists could not be prohibited from the use of any public thoroughfares including parkways "by any local regulation." For violation of any provision of the act, the offender would be fined $25. There were a reported total of 40 physicians and surgeons in New Jersey that used autos in paying professional calls and most of their work was in the cities.[72]

As of February 28, 1903, the Automobile Club of America had a total membership of 418, of which 346 were active members and 72 were associate members. Those members then owned a total of 542 automobiles and they had a total of 147 cars on order.[73]

Automobilists of Fremont, Nebraska, organized a club for self-protection in the spring of 1903. One of the club's bylaws provided for a council board of three members whose duty was to examine every accident involving an auto. If the group found the driver was to blame he would be disciplined by the club. If he was found to have observed the rules of the road but was sued for damages the club would defend him with legal counsel.[74]

According to a reporter the American Automobile Association adopted a plan for the formation of state divisions which would make it possible to follow more closely the trend of legislation in the different states and do more "effective work in this line." Almost simultaneously the New York State Association of Automobile Clubs was formed to do much the same work. That latter organization combined practically all the local clubs outside New York City while only three clubs in New York State—the ACA, the Long Island Automobile Club, and the Rochester Automobile Club—were not then members of the AAA. At that time, in the fall of 1903, there were about 100 automobile clubs in the United States. With the clubs of the New York State Association AAA had a membership of about 15 clubs "but these are nearly all important clubs" and the voting membership of the AAA will probably be nearly one-half of the aggregate club membership of the nation.[75]

Chapter 5

Speed, 1895–1901

The first issue of the trade journal *The Horseless Age* appeared in November 1895. Beginning as a monthly but soon becoming a weekly, it vigorously lobbied for all things automotive and relentlessly attacked anything it perceived as even vaguely anti-automobile. Its editor and proprietor was E.P. Ingersoll. In the publication's second issue, Ingersoll commented that speed was of ever-growing importance because "the pressure of the age demands it." Still, he admitted, speed was then limited but "at some future day, when roads are universally good and motor vehicles are no longer a novelty; when people are accustomed to managing them and taking them into account as a factor of danger in street life, high rates of speed will be permissible, where road conditions are favorable; but for the present it is neither necessary nor desirable."

Prudently, he observed, "Legal measures, limiting the speed of motor vehicles, are as much needed as measures regulating the speed of bicycles and horse-drawn conveyances, and for the same reason, namely, the public safety." Fines for speeding were well established before the advent of the motor vehicle. During his term as United States president (1869–1877), Ulysses S. Grant was stopped on 14th Street in Washington, D.C., for speeding. He was driving along at a comfortable gait when another horse team passed him. That caused Grant to speed up and overtake the other team. A policeman observed the scene and pulled Grant over. The president paid a fine, unspecified in this account.[1]

Automotive pioneer Charles Duryea was president of the American Motor League when he commented on an upcoming auto road race. The awards in that race were to be made on a point basis as follows: speed 50; construction 25; operation 15; and cost 10. Duryea opposed that point system because he believed it offered a premium for speed, "whereas the crying need of to-day is not speed, but better construction and better operation, and possibly, to suit the desires of the masses, less cost." The fact that the winning machine made 7.5 miles per hour over roads far too bad to permit "any such speed for horse flesh, indicates that the speed of the present motor vehicle is already up to the legal limit allowed in cities, and up to or nearly as high a limit as safety will permit, even in the country."[2]

An early article in *Horseless Age* discussed the differences between the road vehicle and the track vehicle [mainly the streetcar]. In the case of the latter the possession of the right-of-way rendered possible the construction of a roadbed suitable for high speed and which prevented, as far as circumstances allowed, the road vehicle from interfering with its progress. Thus, it was argued, the speed of the track vehicle is greater than is possible for the road vehicle to attain in crowded streets. The article went on to discuss speed for motor vehicles, noting the motor vehicle was a road vehicle "and must be governed by the same general rules and conditions that now apply to the horse vehicle.

"Where roads are good and few vehicles are encountered, high speeds will be permitted, but where there are many vehicles to share the common rights of the road, or where the obstructions lie only on the road itself, high speed is not to be thought of." Thus, it was concluded, the demand for speed can only be satisfied by an improvement of the roads on which the vehicles must travel, and by reducing or eliminating the obstructions in their path. Even at that early date the demise of the streetcar to favor the automobile was envisioned. It was also concluded that before any increase in speed was gained for the automobile, roads had to be improved.[3]

The first reports of speed complaints seem to have been made in the summer of 1898. At that time a reporter observed, "Several motor carriages are in use in Cleveland, O., and the citizens are beginning to complain of the excessive speed at which they are run." Continuing, the newsman declared, "The sensations attending the operation of a motor carriage are so strangely exhilarating, and the sense of reserve power so great, that it is hard for the driver of the motor to restrain himself, and keep the every day jog of the horse in mind, but in the interests of all it must be done."[4]

Horseless Age commented on speed limits that were implemented in France in the summer of 1898. "The result of the agitation at Paris against the reckless speed of motor carriages is the fixing of a speed limit of 12 miles an hour in the city, and 18 miles an hour in the country. This is certainly very liberal treatment." The publication added, "The chauffeurs are virtually left free to use their own discretion as regards the speed to be taken at any given time and place. They will have nobody but themselves to blame if the authorities shall find it necessary to take further action in the matter." For this journal, it was obvious that class interests were involved, because it concluded, "The Automobile Club numbers among its members many of the wealthiest and most influential men in France, and to its intercession the lenient course of the police is undoubtedly due."[5]

In February 1899 *Horseless Age* smugly reported, "During the past three years warning notes have been sounded … time and again at the disposition to scorch [speed] manifested by motor vehicle drivers, both in France and the United States. It was pointed out that the evil would finally become so aggravated that serious accidents would result, and the attention of the authorities be directed by public sentiment to the regulation of the speed of all motor vehicles, on a basis that could hardly be satisfactory to enthusiastic lovers of this new sport."

Reportedly, that critical period had been reached in France. The Council of State had reiterated its sanction of a speed of 12 miles per hour in Paris and 18 miles an hour in the country. But police officers in plain clothes and mounted on gasoline-powered tricycles were to be detailed to watch for offenders and in case of an attempt by the speeder to escape, "they will be enabled to overtake any ordinary four-wheeled vehicle with comparative ease. If the experiment is a success, numbers of those mounted policemen will be assigned to the boulevards and principal thoroughfares, to see that the law is obeyed."[6]

Six months later news came from Paris about a contemplated crusade against fast driving of cars. A resolution to suppress auto races was introduced in the General Council of the Seine et Oise and steps were to be taken by the chauffeurs themselves to regulate the speed of automobiles for their protection. "It seems that a strong sentiment against the new vehicle is forming in Paris and the suburban districts on account of the reckless speeds at which motor carriages are driven, particularly by novices," reported a newsman. "The gendarmes are powerless to control the crazy chauffeurs in the city, and in the country many hostile demonstrations against offenders have been made, impediments having been placed on the road or stones hurled at them in some instances."

Because the orderly element had to suffer for the sins of the lawless, the members of the Automobile Club "are beginning to see the necessity of taking a stand in favor of a reasonable regulation of speed." Given those developments, the journalist thought "A useful lesson, however, may be brought home to this side of the Atlantic." American automobile clubs should profit from the French experience and set a better example to their members by taking a firm position on reckless driving.[7]

It was in the spring of 1900 that the issue of speed began to become more prominent in America. New York City newspapers were among the first to cover the issue. In May the editor of the *Sun* remarked drivers of cars "are being criticized on both sides of the Atlantic for going through the streets at a greater pace than people are used to, or the law allows." Many of those complaints originated in Paris but "from Chicago, Washington, and other large cities come similar complaints so that the 'scorching' automobilist has replaced the wheelman [bicyclist] as a target for public dissatisfaction."

The editor found it not surprising that the new carriages excited protest. He pointed out that streetcars were protested in the beginning but all were used to trolley cars by the time he was writing. There was something similar for the first few years that bicycles were used extensively, he believed. Paris, he reported, had imposed a speed limit on cars of five miles per hour, the same rule that applied there to other vehicles—within the city limits. Concerning the United States, the article declared, "It is to be hoped, however, that as the new carriages increase in number, their superior speed will impose admiration rather than fear, and that they and the community will adjust themselves each to the other as have the people, the bicycles and the trolleys."[8]

During that same month, a different New York City newspaper reported that the West Side Association of that city had made special efforts to have the police compel cars to go at a slower rate of speed on the Upper West Side streets and avenues. Members of the association complained that those machines were run at a speed dangerous to pedestrians. John L. Brower, a member of the association, stopped a Locomobile run by John Brant in the employ of the American Locomobile Company, who said he was willing to appear in the West Side Police Court in answer to a summons to make a test case. Accordingly, Brant appeared before Magistrate Mayo. He told Mayo he had been arrested before and arraigned before Magistrate Meade who discharged him on the grounds that there was no law covering locomobiles and automobiles. Mayo then adjourned the case to confer with Meade. A couple of days later Mayo decided cars came under the law and fined Brant $3, which the West Side Association paid, as Brant had been so accommodating about the case.[9]

For several days in June 1900, there was much talk in Newport, Rhode Island, regarding the new automobile of William K. Vanderbilt, Jr., "and the rapid speed with which he has been driving it in and about the city." It was a gasoline-powered machine imported from France and "makes a great noise while in motion and is said to be equal to a speed of sixty or more miles an hour." On June 12 Vanderbilt called at the police station and talked with Police Chief Kaull, who informed his visitor of the complaints made about him "and gave him to understand that the law regulating fast driving must be complied with." The chief interpreted that to mean a speed not exceeding 12 miles an hour outside the compact part of the city and a much lower rate of speed within those limits. According to a report, "The entire interview was of a friendly nature, and upon leaving the place Mr. Vanderbilt and Chief Kaull shook hands in a cordial way, apparently with the best of understanding as to the course to [be] pursued by each in the future."[10]

One day later, "As a result of the automobile agitation in Newport," an ordinance was passed at a special meeting of the City Council that was intended to prevent fast driving in the future. That ordinance provided that in the compact part of the city speed must not exceed six miles an hour and outside the city proper, the limit was 10 miles per hour. Violation of the ordinance provided for a fine of $20 or 10 days in jail, or both. The ordinance covered all kinds of automobiles, bicycles, or any vehicle the propelling power of which was within itself. The matter of licensing auto drivers did not arise.[11]

A month later an editorial appeared about the Vanderbilt case. The piece began by arguing that it was to be expected that "hoodlums" would be persistent lawbreakers and "nobody is surprised when repeated warnings fail to induce some rough fellow on a bicycle or other vehicle to repeat the rules of the road and have regard for the safety of his fellows. Better things, however, are looked for from educated young men of wealth and social standing.... The law protects men of millions in the enjoyment of property which many envy and would be glad of excuse to loot. The millionaire who of his own notion shows them that he thinks laws are annoying things, to be broken at pleasure, is uncommonly thoughtless or uncommonly stupid."

Those remarks were prompted by the experiences of William Vanderbilt while on an auto trip from Newport to Boston and return. He was said to have gone through town at a rate of 65 miles an hour. At first, the police contented themselves with warning him. On his return trip, in defiance of the warning, "he persisted in speeding and was arrested and detained. The fine imposed, of course, meant nothing to him." In conclusion, the editor stated, "Our leaders in automobile driving should have more self-restraint, and their friends should seek to influence them in that direction if they do not wish to see more vigorous measures than fines employed to stop their dangerous practices."[12]

Even the *Horseless Age* weighed in with an editorial about the behavior of William Vanderbilt, Jr., although he did not specifically name the man. "One of these multi-millionaires, whose residence is in Newport, R. I., has been amusing himself, whenever the humor pleased him, by mounting his French racing machine and smashing records over the roads to Boston to the consternation of the citizens and the discomfiture of the authorities en route." Police were only able to detain him on his return journey when he was moving at a much slower rate of speed. According to the report, "Time and again the young Croesus has been brought before the bar and fined for reckless driving." Any fine was meaningless to Vanderbilt and he could have it many times over in a single day. "But what of the right of his fellow citizens, whose property and lives are imperiled by his recklessness? And what of the automobile industry, which must bear the stigma of his bad example and be still further restrained of the rights upon the road? If excessive and dangerous speed are indulged in by automobilists upon the common roads, legal restriction will be correspondingly irksome and unjust, and automobilists will have no one but themselves to blame for the curtailment of their liberties."

The editor stated the *Horseless Age* was flatly opposed to such behavior, calling it the "contraband sport" of road racing and declaring if it was "to be carried on by rich enthusiasts in this high-handed manner because the fines that can be levied under existing statutes are too small, we trust the penalty will be increased until the roads are completely rid of this nuisance."[13]

A report from a St. Louis newspaper on Christmas Day of 1900 observed that it cost Vanderbilt about $57.23 a ride to take pleasure jaunts in his car through the roads of Long Island, according to conservative estimates. He was said to collide often with teams and other vehicles. Whenever he did so he stopped his car, apologized, and told the owner of the other vehicle to send the bill to him. The bill was promptly paid. This article was humorous and tongue-in-cheek. It told of farmers in the general area where Vanderbilt traveled, fighting over the privilege of having their horse killed first.[14]

William Vanderbilt, seated in car, 1906. He was one of the more notorious speeders from the wealthy class. A fine of a few dollars was no deterrent to him or other members of that class.

Vanderbilt had been tearing up the roads around Newport. A reporter remarked that he "has broken many records and the laws of several States with his wonderful, monstrous-looking automobile the 'White Ghost' [and] had decided to get an even faster machine." He was annoyed when he learned some of his rivals in racing were planning on obtaining machines that could outdo the White Ghost, said to have a top speed of 55 miles per hour. Vanderbilt cabled the French makers of his machine asking if they could produce a vehicle that could run half again as fast as his current machine. The answer was yes. For 60,000 francs the French were prepared to deliver to Vanderbilt a machine with a guaranteed speed of 77 miles an hour. Immediately Vanderbilt cabled back to the maker, "Build it."[15]

A lengthy article pointed out that racing in automobiles was a "sport for rich men" and discussed how it felt to ride at top speed. According to the reporter, auto racing was the news that Americans had introduced in the year 1900 from France, Austria, and Germany, and that "promises to be the proper sport for rich men next season." A racing machine cost in the neighborhood of $10,000. "It is a rich man's sport, at least until the price comes down, but they regard it as worth the money." The article portrayed rich men racing about in cars as glamorous, daring, and exciting. The reporter presenting the story took a trip in a car driven by government "auto expert" Peter J. Fisher, Jr., who sneered at the idea the reporter had never traveled faster than eight miles per hour. Fisher had reached speeds of about 60 miles an hour. With the reporter as a passenger Fisher whizzed through the busy streets of New York City, including Wall Street, causing pedestrians to scatter in his wake. The tone of the article was positive, even ignoring any danger to which pedestrians had been subjected.[16]

In New York City the Committee on Law of the Board of Aldermen held a public hearing on a proposed ordinance to regulate the speed of cars. Alderman Otten of Queens condemned the speed of the automobiles in his borough. He even reached outside of his borough to attack Vanderbilt. Otten said, "Why, those automobiles go at least twenty-five miles an hour in Queens. I never saw them go less. There is one called the White Ghost, owned by Mr. Vanderbilt. It goes like greased lightning, and when it runs down a team and kills a horse, Mr. Vanderbilt turns around and goes away, and only says to have the bill sent to him and he will buy a new horse." Otten wanted an ordinance to limit the speed to a maximum of eight miles per hour in all parts of New York City. It was said that horses went at a speed of roughly five miles an hour. No decision was made at the hearing.[17]

Vanderbilt was summoned to the police court in Newport, Rhode Island, on August 31, 1901. He was fined $10 and costs for allowing his car to exceed the speed limit set by the city's ordinance. He promised the court he would observe the law hereafter. One day earlier in the same police court, Foxhall Keene (another extremely wealthy member of the Gilded Age) and Reginald Vanderbilt (part of the Vanderbilt family) were each fined for speeding.[18]

Toward the end of 1902, William Vanderbilt, Jr., was being interviewed about upcoming automobile races and he happened to mention speeding laws in passing. Vanderbilt said the laws regulating the speed of vehicles in the United States were "absurd."[19]

The village Trustees of Tarrytown in New York State passed an ordinance restricting the driving of automobiles and similar vehicles in the streets and public places of the town to a rate of speed not greater than eight miles an hour. Any person violating the ordinance was liable to a penalty of $25 for each offense. It was also provided that a violation of the ordinance would constitute disorderly conduct. As a newsman explained, "The machines are common in the neighborhood of Tarrytown, owing to the large number of wealthy residents and an automobile factory. Frequent accidents occurred and public sentiment led the trustees to take measures to restrict speed. The police have been ordered to see that the ordinance is 'strictly enforced.'"[20]

In September 1900 a court case was heard in Binghamton, New York, in the case of an automobilist arrested for exceeding the ordinance speed limit of eight miles per hour. The police officer making the arrest estimated the vehicle was traveling about 15 miles per hour, based on the amount of time it took the car to travel between two points that were later measured. Four other witnesses "were furnished" willing to swear it was their belief the machine was moving at under five miles an hour. A newsman sneered at the policeman's statement, declaring "Automobilists in the city were at once impressed with the ridiculousness of it."[21]

Harry Burhaus, a driver for the Duryea Power Company of Reading, Pennsylvania, was arrested for fast driving in the streets of Reading and sentenced to pay a $10 fine. Burhaus addressed a letter to a Reading newspaper explaining the ordinance under which he was convicted was unsuitable as applied to autos. Said the letter, in part, "The conviction was made under an ordinance passed in 1876 making it a misdemeanor to ride or drive on the streets of Reading at a speed 'faster than a common trot." An editor with the *Horseless Age* argued, "It is recognized that the highest speed possible, consistent with safety, is the speed most beneficial to the public." For this newsman, the ability to stop quickly, rather than the speed of travel "is the feature most insuring safety to the public."[22]

Assemblyman Woodruff of Orange, Connecticut, introduced a bill in the Connecticut Legislature that involved vehicles. Under the bill, no vehicle, auto, bicycle, two-, three-, or four-wheeled, propelled by electricity, steam, gasoline or any other power shall run on the highway at a speed that exceeded 12 miles per hour. Within the city limits or any city in the state, the maximum speed was not to exceed eight miles per hour. The fine for each offense was a fine of not less than $10 nor more than $100.[23]

In February 1903 the *Horseless Age* editorialized a warning: "The growing hostility of the people to the unlawful speeds of automobiles is beginning to find its legitimate outcome in restrictive legislation governing the speed of automobiles on the highway. These laws, as was long ago pointed out in our columns, are generally oppressive in their nature, reducing the speed of motor vehicles to a maximum below the limit at which an automobile can with safety be run through the streets of a settled community."

The editor did admit to the prejudice that had been engendered in the community by the recklessness of a few hotheads could not easily be removed. "If automobile legislation is to be influenced favorably to the industry steps must be taken at once by those having its interests at heart to rebuke the tendency to excessive speeds...," he concluded. And, he believed the first steps had already been taken by the Automobile Club of America. That organization had taken a "firm stand" against the scorcher whether he was a member or not a member of the club. That was an example the editor felt must be soon followed by all the other automobile clubs on the continent, "The worst obstacle in the path of a new industry is prejudice, and the worst enemy of that industry is one who fosters prejudice."[24]

At Mineola, on Long Island in New York State, a mass meeting of taxpayers was held. At that meeting, according to a reporter, "a strong protest was made against the excessive speeds at which automobiles are run by well-known automobilists of New York and Brooklyn on the main roads of Long Island, and a bill was prepared and endorsed giving the county supervisor power to limit the speed of automobiles within their jurisdiction. It is suggested in the bill the speed limit be fixed at 8 mph and that every automobilist be compelled to stop at a sign from a driver of a fractious horse." And that brought out the automobile lobby.

On hearing of that proposal, "Leading members of the Automobile Club of America were up in arms when they heard of the proposed action." A conference was immediately held between members of the group's Law Committee. The result of that conference was the drafting of a bill to be presented at Albany urged to be used as a substitute by the legislators. It was reported, "The club wishes to discountenance excessive speed, but objects to promiscuous legislation on the subject, such as would follow the enactment of such a law as proposed." Proposed instead by the Automobile Club of America was a speed limit of 14 or 15 miles per hour and "considerably less" in "thickly settled districts." Following the example of the Automobile Club of Great Britain, "the board of governors has passed a resolution to the effect that the abuse of the highways by drivers of automobiles should be and is disapproved by them, and that any member of the club who can be proved to have committed such an offense shall be suspended or dropped from the rolls."[25]

In the wake of such proposed laws as cited above, the *Horseless Age* was getting increasingly worried about the authorities clamping down on the automobile industry. At that time, in February 1901, the automobilists were still overwhelmingly a collection of rich men. The editor declared the auto trade was faced with the speed question in several states, among which were Massachusetts, Connecticut, and New York. In some cities in the Middle West, "it has been found necessary to raise a warning voice against reckless speed." In that emergency, the editor warned, "the duty of the automobile clubs throughout the country seems plain. They should follow the example of the Automobile Club of America and call to a strict account any of their members who are guilty of offending against the public order in this way, whatever their social position may be. The integrity of the industry demands it."[26]

At the same time in Chicago, city electrician Elliott, who was responsible for issuing automobile licenses, found it necessary to send out a warning against excessive speed to all holders of the city of Chicago auto licenses. In those warnings, the license holders "are especially enjoined to check the speed of their vehicles at all street crossings, and the police stationed at such places have been instructed to see that the law is enforced. One license has been revoked."[27]

At a meeting of the executive committee of the NAAM (National Association of Automobile Manufacturers) the matter of the restrictive legislation then before the New York State Legislature in the form of a bill by Assemblyman Smith the organization passed a resolution. The group resolved to endeavor to obtain a "special Hearing" on the speed bill then in the hands of the Assembly's Committee on Internal Affairs.[28]

Later in February representatives of the leading automobile clubs in the New

York State area began to appear before the Committee on Internal Affairs of the New York State Assembly to protest against the passage of the Smith act which would give to county supervisors in districts adjacent to cities of the first class the power to regulate the speed of cars within their jurisdiction. Those auto lobbyists favored a substitute bill providing for a uniform speed throughout the state. Their proposed speed limit was 10 miles an hour in cities and 12.5 miles per hour in the country. The Smith act proposal also required a driver to stop his machine on a signal from the driver of a frightened horse. Lobbyists for the industry included George F. Chamberlin, chairman of the Law Committee of the Automobile Club of America, and James C. Church, chairman of the Law Committee of the Long Island Automobile Club and counsel of the National Association of Automobile Manufacturers.[29]

The Law Committee of the Automobile Club prepared a substitute speed bill for the Smith measure that was then before the Committee on Internal Affairs of the New York State Assembly and submitted it to that committee. At the same time, it was reported, "the delegates of the Automobile Club afforded the legislators an opportunity of testing the control of the different kinds of automobiles, taking them to ride and giving demonstrations of the ease with which an automobile can be stopped at relatively high speed. All the members of the Committee on Internal Affairs are said to have availed themselves of this privilege." The club proposed that the speed limit be 10 miles an hour in built-up areas and 15 miles an hour outside such areas. One other section of the proposal was that no person owning or operating an auto would be required "to obtain any license or permit pursuant to the provisions of any local or municipal resolution or ordinance."[30]

Denver's city authorities passed an ordinance that prohibited operating an automobile at a speed greater than six miles per hour and, wrote a reporter, Denver "employs mounted policemen to enforce it."[31]

Editorials in American newspapers on the problem of speeding automobiles continued to appear in print. One from a New York City paper remarked, "There is an increasing tendency to run horseless vehicles at much higher rates of speed than the law permits in the case of horses, and indeed to claim for them and to concede to them the right thus to be run. It is difficult to conceive any convincing ground for this discrimination in favor of the horseless vehicle, and it is to be believed that the safety of the public will best be served by making and strictly enforcing a uniform rule for both classes of vehicles." The editor added, "It has yet to be demonstrated that a motor can be steered more surely and sharply or can be stopped more quickly than a horse. And there is to be set down against the horseless vehicle the fact that it is governed by only one intelligence instead of two."

Accidents were averted every day by the horses themselves which checked their speed or swerved to avoid obstacles, despite the urgings of a careless or inattentive driver. This editorial also argued for a higher penalty on car drivers who fled the scene of an accident. That was in an era with no license plates.

He reiterated that a maximum speed should be set that applied to all vehicles, whether horseless or horse-drawn.[32]

An editor with the *Horseless Age* penned a worrying piece about the number of automobilists driving at excessive speed recklessly and who flaunted their behavior by speeding away from any pursuing police officers. As far as the editor was concerned such people were forgetting other people had rights as well as themselves: "If automobiles wish their own rights to be respected they must avoid infringing the equal rights of others." Editor Ingersoll was especially annoyed with the Automobile Club of America. "And what of the Automobile Club of America and its high sounding resolutions? The question is no longer whether the automobile is to have its rights upon the road, but whether the automobile is to become a public nuisance and lawbreakers are to flaunt the club's banner as a protection for their crimes." The time had come, he argued, for the club to decide if it was to retain the confidence of the public. If it wished to do so "it must stiffen its back and wield the rod of discipline with no unsparing hand."[33]

A bill to regulate the speed of St. Louis autos came up before the city council in August 1901. It was reported favorably by Chairman Boyce of the Ways and Means Committee. The proposed bill required owners of such vehicles to pay a city license of $10 per annum. As well, it specified the speed of autos was not to exceed six miles per hour in parks and public places, nor eight miles an hour on streets and thoroughfares. Reportedly, "Automobile owners consider the proposed regulations as to speed and license unfair and inequitable, and they propose to fight the bill in the House of Delegates if the Council should pass it."

H. Edgar French was described as a "prominent" member of the St. Louis Automobile Club. He said, "In St. Louis there are now only about eighty motor vehicles and restraints such as are proposed could certainly result in quelling enthusiasm for the modern carriage. So far as speed is concerned, there should be no regulations. Speed is not limited in New York, Paris, Chicago, or other cities. Six miles an hour would be snail-like progress." French went on to add, "In New York owners of automobiles are not obliged to pay [for a] license. The city merely demands a registration fee of $1. The city of Chicago gets a fee of $3 the first year and $1 each subsequent year. The highest fee exacted by any city is much less than the license proposed for St. Louis automobiles.... St. Louis should not attempt to banish the automobile and be behind the times."[34]

That same month the Board of Supervisors of San Mateo County in California adopted an ordinance regulating the driving of automobiles on the county roads. The maximum speed allowed was 15 miles per hour. Upon approaching a vehicle drawn by horses or pedestrians leading horses, and when within 500 feet of such horses, the car operator had to slow down to six miles per hour and maintain that speed until such vehicle or pedestrian and horse had passed, and if required he had to stop the car and remain at a standstill until all danger of frightening animals had passed. The automobilists were also required to carry bells, gongs, or horns and to be equipped with a light when operating the vehicle at night.[35]

The Police Commission of Newport, Rhode Island, held a meeting on August 23, 1901, and the following resolution was passed, addressed to the National Automobile Racing Association of Newport: "We are of the opinion that the resolution of the City Council of Newport in relation to the use of certain streets by your association for the purpose of holding races does not contemplate nor authorize the speeding of machines in such races beyond the limits of the law. We do not, therefore, anticipate that it is our intention to become lawbreakers by exceeding such limit. Nevertheless, as it is commonly reported and believed that some of the machines taking part in the race will greatly exceed the legal limit we feel it but just that the board should notify you that any contemplated violation of the law governing the speed of such vehicles meets our disapproval, and that we shall take all reasonable steps to enforce the law."

That resolution was passed shortly after the secretary of the National Automobile Racing Association appeared before the Police Commission of Newport and asked about the detailing of the policemen. He was informed the police would not assist them in any way, but that men would be sent to protect the citizens of Newport.[36]

An editor with a Lincoln, Nebraska, newspaper was another who was in favor of speed. He remarked that European car race winner Henri Fournier was an idol in his home country of France. However, in the United States, "when Mr. Alfred Gwynne Vanderbilt attempts to race his sixty horse power car in Newport, he is arrested and fined." More generally the editor argued, in the United States, "the police keep a suspicious eye on owners of fast horses and fast gasoline carriages and if they are sped faster than the law or than the safety of the American pedestrian allows, the owners are arrested and fined and assessed the 'costs' of their own prosecution."[37]

Village authorities of Winnetka, Illinois, were adopting "strenuous measures" to put a stop to the excessive speed of cars through their streets. A village ordinance limited the speed of cars to nine miles per hour but it was asserted that speeds as high as 20 or 25 miles per hour were maintained through those streets by reckless drivers. Accordingly the president of the village board of trustees stationed sentinels at various points along the road on Sundays and holidays and devised a cable stretching across the street from tree to tree and guarded by men who warned the approaching automobilists of their danger and forced them to stop, when they were arrested and taken to court.[38]

Around the same time, the New York City Council demanded special ordinances be enforced—as a direct result of New York Police Department Officer John Hoey's death from injuries received after being run down by an automobile owned by Mrs. Bernard M. Baruch, whose husband was a famous member of the plutocracy. Council was urged to make efforts to better protect the public from the dangerous speed of automobiles. Thus, when the city council met, President Randolph Guggenheimer introduced a resolution that was promptly approved. It called attention to the numerous casualties and especially the killing of Policeman Hoey as the result of the high speed of automobiles. The resolution declared that the use of those vehicles made the use of the streets unsafe for foot passengers, as well as those in vehicles drawn by horses. However, it was a weak resolution, as the only thing it called for from the Police Department and the Department of Parks was to enforce with "greater vigilance" the rules and laws relating to the use of cars on the streets of New York City and in their parks.[39]

When a meeting was held in Mineola, Long Island, New York, it contained both pro and anti-auto forces. The meeting was called to consider ways and means of moderating the speed of cars in that section of Long Island. Among those present were Secretary Butler of the Automobile Club of America, Senator William Cocks of the New York Legislature, who was influential in securing the passage of the auto laws then in force in New York State, and S.D. Ripley, "a wealthy amateur residing in the vicinity." After considerable discussion with little or no progress made a committee consisting of Cocks, Butler, Ripley, and Benjamin D. Hicks was appointed to make a report at a future meeting of the most feasible means of "abating the nuisance."[40]

The question of automobilists strictly observing the speed regulations troubled the *Horseless Age,* yet again, at the end of October 1901. The editor noted that the Automobile Club of America agreed with the idea and then noted the *New York Herald* newspaper came up with some suggestions intended to increase the safety of both the driver and the public. White, the editor, felt some of those suggestions were to the point but "others seem of questionable policy." The New York paper pointed out the dangers of neophytes, inexperienced drivers learning to drive on the street on their own. As a remedy the publication suggested all drivers should be required to obtain personal licenses, granted after a successful examination as to their ability. A similar remedy was suggested to counteract the tendency of cheap construction. That is, every auto should be inspected and pronounced safe. The *Horseless Age* dismissed the second point by declaring no maker would sell a car he knew to be unsafe, either in principle or for want of proper material, and likewise, an owner would not be expected to mount a machine which he knew to be unsafe.

The editor whined, "Could we expect a municipal bureau with officials better qualified in this matter than either the manufacturer or owner?" He concluded, "The present automobile law of the State fully meets the necessity for legislative regulation of automobile traffic, and if there are still speed excesses and other abuses in the streets and on county roads it is not because the law is inadequate, but because it is not enforced with sufficient strictness."[41]

The issue of speed became increasingly important in 1902–1903. That was due to the dramatic number of auto accidents that occurred in America. Using the Chronicling America historical newspaper index (Library of Congress) the term "automobile accidents" produced 19 hits in total for the years 1895 to 1899. For the years 1901 to 1902 the total number of hits was 160. Finally, for the years 1902 through 1903 the number of hits was 1,524. As accident totals increased so did the death total.

Chapter 6

Speed, 1902–1903

As 1902 began the *Horseless Age* worried even more about speed regulations in New York State. "The temporary parole which automobilists of New York State received when the present measure became a law was destined, as we feared, to be of short duration. The intercession of the Automobile Club of America and its assurance that offenders were few and that its influence would thenceforth be wielded against excessive speeding on the public highways, even to the extent of expelling members found guilty of the offense, pacified our lawmakers for a time."

Meanwhile, the drivers of cars came under the strict surveillance of the public so that the sincerity of their protestations of innocence and good intent might be determined. "It was with regret we confess that at numerous and flagrant instances their conduct has been most disappointing to friends of the industry and irritating to the public at large." Cars, the editor noted, were rapidly getting bigger and gaining more horsepower. That meant they were capable of more speed and that led to more accidents and increasing severity of injury in those higher-speed crashes.[1]

The editor went on to blame "a sensational press" that harped on the speed of cars. Even many of the auto clubs had organized track races, off-street, and while legal "are nevertheless harmful in their tendencies; because the faster the speed mania stimulates the production of machines that had more and more horsepower—going full speed always violated the speed laws ... So far as the moral or deterrent influence of the automobile clubs is concerned we have yet to hear of a single case of reprimand or expulsion of any member while examples of law breaking so habitual and defiant as to have become a public scandal have been reported against them."[2]

He believed that what had happened was just what any student of human society might have anticipated. "The privileged few, unaccustomed to think of the rights of the many and full of the zest of a new pleasure, have persistently ignored the rights of the road. History from the dawn of the society shows that under such circumstances the many combine against the aggressors and curb their power." The editor lamented the fact that anti-speed bills at Albany were plentiful. That was so, because "of the lawless acts of automobilists themselves." The wealthy chauffeur "cares nothing for a fine of $25. In fact, he finds a certain satisfaction in paying it occasionally. It appeals to his pride and separates him from the common herd who cannot afford such indiscretions." A heavier penalty was needed, he argued. "The millionaire must be brought face to face with a punishment that will deter—a term in jail." A few such convictions, he believed, would do more to stop reckless automobiling than anything else by far.[3]

When George F. Chamberlin, chairman of the Automobile Club of America Law Committee was interviewed about the situation in New York State he said, "I think a penalty should be imposed sufficiently severe to effectually prevent racing on the public highways with motor carriages.…" To make any infraction of the law a misdemeanor may seem harsh, but perhaps nothing short of a fine and imprisonment will deter some drivers of automobiles. Chamberlin concluded, "The club is not opposed to any reasonable measure which will tend to make the public roads safe and prevent their use as speedways, even if some drastic measures become necessary."[4]

The Board of Supervisors of Westchester County, New York, took up the question of regulating the speed of cars on county roads. To that end, "The Judiciary Committee of the board has been directed to confer with representatives of the Automobile Club of America with a view to framing such rules and regulations as may be deemed advisable."[5]

A letter to the editor from David Provost was published in which he requested the support of New York State Assemblyman Julius H. Seymour (New York 19th District) for a bill introduced by Senator Cocks of Long Island regulating the speed at which autos could be driven in rural districts at 15 miles per hour and making a violation thereof a misdemeanor. Seymour said to Provost, "I am not in favor of the bill." When asked in whose interest Provost replied, "In the interests of the automobiles and the automobile people." He went on to explain what a menace to human life were these drivers when they got into the county, especially in danger were the lives of children. Seymour replied, "Keep your children off the roads then." After making a passionate plea for the bill and that it should be strongly supported, Provost concluded, "The automobilist and the automobile manufacturers who are now endeavoring to prevent the passage of this bill simply put themselves on record as not desiring either the passage of a just law or obedience to it."[6]

A new state law in Connecticut was enacted to regulate automobile traffic. Provisions in that law included a speed limit of 12 miles an hour in cities and 15 miles per hour elsewhere. Compulsory speed reductions were imposed at crossings as well as complete stops when horses hitched to vehicles showed signs of fright. That state law deprived cities, towns, and boroughs "of all rights to regulate automobile traffic, going much farther in that respect than the New York law," concluded a journalist.[7]

Assemblyman Holden of Woonsocket, Rhode Island, introduced into the Rhode Island Legislature a bill fixing the speed of motor vehicles on the highways of his state. It provided a speed limit of 12 miles per hour in Providence and 15 miles an hour on the country roads. Also, town councils and boards of alderman could grant, for a specified date, the privilege of operating motor vehicles at a more rapid speed—it was a proviso to allow for motor vehicle races. The bill was referred to a committee.[8]

E.S. Matheson of Denver, Colorado, was fined $25 and costs in police court in that city for violating the ordinance against fast driving. He appealed his conviction and was going to test the law on the ground that an automobile was not a horse and buggy. In testimony, Matheson claimed he was traveling at eight miles an hour and had perfect control of his vehicle, could stop it suddenly, and was not endangering life or property. Others testified he had been driving at about 20 miles per hour. Many complaints had been made against Matheson in the past and a year earlier he had been in court on a similar charge but escaped with a reprimand. Matheson was an employee of George E. Hannan, a Denver automobile dealer.[9]

In February 1902 a petition was filed by the members of the Stable and Carriage Owners' Association of San Francisco supported "by a large number of other signers," asking that immediate action be taken "to rectify the reckless and dangerous manner in which automobiles are driven over the principal streets of the city and county." It was asked that provision be made to regulate the speed of cars and to compel drivers to stop completely when necessary to prevent the frightening of horses. It was further asked that autos be numbered in such a manner that the police could identify owners or drivers who violated the proposed law. It was observed that cars were a great danger to pedestrians from the high rate of speed. Also remarked was that everybody, breeders, farmers, liverymen, horseshoers, harness makers, hay and grain dealers, wagon and carriage makers, "are all interested in the horse, but that the automobile is a stranger, a fad of the very rich."[10]

From a newspaper in the nation's capital late in March 1902, came an editorial on the topic of speed. It began by stating, "The attempts made to regulate the speed of automobiles in cities and on suburban driveways are meeting opposition from some of those who indulge in this sport. It is claimed that the restrictions placed on the running of these machines by bills now before state legislators will ruin the business by discouraging purchases." The editor concluded, "Automobilists must remember that there are several thousand people to each automobilist, and that while it is inspiring to look from a safe distance at an automobile dashing down Lancaster Avenue at the rate of twenty miles an hour it is not a humorous affair to those who are on the street and in the way of the machine. It is against the rash and not against the discreet automobilists that legislation is now proposed."[11]

A delegation from the Automobile Club of Massachusetts called upon state Governor Winthrop Crane to request him not to sign the bill, then before him, to regulate the speed of cars on public highways. It was pointed out to him the legality of the bill was doubtful in its provision requiring the automobilist to stop when a horse showed signs of fright. It was suggested Crane submit the bill to the Attorney-General of Massachusetts. The lobbying effort worked. One week later it was reported that Crane "has asked the Automobile Club of Massachusetts to draft a bill which, in their opinion would be as desirable for the one which recently passed both houses of the Legislature, but has not been approved by him in consequence of the opposition of automobilists."[12]

An editorial on speed appeared in a New York City newspaper in April 1902. It began, "The epidemic of speed law violations, if we may so describe it, on Sunday last was highly significant. It was from one point of view disheartening to lovers of law and order, inasmuch as it followed closely upon the enactment of a measure generously framed in the interest of fast driving. Certainly it seemed most ungrateful for men to celebrate the increase of the legal limit of speed by grossly and wantonly exceeding that increased limit." However, the writer was heartened by the disposition manifested by the magistrates to inflict rigorously the full penalty of the law upon all offenders. He worried, though, about the "manifestations of the mania which we may call speed madness, which seems to possess a considerable part of the community. This is a craze for going faster than the law permits."

It was, the editorialist suggested, the forbidden fruit concept, that whatever the speed limit was, those afflicted with speed madness would go faster. Of Sunday's offenders he wrote, "The personality of some of Sunday's offenders was ominous. There were among them members and even an important officer of an automobile club which has been cited in its professions of a respect for the law and in its declarations that it would sternly discountenance violations thereof. We have hitherto believed such declarations to be sincere, and have thought the best hope of the situation to lie in the authoritative influences of such organizations and of the law-abiding majority. The incidents of Sunday did not destroy that belief, though it would not be strange if they had shaken it, and if hope began to be based not so much upon voluntary moral suasion as upon inflexible enforcement of the law."[13]

George F. Chamberlin, chairman of the Law Committee of the Automobile Club of America, said in an interview with a journalist that he believed there would be difficulty in securing convictions for infractions under the anti-speed law and that unwarranted arrests were likely to be made unless some suitable method was adopted by the authorities to secure positive proof of the speed at which automobiles traveled. Said Chamberlin, "The word of a policeman that an automobilist exceeded the speed limit is not sufficient evidence, and his charge of an infraction of the law must be supported by corroborative testimony that can be sustained. Otherwise the assumption of innocence should prevail." Chamberlin also thought that magistrates' decisions, based on the unsupported testimony of police officers, if adverse to automobilists, would lead to frequent appeals to higher courts.[14]

In the middle of April 1902, it was reported that a police crackdown on speeders would take place in New York City. Both mounted and bicycle policemen had been instructed to keep a sharp lookout for speeding automobiles and to take offenders to the station "without hesitation." According to the police, there had been much uncertainty regarding the new speeding ordinance and that was the reason that so few arrests had been made. Police Commissioner John Partridge sent general instructions to the police force general commanders to see to it that the patrolmen under them were carefully instructed in the details of the crackdown on speeders. "Since the passage of a recent act in regard to automobiles, the police have been at sea in regard to their duties. Automobile owners, generally, are able to employ counsel and to make it disagreeable for any policeman who makes a false step in arresting any one of them for what he thinks is a violation of the law," remarked a newsman.

The instructions from Partridge stated, "You will see that the members of your command are properly instructed as to their duties, and will insist upon arrests being made when the legal rate of eight miles an hour is disregarded by those in control of automobiles." Concerning the new law the New York City Corporation Counsel gave the following opinion: "For driving an automobile at a speed greater than is reasonable he is liable to a civil action and a criminal prosecution as well. For not providing suitable brakes, bells, and lights he is liable to prosecution, both by a civil as well as a criminal action. For not stopping at the request of a person driving or riding a restive horse, he is liable to a civil action only, unless the automobilist's conduct should be disorderly. For not having the initials of the owner in a conspicuous place on the back of the automobile, the owner is liable to civil action only."[15]

That same month Richard Sylvester, superintendent of police in Washington, D.C., received from a number of large cities copies of recent laws or ordinances regulating the speed of automobiles. New York had speed limits of eight miles and 20 miles an hour (cities and country) while Newport, Rhode Island, had a limit of 10 miles an hour and St. Louis had a speed limit of seven miles an hour. Sylvester forwarded the information to the District of Columbia Commissioners.[16]

Another editorial on speed appeared in *Horseless Age* in the spring of 1902. "The reckless driving of automobiles in city and country by operators suffering with the speed mania is resulting in anti-automobile legislation all over the country. Accidents are occurring frequently…." The opportunity for accidents at 15 or 20 miles an hour or more was greater. "The public therefore receives the impression that automobiles are a menace to the safety of other users of the road and that practically all automobilists habitually run at law breaking speeds whenever they are out in their vehicles. The public thus becomes prejudiced against automobiles, and wherever ordinances or State house proposals to regulate automobile traffic, public sentiment is strongly opposed to the cause of the automobile."

Thus, the editorial continued, the proposal to raise the speed limit in New York City from eight to ten miles an hour "has met with determined opposition. A political club which sent out postal cards inquiring of residents of its district as to their position on the question received over 1,000 replies from persons opposing the change, while the number of favorable replies was only about 100.... Thus the unscrupulous scorchers seem to have spoiled the chances of the legal speed limit in the city being raised above the present very low 8-mile limit."[17]

The first test case under the New York State auto law was tried at Brighton, a suburb of Rochester. Harry S. Woodworth, described as a "prominent" citizen of Rochester, faced a charge brought by C.B. Parsons, a Brighton mail carrier. Parsons claimed Woodworth drove his car at a speed greater than 20 miles an hour and in doing so frightened a horse Parsons was driving. That caused a runaway and resulted in mail being scattered along the road. One question raised was how Parsons determined the rate of speed at which Woodworth was driving. The case was adjourned.[18]

Minneapolis Chief of Police Fred Ames had a plan for catching reckless automobilists. He wanted his officers to use motorcycles to catch them. He explained that the rapid increase of drivers in Minneapolis "and the persistency with which many of them break the fast driving ordinance" had forced home to the police the necessity of regulating their speed. "Mounted officers on the boulevard have reported their inability to keep within speaking distance of autos...." In Minneapolis, horseless carriages came under the ordinance limiting speed to six miles per hour. Policemen on foot had no chance to stop an auto with the driver speeding away from the foot officer often turning to "laugh back derisively." The bicycle officers also reported their inability to keep pace with cars. The most reckless driving of cars in Minneapolis occurred on Nicollet Avenue, where Ames remarked that the normal speed seemed to be 15 miles an hour.[19]

An ordinance was passed in the Missouri community of Belleville that regulated the operation of cars inside the city limits. All machines had to be equipped with bells or gongs which had to be sounded within 50 feet of a crossing. The speed limit was 10 miles an hour, except at crossings, where the limit was reduced to five miles an hour. According to a news item, "From time to time the attention of the city fathers has been directed to the speed at which some owners of automobiles in Belleville have been accustomed to driving their machines. It has been said that a number of serious accidents have been barely averted and that all were due to recklessness of the right of pedestrians and others on the part of the chauffeurs."[20]

According to a report from Freeport, Long Island, New York, District Attorney P. Nieman had begun to enforce the speed limit in that vicinity with what was likely America's first speed trap. On the Merrick Road, a quarter-mile stretch was laid out and policemen were stationed at each end. When a vehicle went across the line a signal was given by the officers at that point and at the other end the time was taken. If the vehicle arrived at a rate of speed that showed it traveled at more than eight miles an hour it was halted and the driver was arrested. Seven arrests were made on Sunday, July 6, 1902. A police justice was on hand and court was held. Two pleaded not guilty and were held on bail for trial at a later date. The other five pleaded guilty and were fined amounts that ranged from $5 to $15. That crusade against speeders in Freeport was expected to continue. In East Moriches, Long Island, there had been considerable friction between speeding drivers and the authorities. As a result, the following notice had been published, "A reward of $50 will be paid for evidence that will lead to the conviction of any violation of the law regarding the speed limit of automobiles on public roads in the town of Brookhaven."[21]

Later that month three speeders were arrested at Manchester by the Sea, New Hampshire. One of those arrested was George C. Cannon, the Harvard student "whose steam racer has brought him notoriety." When asked what made the police successful in those arrests a newsman remarked, "Stop watches and a measured road did the business." Meanwhile "prominent" citizens of Merion and Paoli Townships near Philadelphia filed sworn statements against 21 other "prominent" Philadelphians who were threatened with arrest unless the speed of their automobiles was moderated.[22]

The speed trap had thus been introduced and it became more popular as time passed. The mayors of the towns along the north shore above Chicago resorted to still more extreme measures to put a stop to scorching. The mayor of Glencoe stretched a wire cable across the road and stationed deputies with stop watches at marked intervals along the way. By prearranged signals, the automobiles were timed, and if the speed was found to be excessive the cable was made tight and escape was banned.[23] On Sunday, August 17, 1902, seven cars were stopped for speeding, and the drivers were arrested by the police of Evanston, Illinois. Each of the seven gave a bond of $50 for his appearance for trial on the following day. The police used a measured one-eighth of a mile course. With the legal speed limit of eight miles an hour that made 56 seconds the minimum time to cover the course. Those seven automobilists were timed as follows, in seconds; 28, 32, 39, 28, 29, 34, and 31. On Monday in court, each of the seven was fined five dollars.[24]

A chauffeur for automobile owner W.D. Guthrie in Oyster Bay, New York State, was named Dietz. He was discharged by Justice Wallace in court at Oyster Bay on the ground that the homemade timing device used by the deputy sheriffs who made the arrest failed to show results with reasonable accuracy. The apparatus used by the police consisted of three posts set one-eighth of a mile apart, and strings stretched from one to another, connected to a bell. When a vehicle passed the first post a deputy there pulled a string that rang a bell at the middle post. The deputy there then set his stop watch, and if the vehicle passed this post too early, he rang a bell at the last post and a deputy there arrested the offender. According to the article the system was proven to be inaccurate by "experts for the defense," although no details were provided.[25]

Lincoln, a town near Boston, passed an ordinance reducing speed in town from ten miles an hour (the Massachusetts state law) down to eight miles an hour. As well, a stretch of road for timing was laid out and a "police trap" was established. An editorial in *Horseless Age* grumbled about the state law in Massachusetts that allowed municipalities to reduce their speed from that mandated by the state. "It is pretty generally recognized that unreasonably low speed limits encourage reckless speeding," he whined. With no evidence or date, he declared, "there is nowhere in the world a more pronounced feeling against automobiles than in England, the land of the lowest speed limit. The conclusion seems justified that there actually is more reckless speeding in England than elsewhere." He argued that the most satisfactory way out of the difficulty "would be an amendment to the State law depriving local authorities of the right to reduce the speed limit in their territory.... And in other States automobile interests should insist on the minimum speed limit being established by the State and not by local authorities."[26]

For a long time, there had been an opinion in the minds of many Akron, Ohio, citizens, it was reported, that automobiles were run in the city at a speed greater than that allowed by the ordinance, which set the limit at 12 miles per hour. No arrests were made, however, until Superintendent A.H. Marks of the Diamond Rubber Company was arrested in the city for speeding. He appeared in police court, pleaded not guilty and the case was continued. When he appeared in court the case against him was dismissed. There seemed to be great uncertainty among the witnesses as to the facts for the prosecution and no case was made against Marks.[27]

When three doctors were arrested, separately, for speeding in Buffalo as they were on the way to see patients, the president of the Buffalo Automobile Club, also a physician, interested his organization in the matter. Thus, it was believed that the pressure brought to bear could influence the police to relax the law to some extent in favor of physicians. In Detroit, around the same time, a physician arrested for speeding had the case discharged by the magistrate when he explained that he was answering a "hurry" call. The journalist reporting the case declared, "Surely a reasonable latitude must be allowed in such cases."[28]

In New York City late in July 1902, the presiding justice of the Court of Special Sessions, in sentencing a chauffeur who had been arrested for violating the speed law, gave public notice of his intentions to inflict upon such offenders henceforth the full penalty of the law, in the absence of extenuating circumstances. The offender before the bench was an employee of a wealthy merchant, who, it was stated, was sitting beside the chauffeur at the time of the arrest and protested to the policeman against detention because he was in a hurry to get to his dinner. According to the piece, it appeared that the employer himself aided and abetted the employee; and in fact, was himself the direct cause of the violation of the law, since he must have given orders to his chauffeur to drive fast so that he might be in time for his dinner.

The reporter argued in such cases it was no more than right that the owner of the machine should be held as at least contributing to the offense if not chiefly responsible. "Many of the chauffeurs who are guilty of habitual excesses are only imitating their employers or basing their hype of immunity on the wealth or station of their employers. In a country where the law is supposed to be enforced without prejudice or discrimination on rich and poor alike it is worthy of notice that some of the very worst offenders of this class have never been arrested. Is it because they are rich?"[29]

In the above-cited case, Justice Holbrook sat as presiding judge in the Court of Special Sessions, with Justices Mayer and Hinsdale as associates. He declared a maximum penalty of a $50 fine on the chauffeur, Harry G. Larcum. The chauffeur was arrested after a chase of 18 blocks. His employer was a woolen merchant who lived in Tarrytown and who declared it was a "shame" to stop him as he was in a hurry for dinner. Larcum paid the fine. It was a second offense and thus an offender was subject to a $50 fine, six months in jail, or both. From the bench, Holbrook declared, "The reckless operation of automobiles in this city is getting to be a serious matter. Chauffeurs of automobiles seem to think that horsemen, pedestrians and others have no rights they are bound to respect. This court is determined to put a stop to this matter of violating the law in this city, if possible.... It seems to us proper that it should be generally known that we have made up our minds to impose a maximum fine in these cases, except under very extenuating circumstances."[30]

With all the incidents of excessive speeds, it had been repeatedly urged in the press that automobiles should be equipped with speed meters [speedometers]. One journalist had reservations about the reliability of such devices. For example, vibrations from the machine might throw speedometers off. Then there was the problem of the cost of such a device added to the cost of the automobile. He added, "The fact that no registering speed meter has yet been placed upon the market indicates either that chauffeurs feel no need of such a device or that the production of a practical instrument of this kind presents great difficulties."[31]

When the *Horseless Age* editorialized on the speed laws in August 1902 it declared, "Aggressive speed regulation, trapping of automobilists by the police and general opposition to the automobile have now become the vogue in the towns surrounding all the larger cities." Cited as examples were Glencoe and Evanston, Illinois, both in the vicinity of Chicago. Both, the editor complained, "have become notorious for the anti-automobile inclinations of their municipal governments, and in the Far West the town of San Mateo, in the vicinity of San Francisco, has just passed an ordinance which for its oppressive nature is probably without an equal in the country. Besides the usual requirements of brakes, bells and lights, the ordinance provides that 'no person shall drive, guide or propel an automobile or other motor vehicle on any street avenue or highway within the city of San Mateo, at a greater rate of speed than 5 miles an hour.'" And on approaching within 500 feet of any vehicle propelled by animal power, or any person leading or driving a domestic animal, a motorist was to slow down to a speed not exceeding 2.5 miles an hour. He grumbled, "There certainly ought to be some way of stemming this adverse municipal legislation by co-operative action of automobilists throughout the country; and the time for action seems to have come." A "correct opposition" of the situation, he thought, could be seen at Wilmette, Iowa, which had recently increased its speed limit to 12 miles per hour.[32]

For some time the board of trustees of the village of South Orange, New Jersey, had been considering an ordinance to regulate car traffic on its streets. That city was the home of many businessmen having their place of business in New York City "and as the population is comparatively wealthy many automobiles are owned there." The ordinance introduced provided a speed limit of ten miles an hour. "This limit was considered rather restrictive by the automobilists, as the streets of the village are comparatively free from traffic, and accordingly Mr. Adams of the Adams-McMurtry Company, who resides at South Orange, gave the trustees an opportunity to acquaint themselves by experience with the various factors affecting the safety of automobile traffic, by taking them out in his machine, and drafted an ordinance raising the speed limit to 15 miles an hour, which has just been adopted," explained a reporter. The journalist concluded, "It is to be earnestly hoped that the Orange automobilists will appreciate the freedom accorded them by their village trustees.... The terms of this ordinance are such as we eventually hope to see in force in all country towns, and the success of this ordinance will hasten the removal of oppressive and unreasonable speed restrictions."[33]

Floyd Palmer was a contractor in Washington, D.C., who was taken into custody in that city for violating the speed law with a horseless carriage. Palmer was arraigned before Judge Bundy of the police court later in the day. After a hearing of the facts, Bundy imposed a $2 fine, which was paid. The procedure illustrated the speed of the legal system. Palmer was arrested by the police at 11 a.m., appeared in court, was convicted and fined, and the story made it into the newspapers on the same day. Policeman McQuade testified he followed Palmer and the indicator on his bicycle showed the car was traveling two miles an hour over the limit allowed by the law. McQuade also noted Palmer did not seem to have control of the machine and nearly collided with a pedestrian. Police officers in many cities by this time had speedometers on the bikes used by the police.[34]

In Canton, Ohio, an editorial in a local paper asserted, "Newspapers all over the state are clamoring for a statute regulating the speed of automobiles. The legislator who introduces such a bill and sees it through will win not only the approbation of the press but the everlasting gratitude of the pedestrian public. There can be no doubt that automobiles, rapidly multiplying as they are, will soon become a real menace unless they are properly restrained."[35]

In another editorial in the *Horseless Age*, the publication again urged the

Automobile Club of America to do more to stop the violations of speed laws "which have been openly flaunted [*sic*] by some of its members." That organization, he argued, would be more effective if it suspended or expelled from membership "prominent members" who had been repeatedly reprimanded or fined for excessive speeding and who openly defied the law and public sentiment. "The greatest offenders are those whose wealth and position make them leaders of the fad worshiping sect, which unquestioningly follows their bad example and holds them up in justification. They have their fun and go scot free, the initiators argue, then why should we hesitate to break the law?" In conclusion, the editor thundered, "Let the leaders of the automaniacs be brought to brook and a wholesome lesson will be learned by all."[36]

In Buffalo, New York, W.J. Schultz was being sued for $1,000 damages by the guardian of an 11-year-old boy who was run over by the defendant's auto when, it was alleged, the vehicle was being operated at an illegally excessive speed. Schultz claimed the accident was unavoidable because the boy ran out in front of the machine. The jury awarded $345 to the plaintiff. Around the same time, the Automobile Club of America and other organizations were preparing to lend their assistance to Felix Warburg, the New York banker against whom $12,070 damages were awarded at Trenton, New Jersey, for causing a runaway with his automobile. It was claimed that no criminal negligence was shown on the part of Warburg's driver and that the verdict was therefore prejudiced.[37]

Horseless Age became almost deranged in an editorial published on April 29, 1902, when it declared that "automania" needed to be viewed in a new light. "The conviction is gaining ground among scientific men that indulgence in extraordinary speeds of transition voluntarily controlled breeds in the human species a form of disease capable of development to the degree of delirium. The disease is generally referred to as the speed craze or speed mania." One proponent of that theory was said to be Dr. Pierre Hatchet-Souplet. He maintained persons in positions to increase their speed at will are simply carried away by the consciousness thereof. "They have no longer control of themselves, they are intoxicated. They then develop characteristics which are foreign to them when in the normal state: boastfulness, combativeness, crabbedness, hatred, mischievousness and violence. Their characteristics vary in form and degree, but may attain a maximum in the cyclist and automobilist."

According to Dr. Edgar Berillon, there was a strong analogy between the "delirious intoxication" of speed and that of morphine. Regarding the conclusions of Berillon and Hatchet-Souplet, the editor then remarked, "Their generalizations may seem rather too sweeping, but several extreme cases of auto mania during the last few years afford considerable substantiation for their argument." He cited the example of a French automobilist who ran over a customs official and was compelled to pay a heavy indemnity to the family of the latter.[38]

In Indianapolis, Indiana, the city council committee on public safety and comfort met to hear opinions on the ordinances to regulate the speed of autos and the speed of electric streetcars. An ordinance for autos was introduced by Councilman Crall and limited the speed to eight miles an hour in the district bounded by North, East, South, and West Streets, and 12 miles an hour in other parts of the city. It also required lights, slowing down in turning corners in the business district, registration with the controller, and the initials of the car owner to be carried on display. Members of the Automobile Club of Indiana were present and made some minor suggestions but described the proposal as "fair and representative of the best judgment of cities and States that had already dealt with the subject." Fred M. Ayres, president of the Automobile Club of Indiana, expressed the thought that 12 miles an hour was a "proper limitation." At that speed, Ayres said he could stop his machine in ten feet. That was somewhat in error. According to the organization nacto.org's chart at ten miles per hour, the stopping distance is 27 feet, and at 15 miles per hour, the required stopping distance is 44 feet.[39]

Police Commissioner Francis Greene of New York City had under consideration the adoption of automobiles to be used in pursuing those who violated the speed law. Plans for the cars, to be built for speed, were said to have been recommended by the Deputy Commissioner of Police in Brooklyn. Arthur P. Sturgis of New York City was discharged from a charge of speeding. The magistrate held that the police officer who made the arrest could not have known how fast Sturgis was traveling as he did not have a watch. In Boston, Kenneth A. Skinner was discharged from a speeding charge when the presiding judge held "the evidence on the testimony of the officers is not sufficient to hold the defendant, in spite of the fact that the machines were timed by stop watches."[40]

E. A. Mulliken of Quincy, Massachusetts, was indicted in September 1902 on a charge of manslaughter in causing the death of A.B. Scott with his automobile. In May 1903 he had his case placed on file by the consent of the court and agreed to pay the cost of prosecution. He had already settled several suits which grew out of the fatality. Meanwhile, in Milwaukee, it was announced that a detective would pursue speeding offenders in an automobile.[41]

In a brief editorial from *Horseless Age*, the writer mused, "how can an automobilist who buys a machine capable of a speed of 50 to 60 miles an hour be expected to remain within the legal limit of 15 or 20 miles an hour?"[42]

Police were about to "wage war" against the violators of Canton, Ohio's speed ordinance. Within the city limits maximum speed was eight miles an hour. Canton Police Chief McCloud commented, "There is not a day passes but what we hear numerous complaints against the excessive speed of street cars and automobiles."[43]

When a meeting of the Indianapolis Board of Public Safety held a meeting on December 9, 1903, Mayor John Holtzman called attention to the fact that many drivers in the city paid "no respect whatever" to the city's regulation of speed and asked the board to attend to the matter. The board issued an order to

TO STOP DANGEROUS AUTO-SPEEDING.

President A.C. Shattuck of the Automobile Club of America, 1903. The ACA suddenly announced it was against racing and the speed-mania gripping the automobilists. That sudden turnaround from sponsoring and encouraging races came about due to the increase in accidents and deaths on the road, and the resultant increased public backlash.

Superintendent Kruger requesting him to see that the law regulating the speed of autos was hereafter strictly enforced. Resident Stoughton Fletcher, Jr., said, "Every man that owns an automobile goes faster than the ordinance allows, if he can.... I know I do. He goes as fast as he can and wants to go faster. Sure the ordinance is a good thing. It ought to be enforced. But it's broken by every man that has an automobile." The speed limit was eight miles an hour.[44]

Pedestrians had long been opposed to the speeding of automobiles but they had a hard time being heard. The automobilists, who were mostly rich or very rich, enjoyed speeding so they got their way. However, the number of accidents and deaths from reckless driving continued to mount. The result was that a more influential group of people began to join with the powerless pedestrians to put a stop to speeding. As the cars got bigger and more powerful the rich themselves were often the victims of accidents and deaths due to the reckless abandon of their class. Auto racing rapidly began to be moved from city streets and country roads, with or without local authorities' permission, onto specific racing ovals that were not public roads. The auto clubs that championed racing anywhere and everywhere and always fought speed limits suddenly changed their tunes.

In June 1902 the governors of the ACA took unanimous action against street races. This was a result of the "terrible accident" during the holding of the record trails by that club on Staten Island, New York, on May 31, 1902. That accident convinced the governors of the Automobile Club of America that it was unwise to hold speed trials with automobiles on public highways. As a result, the ACA would not hold or consent to the holding of any such contests by the club. In that Staten Island race, a contestant's vehicle went into a crowd of spectators resulting in two deaths and nine people injured.[45]

Reportedly, the Automobile Club of America was the first organization to encourage the sport in the United States and it was also the first organization to come out earnestly in favor of a discontinuance of fast speeding on the highways.[46]

MILLIONAIRES IN CRAZE FOR SPEED
DAILY RISK LIVES ON RACING AUTOS

Men on Whose Safety Depends the Investments of Thousands Pay Constantly Increasing Price for Machines.

MEN WHO PLAY WITH DEATH IN AUTO RACES.

Here are the names of some of the millionaires who play with death by using the fastest obtainable racing machines:

SENATOR W. A. CLARK, AUGUST BELMONT,
WILLIAM C. WHITNEY, O. H. P. BELMONT,
GEORGE J. GOULD, JOHN W. GATES,
WILLIAM ROCKEFELLER, CHARLES A. DRAKE,
HENRY CLEWS, CHARLES M. SCHWAB,
E. R. THOMAS, ROYAL PHELPS CARROLL,
BERYL PRESTON, ROBERT GOELET.

Many Narrow Escapes.

A 1902 article about millionaire autoists and their craze for speed. Illustrations included three auto crashes involving the rich. Fourteen men were named who "played with death." All were from the wealthy class.

Responding in a slightly different way was the American Automobile Association. The AAA endorsed the popular movement for a specific race track. "The plans are a result of a national movement now under way to put a stop to the speeding of the death-dealing flyers on the public highways of America."[47]

The efforts of local authorities in various parts of the country "to put a stop to the speeding of automobiles along country roads to the continual risk of life and limb of foot passengers" had the endorsement of the ACA. Club President A.C. Shattuck said his club regarded "the unlawful speeding of autos as the greatest menace to the existence of the sport in this country."[48]

Another lengthy article on millionaires appeared less than two years after the first one. This second article was much more sober in tone. It did not admonish the rich for their foibles nor did it mourn the injuries and deaths among hapless pedestrians who were run down by the millionaire automobilists. It did mourn the more recent events in which the millionaires themselves were sometimes injured or killed in those accidents. That was serious and it posed a potential economic disaster because so many people were invested in these large companies run by the millionaires. A loss of such key figures could put their investments at risk. The piece named 14 of the millionaires "who play with death by using the fastest obtainable racing machines." Those named were: Senator William A. Clark; August Belmont; William C. Whitney; O.H.P. Belmont; George J. Gould; John W. Gates; William Rockefeller; Charles A. Drake; Henry Clews; Charles M. Schwab; E.R. Thomas; Royal Phelps Carroll; Beryl Preston; and Robert Goelet. One tragic accident stood out and turned a lot of the rich away from the reckless driving lifestyle. Charles Fair and his wife were killed in a single-car accident near Paris, France, in which Fair lost control of the machine and it crashed into a tree. He was a brother-in-law to W.K. Vanderbilt, Jr. Not long after that accident Vanderbilt, notorious for speeding, announced he was abandoning car racing. He sold his stable of high-powered vehicles. That was shortly after the death of Fair. Edward R. Thomas, who bought the "White Ghost" auto from Vanderbilt, had not owned the machine a fortnight before it killed a child and had been in several collisions.[49]

Chapter 7

Accidents, Deaths, Insurance

One of the earliest editorials in *Horseless Age* that fretted about the future was published in June 1898 and concerned the topic of recklessness and legislation. "Time and time again has the note of warning been sounded in these columns against the reckless driving of motor carriages. The practice has been condemned not only because of the direct danger to the persons indulging in it, but also because of the antagonism it will surely arouse in the popular mind against the whole motor movement, leading to restrictive legislation which will seriously hamper the new industry."[1]

The idea of automobile insurance appeared in print in January 1900. It was contained in a letter to the editor from Horace Brown of Boston. Brown explained he had noticed from time to time discussions of the liability of owners and drivers of horseless vehicles in case of accidents resulting from frightened horses. "It seems strange to me that no mention has been made of the fact that there are companies that insure one against all liability in case of accidents of this kind." The company takes the entire responsibility of conducting the case, wrote Brown, "and pays any and all damages awarded." He had personally such a policy "and recently caused an accident by frightening a horse ... although I do think I was not in any way to blame." Brown added, "The policy of the company is to fight a case of this kind rather than settle out of court, in order to strengthen the precedent."[2]

Another editorial in *Horseless Age* cited a New Jersey publication (the *Journal* of Jersey City). "Not one day passes now without its chapter to be added to the record of automobile accidents; and the automobile is getting a black eye for something it does not deserve to have charged against it. It is safe to venture the assertion that not one per cent of the 'accidents' have been accidents due to the machine. Ninety-nine per cent of the mishaps are due solely to the blunders of the operators." The editor fully agreed with those sentiments. However, in prior months he had regularly argued that auto drivers were so much better drivers than the horsemen. He concluded, "we could name metropolitan journals which have sensed the situation as to accidents far less intelligently than the paper quoted from above."[3]

A Washington, D.C., newspaper editorialized on the subject. It noted that several accidents, more or less serious, had been recorded in Washington during the previous few weeks "as a result of reckless running of automobiles." An elderly man was struck as he stepped off a streetcar, for example. "The automobiles are, of course, subject to the speed regulation of the Commissioners and yet, despite violations which are palpable to anyone who watches the streets for a few minutes any day, only one case has been presented to the Police Court thus far." And, he added, "The police authorities should instruct the bicycle squad to keep a particular watch upon these machines and to make arrests whenever the speed rules are being clearly violated."[4]

An article in May 1901 noted that "Owing to the frequency of accidents there is in vogue among French automobilists a practice of insuring themselves against accidents, the policy covering damages sustained both by the owner and by outside parties for which he may be held responsible. It is thought that the consciousness of freedom from liability from any damages that may be caused by disregard of ordinances for the public safety increases the recklessness of many operators. If this be the case, the insurance system is certainly not working for the benefit of the industry."[5]

An editor with *Horseless Age* reported that the trade publication "very frequently" received inquiries from users of autos as to where these vehicles could be insured against fire on the road or other accidents. "The ordinary fire insurance is only effective while the vehicle is in the stable," and often the owner thought it desirable to insure against other risks. "It appears that the insurance companies in this country have so far not given any consideration to the extension of the insurance business which the automobile movement is bound to create."

The case, the editor explained, was different in Europe. In France a company had been in that business for two years, insuring owners not only against accidents to their vehicles through any cause, but also against any accidents that may be caused to outside parties, or that may happen to hired drivers, for which the owner could be held responsible. In Germany, the Mid–European Motorwagon Association recently made arrangements with an insurance company in Stuttgart whereby the latter agreed to insure the vehicles of all members of the association at special rates. The editor thought auto usage was pervasive enough in America that some potential owners declined to purchase after assessing the various risks and problems associated with car ownership. Therefore, "Here is an obstacle to the progress of the industry which a rational and comprehensive insurance system could remove. The time is ripe for a progressive insurance company to enter this field."[6]

Insurance companies were said to be looking into the subject of possible fire risks from the storing of automobiles. Reportedly, when a man wished to insure a shed or barn he was generally asked whether an automobile using gasoline fuel was stored therein, and that companies were inclined to increase rates, especially if the vehicle also was to be insured. A report from Hartford, Connecticut, an insurance center, stated that in that city cases were few in which the insurance

Photographs of the Staten Island, New York race tragedy that left several dead and injured, 1902.

rate had been increased on account of cars. That increase was only imposed when the number of vehicles in a building was greater than three.[7]

When a speed test for automobiles was held in Staten Island, New York, on May 31, 1902, it ended in tragedy. The subhead declared, "Motor car going over a mile a minute crashes into line of spectators at speed test." That race was sponsored by the Automobile Club of America. Two people were killed and about 10 more suffered serious injuries.[8]

That tragedy sparked a great deal of negative press. Within a short time W.C. Baker, president of the Baker Motor Vehicle Company that built the machine that crashed at Staten Island, was held on $20,000 bail to answer charges of murder. Chauffeur Denzer, who was with Baker in the automobile at the time, was held on the same amount of bail.[9]

Also a few days after the crash the ACA came out against speed races. J. Bayard Backus, chairman of the Committee of Fifty, opposed increasing the legal rate of speed of vehicles in the congested streets of New York City. Backus saw the Committee of Fifty as a committee of public safety. He said his group "is not opposed to automobiles, but it is opposed to the streets of the city being used with an utter disregard for others. This has got to be stopped." He added, "The automobile, and especially the larger and heavier ones, are certainly the greatest menace to life and limb.... A horse may knock you down, but an automobile will go over you. They are especially dangerous to the aged and infirm, and to women and children—the weaker portion of our citizens."[10]

Around the same time a horse, frightened by the rushing of four autos and the blare of their horns, became a runaway. The animal dashed through the gates at the railway crossing and an express train struck the carriage, killing a boy in the carriage and injuring another boy and the driver of the carriage.[11]

Another automobile tragedy that garnered even more media attention was the previously mentioned crash that killed Charles Fair and his wife. The couple, from San Francisco, were part of the American plutocracy and were spending the summer of 1902 in France. On the afternoon of August 14, the couple were killed in a single-car auto accident some 50 miles west of Paris. Charles Fair was driving the car at a high rate of speed. He lost control of the vehicle, went off the road, and struck a

A sketch of the Staten Island crash. It was an event that turned the public even more hostile to the rich speed-obsessed automobilists.

tree. He and his wife both died although their chauffeur (in the car but not driving) survived with injuries. The Fairs had a very fast 45-horsepower machine. It was said they were traveling at a speed of 62 miles an hour, in a machine that was capable of speeds of 74 miles an hour. Mrs. Fair was the sister of Mrs. W.K. Vanderbilt, Jr.[12]

The first day Fair received the car was June 23, 1902. That very day he had an accident in Paris on the Champs-Élysées, colliding with another car, although in that instance, there were no serious injuries. The death of the Fairs set off a lengthy legal battle among the heirs. The issue was which of the couple had died first.[13]

Later that year the wife of United States Senator W.M. Stewart of Nevada was thrown to her death from an automobile when the driver lost control and slammed into a telegraph pole. Two other people were in the car, H. Ben Taylor (driver) who was injured, and Henry S. Foote (brother of Mrs. Stewart) who was uninjured. The car was trying to swerve around another vehicle in its path, lost control, and crashed into the pole. Reportedly, the vehicle was not speeding.[14]

Antonio Peerer, a Rye, New York, contractor, was riding a bicycle on the Boston Post Road on June 5, 1902, when he was killed while trying to get out of the way of a speeding automobile. The car contained four people, two men, and two women. The car did not stop after the man was down but continued through the village at a speed of 40 miles per hour. "The dust was so thick that the initials on the rear of the machine could not be distinguished." According to the reporter, "The authorities of West Chester are thoroughly aroused over the way automobiles are run at an express speed along the Boston Post Road. As many runaways have resulted, there is a plan on foot to patrol the road and arrest every violator of the law."[15]

Charles Fair and his wife were killed in a single-car crash near Paris France, 1902. Speeding was the cause. The Fairs were part of the Vanderbilt clan. This crash drew extensive media coverage and also turned the public against the rich speeders.

In Chicago a company was said to have entered the business of insuring owners of automobiles, guaranteeing to fight all damage suits brought against the holder of the policy. The policy covers damage suits on account of accidents to any person or persons claimed to have been caused through the negligence of the insured or his chauffeur. Those Chicago automobilists who favored the idea maintained that it would check wanton persecution of automobilists. Auto owners "are generally thought to be wealthy and there are always some unscrupulous persons who regard them as legitimate prey. Claims may be brought against automobilists in cases of accidents for which they were not in the least to blame and it is to protect them against the annoyance of such claims that accident insurance might prove a desirable institution!" Opponents declared that it would necessarily make a driver less cautious and that caution was the best safeguard the driver of an automobile could have. Moreover, insurance gave the driver a false sense of security.

"In case of a serious accident a charge of criminal carelessness might be brought and the fact that the driver was insured would be a strong point with the lawyers for the prosecution. It would be likely, also, to prejudice the jury against the defendant." The editor of *Horseless Age* concluded, "It is necessary

Illustrations around the 1902 single-car accident that caused the death of Mrs. Stewart, wife of United States Senator William Stewart.

at the present time that all operators of automobiles should constantly be possessed of a sense of responsibility, which will save them the trouble and annoyance individually, and protect the interests of users as a whole and of the industry at large. This damage claim insurance scheme is therefore not to be encouraged."[16]

The New York accident and insurance companies had reportedly again increased the rate of auto insurance, as of July 1902. All of them reported that they had lost money in the business and were not especially eager for auto insurance even at the new rate, which was $100 per vehicle as compared with $25 just 18 months earlier. Whereas there were ten companies writing auto insurance in New York a year earlier, only four were then said to be paying any attention to that section of the insurance business. The usual policy carried a limit of $5,000 where the injury was confined to one person and $10,000 where several people were injured.[17]

Journalist Edward Sephton mentioned the increasing frequency of auto accidents. He felt it was not just the result of the increasing number of cars on the road but was due also "to the mania for racing which seems to have possessed many auto owners and hurried several of them to untimely deaths." He mentioned the death of the Fairs and then 12 days later F.J. Matthews and a lady companion were killed in a similar accident in New Jersey with high speed involved. Sephton argued the persistence of such accidents showed something was radically wrong, both with the machines and in the manner of using them. He noted the

A 1902 sketch of the "automobile face." Included are William Vanderbilt in his notorious "Red Devil" racer.

renunciation by Vanderbilt of such speeding activities after the death of his family members but since that renunciation, he had been arrested for speeding on the streets of Newport, Rhode Island. It was one thing to have laws about speed limits, he felt, but it was another thing to enforce those laws. "A strict enforcement of the laws, with the substitution of imprisonment for a fine (which the millionaire drivers of automobiles only laugh at) will reduce the number of casualties on our highways."[18]

In the wake of increased agitation against speeders, more drastic action was taken against W. Byrd Raymond, described in the media as a "rich automobilist." He was sentenced to six months in jail but spent only one night in jail before his lawyer came along and got him released when the warden was served with a writ of appeal. The sentence was imposed on him by Judge Kellogg of Yonkers for crashing into a streetcar and injuring 22 people. That sentence excited the "indignation" of automobilists who came to his aid. Both the ACA and the NAAM pledged their full support for Raymond. Although he spent just one night in jail it was enough time for prison authorities to shave off his hair, much to his embarrassment.[19]

Mrs. James E. Shannon of San Francisco was struck by a car as she left the sidewalk to catch a streetcar. She was tossed in the air and the vehicle passed over her body. However, she escaped without serious injury. According to witnesses, the car was going at a high rate of speed, estimated at 20 miles an hour. The driver didn't stop. Mr. Shannon chased him and caught him after a block. That case illustrated another problem with accidents in the early years. The hit-and-run driver could often escape completely. And the means of identifying car and driver were often sorely inadequate.[20]

W. Byrd Raymond was a young, rich speeder who was sentenced to jail in 1902 for speeding. He was in jail less than 24 hours before being bailed out. However, it was enough time for prison authorities to shave his head, much to his embarrassment.

H. W. Dupuy, a senior at Yale University, settled with the estate of Ditmas Thorpe Munro. The latter died in July 1902 from injuries inflicted by Dupuy's automobile several weeks earlier. It was said that Dupuy paid $5,000, the full amount allowed by the statutes of Connecticut for damages for the death of a human being when caused by the carelessness or negligence of another.[21]

In Paterson, New Jersey, the suit brought by Lizzie Whiteman against Robert B. Holmes of Orange, New Jersey, came up for trial in Passaic, New Jersey. The suit arose out of an accident in which the son of Whiteman, who was riding a bike, was struck and killed by an auto driven by Holmes.[22]

In New York City an automobile knocked down a horse, ran over it, and broke its leg at Broadway and 26th Street. The car did not stop. The only person in the car yelled out the window of his car as he sped past after striking the horse. He yelled his name was Sweeney and he lived at 428 56th Street in New York. All that information proved to be false. The Society for the Prevention of Cruelty to Animals had to be called. When its agent arrived he shot the horse dead in the street. When the car struck the horse it threw the animal some 20 feet forward.[23]

Arthur Anson of Cincinnati, aged 17, was placed under arrest on a charge of murder alleged to have been committed by an automobile. On the evening of June 17, 1903, Anson drove a car belonging to his employer, A.L. Rich, and at an intersection in Cincinnati, his car collided with Mary Niemeier, inflicting a serious injury from which she died the next day. At first, Anson was placed under a charge of reckless driving and released on $1,000 bail. But after the woman died he was arrested again and charged with murder. Rich, Anson's employer, said at the time of the accident Anson was running the machine for pleasure. That is, he was not on the clock and doing so without the employer's consent. Before the accident a police officer had tried, and failed, to stop Anson for speeding. Anson did not possess the required license to operate a car. He had been an inmate of the House of Refuge, where he was sent on the complaint of his mother, who declared she was unable to contend with her son.[24]

WOMAN BARELY ESCAPES DEATH
UNDER WHEELS OF AN AUTOMOBILE

Struck by Machine as She Leaves the Sidewalk to Catch a Car, She Is Tossed in the Air and the Vehicle Passes Over Her Body, but She Miraculously Escapes Without Any Serious Injury

MRS. JAMES E. SHANNON, wife of a commercial traveler and sister-in-law of Dr. O'Connell of this city, who resides at 1025 Valencia street, was knocked down yesterday afternoon at 4:30 o'clock by an automobile, which was being run by W. F. Eichbaum, manager for Henry R. Worthington, 148 First street, and who resides at 815 Haight street. The accident occurred at the corner of Powell and Market streets. Mrs. Shannon sustained injuries to her legs and left hip.

Her husband stated last night that his wife, Dr. Henderson, Dr. O'Connell, Dr. Reagan and himself were standing on the corner waiting for an outward bound car. The car came in sight and before he could realize it his wife had stepped from the sidewalk to catch the car. The next moment she was struck by an automobile, which had approached at high speed and thrown into the air and the machine then ran over her.

"It must have been going at the rate of

WOMAN WHO WAS PAINFULLY INJURED BY AUTOMOBILE, AND SCENE AT TIME OF ACCIDENT.

stopped voluntarily within a few feet of where the accident occurred.

J. J. Richsteen, clerk in J. S. Potts' drug store, stated that Mrs. Shannon seemed badly shaken when she came in and very nervous, but he did not consider her injuries were serious. He said that he heard Dr. O'Connell say that he would not be able to tell for two or three days whether she was injured internally or not. From outward appearances he did not think Mrs. Shannon was badly hurt.

POLICE WATCH CHAUFFEURS.

Will Arrest All Who Trespass on Forbidden Drives.

The park police, under Sergeant Helms, are determined to punish a class of of-

In 1903 Mrs. James Shannon was run over by a speeding car. Luckily, she escaped with no serious injuries. It was one of many accounts from an increasing number of accidents. That led to a growing demand for authorities to do something.

A coroner's jury at Oshkosh, Wisconsin, held Dr. Henry H. Muggley, of the National Automobile and Motor Company, responsible for causing the death of Alfred H. Tuttle, of Oshkosh, by running into him with his automobile on July 3, 1903. Witnesses testified the machine was traveling at a speed of eight to ten miles an hour.[25]

In that same month fatal auto accidents had happened in the vicinity of Brooklyn and Schenectady, New York, and Providence, Rhode Island. In at least two of those cases, recklessness on the part of the driver was the cause. A reporter blamed the speed craze and inexperience on the new form of locomotion. "It is needless to say that a fatal accident makes a profound impression upon the community and is bound to do a great deal of harm to the automobile business...." He urged automobile clubs and trade associations to take concerted action and suppress scorching.[26]

Auto pioneer Charles E. Duryea wrote a letter to the editor in response to a piece on accidents. Duryea argued the heavier vehicle and not the lighter one was the cause of the problem. That is, the little vehicle "being more harmless should not be so strongly restricted," and such things as identification numbers, lamps, and so forth, should be applied only to the large, high-speed cars, leaving the little, lightweight cars in the same class as other vehicles—unregulated.[27]

At the end of 1902, a report from New Haven, Connecticut, observed that several insurance companies had recently undertaken to insure owners of cars against damages that might be found against them as the result of accidents to individuals or horses, or other property arising from the use of horseless carriages. The policies were issued to cover losses in a single instance and either for $5,000 or $10,000. Should the owner of an auto feel that he might need insurance against more than one accident, or that on any single occasion, he might cause damage over $10,000, he was permitted to take out what was designated as "an excess liability policy" at half the original rates. According to the article, it was felt unwise at the time to offer rates to owners of steam-propelled vehicles. That distinction was made not because that class of automobile was in itself dangerous to drivers or less susceptible to control. It was made because it had been demonstrated by the record that more accidents had resulted in horses becoming frightened by the escaping steam than from any other cause. An electric automobile could be insured against damages to one person not to exceed $5,000 at a rate from $50 to $75. The gasoline-powered vehicles came higher. The rate for the same amount of insurance ran from $60 to $90. Policies paying out for damages to more than one person were available but total liability was limited to $10,000. Those higher value policies were available for both gas-powered and electrics.[28]

Chapter 8

Licenses

The issue of taxing the new horseless carriages and licensing them in some way arose early in the development of the automobile. In May 1899 authorities in Philadelphia debated the question of taxing motor vehicles, especially those that competed with horse-drawn vehicles, from which the city extracted a license fee. A bill had then been introduced in the Philadelphia City Council requiring a license fee of $10 for every motor vehicle. Other municipalities were also reported to be considering the same question and it was considered more than probable that a tax or license would be demanded in the case of public vehicles. A reporter exclaimed, "for this there is apparently just ground if horse vehicles of the same class are so treated. But the proposition to license or tax all motor vehicles is without justification, and would surely be contested by the progressive interests affected. No plea in favor of taxing or licensing motor vehicles can be advanced that does not apply equally or more forcibly to horse vehicles or even bicycles for there is notorious carelessness in the handling of both of the latter classes of vehicles."[1]

This reporter was writing for the *Horseless Age* and was biased. He continued by declaring, "As between the two—drivers of horses and motormen—there can be no question that the former are more in need of regulation. Many of those employed to drive horses in cities are mere boys or men of intemperate habits, because the labor is looked upon as unskilled and is poorly compensated, competition among the unemployed forcing the wages down to a low level. On the other hand, in the present state of the motor vehicle industry, motormen may be classed as skilled labor, constituting a class more careful and more intelligent than the average driver of horses. For this reason, if any discrimination is to be made it should be made in favor of the motor vehicle, the operation of which demands a better class of labor, and which is more readily controlled by a practiced hand than any horse possibly could be."[2]

This journalist argued that the proposition to tax all vehicles, motor and horse, "seems hardly likely to meet with general approval," while admitting it was true that the dangers of the streets were increasing as traffic increased. "The remedy for this congestion," stated the reporter, and its attendant danger to life and limb, "is to be looked for rather in the removal of surface tracks from the streets, and in the classification of traffic on the main thoroughfares." This was an early example of the automobile industry, which barely existed, already trying to get rid of streetcars—which that industry did not finally accomplish until the post–World War II years. As for bicycles, the journalist asserted, "They should be kept off the congested streets and special paths built for them when necessary." Yet this publication had often argued that every vehicle had a right to be on the road—when it suited the trade journal and was seen as a method to defend motor vehicles. He also argued that pedestrians should not be obliged to cross crowded streets. Although he did not suggest how to solve that particular problem.[3]

One month later it was observed that the aldermen of Boston were wrestling with an ordinance to compel the licensing of all motor vehicles. The ordinance that had been introduced at a city council meeting read, "Nor shall any owner or driver of any vehicle drive it or permit it to be driven on the streets of Boston by power of steam, gas, gasoline, naphtha, compressed air, electricity or condition of any or all without a permit from the Board of Aldermen." That provoked a response from the auto lobby that declared, "There is no shadow of justification for the licensing of motor vehicles, unless all vehicles are to be licensed. The motor vehicle is not a road destroyer like the horse, but a road maker; it is safer and more manageable than a horse; it will relieve the congestion of the streets and facilitate travel and traffic in general. How, then, can it be rightly subject to restrictions from which the horse vehicles are exempt?" Not mentioned by this auto enthusiast was the extra speed and power of motor vehicles and the other inherent dangers such as carrying gasoline on board and in the building and maintaining a fire in a steamer, and so on.[4]

Reportedly, in July 1899 "the motorphobia has struck Chicago like a cyclone. No sooner does the South Park Board direct a vicious sally at the motor vehicle [banned from city parks] than the other civil authorities are stirred to action and the mayor himself takes a hand in the onslaught. He has just directed the Law Department to draft an ordinance requiring all drivers of motor vehicles using the public streets to be licensed." And, "It is reported that applicants for licenses will be subjected to a rigid examination under the supervision of the civil authorities.... The examination will consist of a physical test and the investigation of the applicant's mechanical knowledge and his ability to operate a motor vehicle." It was declared, "The reason assigned for this radical action is that several accidents have happened through the incompetence of drivers of motor vehicles."[5]

Editor Ingersoll of the *Horseless Age* wrote that the logic of that procedure was worth following closely. It was contended that because many accidents had occurred, he reasoned, "through incompetent drivers, all motor vehicle drivers should be licensed. How then about horse drivers.... It has been repeatedly asserted in these columns and can easily be proved that motor vehicles are more easily controlled than horses." Ingersoll added, "It has also been admitted that there is among motor vehicle drivers a disposition to exceed the limit of speed which can safely be taken in crowded thoroughfares. The proper method of regulating this, however, is by an ordinance limiting the speed of motor vehicles within city confines, and not by compelling motor vehicle operators to take out a license when in strict justice horse drivers are in greater need of restraint."

Ingersoll concluded, "The law the mayor of Chicago contemplates enacting is too unfair to long burden the statutes if it should be pursued. It is an abuse of the law-making power, born of ignorance of the subject with which it deals, laying onerous burdens and unnecessary restrictions on one class of users of the highway and allowing another class to go scot free. It will not stand the scrutiny of the courts."[6]

The mayor of Chicago and the city electrician, "who are leading the opposition to the motor vehicle in that city," according to one journalist, had drawn up a letter embodying the reasons for their action. According to the reporter the pair were laboring under the same misconceptions that prompted the introduction into the New York Assembly of a similar bill requiring that none but skilled electricians should operate electric vehicles. The reporter argued problems ensued when the construction and maintenance of a machine were not separated from the operation of such a machine. A second assumption was also founded on an error "for it is evidently based on the assumption that the percentage of accidents caused by motor vehicles is greater than that caused by horse vehicles." The Chicago letter argued that "accidents have happened through careless or incompetent drivers of motor vehicles." Admitting this was a statement that could not be denied, the journalist insisted "it was incumbent upon the authors of this bill to prove that motor vehicles are extra hazardous and that the control of them is more difficult than the control of a horse."[7]

He decried that public officials would not take the time to enlighten themselves on those points "and thus be able to legislate intelligently, but, influenced solely by prejudice, they plant themselves stolidly in the path of progress. The relative manageability of the motor vehicle and the horse can easily be determined by investigation and experience, and can be decided in one way only—overwhelmingly in favor of the motor." Hammering on points made in the past about boys of 14 to 16 and drunken men in charge of horses in all the large cities, driving with loose reins (a sign of not being in control) and at unlawful speeds, "the officials will see horses in constant use that are habitual runaways, liable at any moment to dash wildly through the streets, carrying death and destruction with them. Then if they will visit the motor vehicle companies and learn the character of their drivers and the wages paid, and get further light by riding in motor vehicles for a few days, they will surely be convinced of their mistaken zeal and lay this bill on the table indefinitely."[8]

The journalist presented no evidence or statistics for his arguments. The dangerous drivers he ascribed to horse-drawn vehicles were the automobile drivers. The drunken automobile driver had no guiding hand applied to the mayhem he potentially caused. The drunken horse vehicle operator if he accidentally tried to drive his horse into the gutter or over a cliff, or into another car, would experience resistance and refusal from the horse. The horse vehicle had two sets of intelligence to guide it while the auto was controlled by only one.

The reporter added another, more bizarre rationale to his argument, when he declared the motor vehicle industry was new "and promises such phenomenal development that attracts to it a higher class of labor and disposes employers to be more careful in the selection of their men." Among the recommendations offered by the Chicago officials the only one of any practical value, in the mind of the journalist, was that limiting the speed of motor vehicles in the city streets to eight miles per hour. He wanted it raised to ten miles an hour but noted that "some such speed limit is needed is generally conceded by the reasonable element in the motor vehicle industry."[9]

Chicago did enact a measure to grant licenses to operate an automobile. As of the middle of March 1900, the city had granted 80 licenses. The first woman to be granted a license was Juliet E. Bracken, who passed an examination conducted by the city electrician and city engineer.[10]

Eleven months later the Chicago authorities had issued 378 auto licenses, of which 226 were for the operation of electrics, 60 for gasoline-powered vehicles, and 92 for steam machines. Reportedly, only 12 accidents in which anyone was injured had occurred and not a single death had resulted. So that the city could have a complete record of all accidents in the future, everyone who received a license was then required to promise that in case of any mishap, he would make a detailed report of the event to the city electrician. Speed on the city streets was limited to eight miles an hour and no two machines were allowed to travel abreast without receiving special permission from the city. Violators of the speed ordinance were subject to a fine of $5 for each offense.[11]

Soon thereafter the Chicago Board of Aldermen adopted a measure providing that every automobile must display identification numbers and letters on the rear of the machine and those numbers had to be illuminated at night. *Horseless Age* worked itself into a rage over the measure. "It is unnecessary to say that the measure was strenuously opposed by the Chicago Automobile Club" but it passed and would have made Chicago "a laughing stock for the outside world" had not Chicago Mayor Carter Harrison IV vetoed it. Analyzing the ordinance, the reporter declared, "There is little doubt that the aldermen were influenced in their action in connection with this ordinance by a desire to court favor with the laboring vote, by imposing annoying restrictions upon 'the plaything of the rich.'"[12]

While the measure was vetoed it was brought up for reconsideration. Originally the measure called for ID numbers eight inches in height. The new proposal suggested letters be four inches high. That was also opposed by the Chicago Auto Club, except by one member of the club who was also a member of the board of aldermen. He supported the four-inch height, fought with other members of the

Privileged sport. This 1909 illustration shows an automobile driven by a chauffeur speeding down a road, surrounded by newspaper clippings with headlines about numerous traffic accidents involving pedestrians struck by automobiles, including one where a chauffeur was charged with first-degree murder in the death of a 13-year-old boy.

Chicago Automobile Club, and finally resigned from the club. The reporter worried that if such a measure was passed it would set a precedent. "For purposes of identification numbers are really less satisfactory than initials.... Owners prefer to carry initial plates and these have been introduced in a number of Eastern States at the recommendation of automobile clubs." That is, the plate of owner John Smith would have the initial plate of JS. In conclusion, the reporter even managed to bring in nationalism. "The initial plate requirement is of American origin, while numbering is a foreign idea; for this reason, and also for the sake of uniformity, it is to be hoped that the Chicago Automobile Club may succeed in preventing the numbering ordinance from being passed."[13]

Licenses for steam-powered vehicles presented a special problem, mainly because an actual fire had to be kept burning in the machine. Even the *Horseless Age* grudgingly accepted a licensing system for them. The editor suggested a graded system of licenses for such vehicles, depending on the horsepower of the boiler and the class of the vehicle, might be advisable. The Red Flag Law was still in force in New York State and Vermont, at the end of 1899. Other states required licenses only when the boiler exceeded ten horsepower or, in some cases, five horsepower. "Here is an opportunity for the Automobile Club of America to exercise its influence," argued the trade journal. Red Flag laws existed only briefly in the United States, in a limited number of jurisdictions. There were enacted mostly in the 1890s and covered steam-powered vehicles. The owner of such a vehicle was required to have a flag man one-eighth of a mile or so in front of the vehicle to warn any livestock on the road of the approach of the vehicle. This was done for steamers and not electrics or gas-powered cars since livestock were much more likely to take fright at the approach of a steamer.[14]

Charles E. Foster, a Washington, D.C., attorney for the Locomobile Company of America (a major maker of steamers), addressed a letter to the District of Columbia Commissioners on behalf of his clients inquiring about the requirements necessary to secure a permit for the operation of a locomobile in Washington. He explained that several such vehicles would soon be in the District "but the requirement that an expert engineer shall be necessary to operate them would greatly hamper their use." He acknowledged that it was recognized that any vehicle capable of running from 15 to 40 miles per hour "whether propelled by steam, electricity or a gas engine, and whether carrying corrosive acids or ignitable liquid, should be under the control of competent parties." Foster added that no objection would be made to a requirement that licenses should be issued to those who, after examination, showed themselves competent to run the vehicles.

He suggested that, without any modification of the existing regulations, an additional regulation be made to the effect that third- or fourth-class engineers' licenses should be granted authorizing the holder to run a motor vehicle whenever he showed himself upon examination capable of doing so. Commissioner Wright concurred with Foster's recommendations, holding also that these vehicles should be limited in speed to 12 miles per hour in the city and 15 miles per hour in the country, as were bicycles.[15]

Horseless Age looked at the issue of steamer licenses in December 1899. The journal declared that steam automobile makers had overlooked the question of licenses and now faced hard facts that were staring them in the face. One question was whether or not licenses would be demanded of all operators of steam vehicles as licenses were then needed by operators of marine and stationary boilers. Or were there good grounds for making exceptions in favor of certain classes of vehicle boilers? The publication admitted that many of the steamers turned out by manufacturers "have fallen into the hands of unskilled operators." And, "The inspectors of steam boilers have been aroused by this sudden appearance of the steam carriage upon our streets and the evident incompetence of some of the operators, and are requiring licenses of one form or another. The interference of the inspectors is already so general that it may be accepted as certain that some form of a license will be demanded of every operator of a steam vehicle." The piece declared the conclusion seemed to be a graded license but "to demand a full engineer's license by the operator of a light steam carriage would be to seriously cripple the industry."[16]

The New York police authorities were, in the view of a journalist, "setting the pace" for the country about the licensing of steam vehicles. "During the past two or three weeks quite a number of engineer's licenses of the third class have been granted to aristocratic New Yorkers who own pleasure carriages provided with vertical shell boilers. Applicants for such licenses are required to undergo a superficial examination in the construction and care of such boilers, but the inspection of the boilers themselves seems to be rather formal so far."[17]

On June 16, 1900, the boiler inspectors of Yonkers, New York, ordered the police to arrest all persons not licensed by the Boiler Inspecting Board who operated a steam automobile in that city. Captain McLaughlin of the Yonkers Police Department asked whether the order meant to arrest a person from out of town who was passing through Yonkers. The inspectors said it did and insisted on the arrest of any person running a steam horseless carriage if he lacked a local license even though he held a license from another city. It was noted that "droves" of horseless carriages passed through Yonkers every Sunday with people going up the east shore of the Hudson River from Yonkers. That night McLaughlin issued orders to his men to stop all steamers and if the operators did not have a local license, to place them under arrest. He declared the police officers would comply and let the courts decide the validity of the issue.[18]

Two weeks later the examiner of Stationary Engineers in Buffalo, New York, announced he wanted to see the present engineers' license law applied to all motor vehicle operators. That would result in restricting the right to use those vehicles to the regular locomotive and stationary engineers and would ban all females from automobile operation. A journalist moaned, "What have stationary engines to do with automobiles anyway, we should like to know.... And what have steam engines to do with gasoline and electric motors?"[19]

New York State Assembly Representative James K. Apgar introduced a bill into the New York State Assembly. His bill applied to all motor vehicles and not just to steam. In general, the measure met with the approval of the *Horseless Age*, which meant that it was weak. "The fee is nominal and on the whole the regulation of motor traffic in this manner, if judiciously administered, may serve as a needed restraint in some cases and correct abuses that would otherwise go unchecked." The journalist then went on to say that since the whole subject of protective vehicle legislation is being discussed, "it is pertinent to inquire why, if motor vehicle drivers are to be compelled to take out licenses, those who daily send out into the streets incompetent drivers or uncontrollable horses to endanger the lives of their fellow citizens should not be held to a stricter accountability."[20]

The Duke of Manchester called at New York Police Department headquarters on December 20, 1900, to get a license to enable him to run an automobile. The Duke was directed to Sergeant Frank Mangin who was the man with the authority in the police department to issue the license. That request was denied by Mangin who told the Duke, "under the law only an American citizen can get a license to run an automobile."[21]

New York City Counsel John Whalen sent his opinion to Commissioner Michael Murphy that owners and operators of automobiles and other motor vehicles for pleasure purposes did not require a license. Following that opinion Murphy sent an order to the police force informing them that vehicles run by other than horsepower—that is, automobiles—could be run without licenses. The only requirement to operate a car was registration with the New York Secretary of State (for one dollar). As well, the owner had to have a license plate on the back of his vehicle. It had to contain the owners' initials with the letters being at least three inches high.[22]

An ordinance was introduced to the Law Committee of the New York City Board of Aldermen on September 4, 1902, by Joseph B. Thompson, who was chairman of the Rights and Privileges Committee of the New York State Division, League of American Wheelmen [cyclists]. He was requested by the executive committee of that division to prepare an ordinance of that type. After review the Law Committee introduced the measure in the New York City Council. Among the provisions was one that stated no person shall operate an automobile until such person has first obtained a license to operate the same. A license was to contain the name and address of the subject, and the kind of vehicle to be operated along with a description of it. The vehicle was to have two lamps affixed and a license tag with vehicle number in numbers not less than 1.5 inches tall. That tag was to be attached to a lamp.

The moths and the flames. Illustration shows a candlestick with flame labeled "Speed Madness" and speeding automobiles caught in the illumination with people falling out of the cars and the wreckage collecting in the basin of the candlestick holder, 1907.

The license fee for any such vehicle operated as a public hack, cab, coach, or for hire, if intended to carry one or two passengers, was $3. If the vehicle was intended to carry more than two passengers then the license fee was $5. For any such vehicle operated for private use, either for business or pleasure, the fee was $10. Anyone caught operating a car without a license could be fined not less than $10 nor more than $50 or could be imprisoned not less than two days nor more than 10 days, or both, for each offense.[23]

In response to that proposed New York legislation, a

journalist pondered, "Just what prompted the League of Wheelmen to take this step, which can only be interpreted as directed against the automobilists is not quite clear, unless it be that decadent organizations the same as decadent individuals, take delight in obstructing the progress of others." He added that some form of auto driver licensing "is not at all objected to among prominent automobilists" but the general opinion was that the matter should be regulated by state law and not by municipal ordinances. As well, he insisted, the ordinance had many defects. Anyone from outside New York City, while in New York City, needed a New York City license. No exemption was made for tourists. Under the proposal, the mayor was empowered to name a commission of three to examine applicants regarding their competency to operate an automobile. The journalist thought that could lead to abuses although he specified none. The section giving the mayor the right to revoke licenses for cause was also a cause for objection. Finally, the requirement that the machine was not to be left in the street unattended "is certainly unreasonable."[24]

A journalist asked a rhetorical question as to how long did a person have to study before venturing out into the road. He answered that under the best possible condition, the brightest man might run an automobile after four lessons of one hour each from an expert chauffeur, "but even then he must be very careful." At that time, in 1901, in France, one was permitted to run an auto with a "certificate" if he was competent. Any police officer could stop any car anywhere at any time and ask to see the driver's license. If it was not forthcoming, the driver went no further. The test for a license in France consisted of two parts. One was a test drive while the other was equivalent to the written test of today. As far as one journalist was concerned, "The great automobile peril in America to-day is that any man who can get possession of an auto is at liberty to run it on the road as fast as he likes—for police regulation as to speed amount practically to nothing." He concluded, "To stop all this recklessness I urge that no one be permitted to run an automobile until his ability has been certified by a competent government expert."[25]

The Board of Works in San Francisco recommended on November 27, 1901, to the city's Supervisors that no examination or license be required of the operators of any class of automobiles. The board took the position that in examining and licensing the operators the city, in a way, would take upon itself the responsibility of insuring the fitness of the licensee, thereby rendering itself to a certain extent responsible for his or her conduct, "while placing an operator on the same basis as any driver puts such responsibility where it belongs and makes the operator more careful. Both of his vehicle and of the safety of others."[26]

Mayor Rolla Wells of St. Louis obtained from License Collector Whyte the first set of licenses for 1902. The horseless vehicle licenses that would be issued after January 1, 1902, were to be the first ever issued by St. Louis. The first vehicle license plates were slated to go to the Bridge Transit Company for the public automobiles operated on a bridge between St. Louis and East St. Louis.[27]

Wreckreation. Illustration shows a vignette cartoon where accidents take place in various forms of recreation; at center is an automobile accident involving a horse-drawn carriage, also scenes from golf and baseball, hunting and fishing, and mountain climbing, 1908.

A notice signed by Joseph P. Whyte, License Collector at St. Louis, told the reader that the annual license tax on all vehicles was due January 1, 1902, and that a double tax penalty kicked in on April 1, 1902, if the tax had not been paid by that date.[28]

Another bill requiring the registration and numbering of all vehicles other than those propelled or drawn by horses or persons was introduced in the Massachusetts Legislature. If the bill passed, then automobile owners had two months to get their vehicle licensed. Failure to do so meant a fine was levied that ranged from $10 to $100. Under the measure, every vehicle had to carry four license plates—one on each side and front and back. Numbers on the plates had to be in Arabic numerals at least four inches high.[29]

New York City Alderman Herbert Parsons prepared an ordinance affecting the owners of automobiles. The proposal limited the speed of automobiles and provided that every owner was required to procure a license "and that every automobile shall be numbered, and shall carry the number in plain black letters on the back. A fine of $50 is provided for violation of the ordinance." According to a journalist "the move for a special ordinance affecting automobiles comes as a countermove to the agitation that has been underway for a more liberal law, the present ordinance limiting the speed in the populous districts to eight miles an hour, which the automobilists assert is unnecessarily low." And he added, "The whole agitation against the automobile comes from the actions of thoughtless individuals who, without due consideration for the rights of others, persist in running their machines through the crowded streets at a rate of speed dangerous to life and limb." The reporter concluded, "the governing bodies of municipalities will do themselves or the people no lasting good by adopting ordinances too sweeping and imposing measures too drastic upon the increasing number who are taking to the automobile."[30]

A worried editor at the *Horseless Age* was concerned in June 1902 when he noted the subject of licensing car drivers was then under discussion in the councils of some large American cities and the prospects were that licenses would soon be generally required. He fretted, "Fundamentally any measure to restrict the operation of automobiles is objectionable. If speed laws and the dictates of common sense in this respect had not been generally violated there would be no occasion for requiring drivers to be licensed, for it is plain that the chief object in making this requirement is to secure an effective remedy for speed excesses in withdrawing licenses rather than to insure that automobiles be operated only by mechanically competent persons."

The editor went on to admit the licensing system in France had been in force for a considerable time, "apparently to the general satisfaction of automobilists." He qualified that by noting, "in France, of course, they are more accustomed to governmental paternalism that we are in this country, and the objectionable feature of such requirements is less apparent there, because the measure is in line with the entire system of government." Fatalistically he concluded, "A system of licensing would tend to discourage speed excesses and would favorably influence the reliability of hired drivers. Whatever may be the disadvantages of the system it certainly offers some advantages in return, and, it is bound to come anyhow, whether we want it or not."[31]

This editor came to believe that since the licensing of drivers "seems to be coming," then this inevitable development should perhaps be a federal initiative. That was because he felt "means must be devised to meet the exigencies of touring." They thought it likely that license laws would be so construed that licenses issued by the authorities in one city would be honored by authorities in other jurisdictions. But he wondered, what about drivers from other jurisdictions in which no license was required? His solution was that "a Federal license law covering the operators of motor vehicles would be most desirable." And, "Moreover, a withdrawal of the license for any cause would deprive the individual of the right to operate automobiles anywhere in the country and would therefore be a more powerful deterrent against careless operators. Finally, political abuses would be much less probable in the case of a national license bureau than with municipal bureaus."[32]

Several months later it was announced that NAAM (National Association of Automobile Manufacturers) believed in the possibility of a national license law for drivers, as an aid to interstate commerce. Following that belief NAAM appointed a committee of one to represent it in Washington and urge the introduction of a license bill in Congress at the earliest possible date. Editor Ingersoll had no objection to that attempt to obtain a national license law but "we believe that the chances of success are very slim."[33]

When a newspaper in New York City commented on the movement then underway in the city to license automobilists a journalist remarked the movement "may be open to criticism in some respects but, on the whole, it is well conceived. Even the automobilists themselves offer no opposition to licensing, providing it is not to be employed to their injury." At that time a license fee of $10 for pleasure vehicles was then under consideration. The newspaper man thought that amount "seems excessive.... The license question is one which calls for careful consideration."[34]

A new ordinance went into effect in Cleveland in September 1902. Under its provisions, all machines had to be numbered with the numbers being of "standard size," 1.5 inches apart, and in the center of the back of the machine. There were then 417 car owners in Cleveland, 210 gasoline-powered, 134 steamers, and 73 electrics.[35]

The Chicago Board of Aldermen enacted a law requiring owners of automobiles to display the numbers of a city license on the lamps and backs of their cars, for identification purposes. In enacting that ordinance the council was unanimous and did not even refer it to committee. President Palmer of the Chicago Automobile Club was a member of the Board of Aldermen and he said his organization was in favor of the identification system. Numbers on the backs of cars had to be at least eight inches high and the numbers on lamps had to be legible at a distance of 75 feet. However, a week later Chicago Mayor Carter Harrison, Jr., vetoed the ordinance. He explained that several months earlier representatives of the park boards had conferred with the city on a uniform system of regulations for cars and as the machines used the park boulevards as well as the city streets, he favored cooperating with the park boards in passing an ordinance applicable to boulevards as well as streets. In general, though, Harrison declared himself "in sympathy with the purpose of the ordinance."[36]

On February 6, 1903, 62 auto licenses were applied for at the Bureau of Boiler Inspection in Philadelphia. Licenses were issued under provisions of an ordinance passed the previous December. New numbers were furnished to each person who applied for a license. Those numbers were on a blue enameled sign seven inches in length and four inches in width. In one corner of the sign was "1903." It was the intention in Philadelphia to issue those plates annually and to change the color each year.[37]

In accordance with new automobile regulations in Washington, D.C., Commissioner Henry West settled on the personnel to make up the Board of Examiners. He appointed E.F. Vermillion, Henry Boesch, and Daniel Johnson, the three members of the board of steam engineers.

That board was charged with issuing licenses to all persons desiring to operate steam engines of any description in the District of Columbia. Also appointed were Walter C. Allen, head of the DC electrical department, W.A. McFarland, superintendent of the water department, and Charles E. Foster, vice president of the National Capital Automobile Club. All board members, except Foster, were connected with the DC government and their duties on the automobile examining board were without compensation.[38]

City authorities in Chicago temporarily suspended the auto license of Albert C. Banker of that city for violation of the speed regulation. Banker applied for an injunction to restrain the city and received at first a temporary injunction that was later changed to a permanent injunction. Chicago officials had threatened to arrest him if he appeared on the streets driving an automobile. The permanent injunction was granted on the ground the city had no authority under State laws to issue licenses and that the Chicago ordinance was therefore unconstitutional. The injunction was to remain in effect until the city could prove the constitutionality of its measure. It was held that all those laws requiring numbering, licensing, and so on were unconstitutional because no such requirements were made for horse-drawn vehicles and therefore those laws constituted class legislation. On the other hand, it was asserted that the withdrawal of licenses was unconstitutional for the reason that it might deprive a person of his means of gaining a livelihood.[39]

Washington, D.C. Corporation Counsel A.B. Duvall submitted his opinion to the DC Commissioners on the right of the Commissioners to establish an age limit for automobile operators. The Board of Examiners had been considering applications from persons desiring to operate motor vehicles. That board asked for instruction from the Commissioners as to the lowest age limit for issuing permits, stating it had refused in two cases to examine two boys aged 15 and 16, and one boy aged 14 had satisfactorily answered questions from the examiners but had not been issued a permit. The Board of Examiners thought that no person under 18 should be allowed to operate a motor vehicle. Duvall gave his opinion that the Commissioners had the authority to prescribe a limitation of age in the matter of granting permits to operate automobiles. But he added that the competency of the operator of the vehicle was not to be determined by an ironclad rule.[40]

Those seeking a driving license from the Massachusetts Highway Commission were asked about their experience. Some had none at all or "rather dubious experience." To cover such cases the Commission desired a provisional license having a restrictive clause as follows. "SPECIAL RESTRICTION. This license is issued subject to the express condition that the licensee shall not operate any motor vehicle unless he is accompanied by a regularly licensed adult operator. This restriction will be removed when the Massachusetts Highway Commission is satisfied that the licensee has acquired the requisite knowledge and skill to operate motor vehicles with safety." That clause was removed when the applicant submitted a special petition, accompanied by an affidavit that the applicant had become a competent operator, then a full license was granted.[41]

Chapter 9

Laws, Rules, and Regulations, 1896–1899

Laws, rules, and regulations governing the operation of motor vehicles began in earnest in 1899 and never let up. However, a handful of rules were put into place or proposed as early as 1896. One of the earliest surfaced in February 1896 and was aimed not at cars but at motorboats. It illustrated some of the problems that would arise in regulating automobiles. Regulations were sometimes imposed to give one of the motive powers an advantage over the others, rather than to advance some general idea of health and safety.

At the federal level, a bill was introduced in the United States Senate providing that all naphtha, gasoline, kerosene, and electric motorboats should be brought under government inspection and that licensed engineers should be required for them as they were for steam launches then. That bill died an early death in the committee room. On February 3, 1896, a similar bill was introduced in the New York State Senate by Senator Simon Seibert and referred to committee. Regarding such measures, a journalist pronounced, "The people are becoming their own engineers, and the knowledge necessary to operate a petroleum boat can easily be gained by any one. The true cause of this antipathy to the petroleum boat is to be found, not in the representation that it is unsafe, but in the fact that it is crowding out the steam launch, which is convincing proof of its safety."[1]

That same month a bill was brought up before the Ohio Legislature that proposed to prohibit any vehicle traveling upon the roads of that state if it was propelled by steam, gasoline, electricity, or any other motive power. However, "by the influence and prompt action of the American Motor League the hearing of this bill was indefinitely postponed. This virtually means the withdrawal of the bill." That same organization brought up the matter of admitting motor vehicles to the Chicago parks "and after considerable agitation the motor vehicle has been admitted to all of the Chicago parks on an equality with other vehicles."[2]

Automobile pioneer Charles E. Duryea was president of the American Motor League at that time. He commented on an upcoming auto road race in which the awards were to be made on a points basis as follows: speed, 50; construction, 25; operation, 15; and cost, 10. Duryea opposed that point system because he believed it offered a premium for speed "whereas the crying need of to-day is not speed, but better construction and better operation, and possibly, to suit the desires of the masses, less cost." He concluded, "The fact that the winning wagon on Nov. 28 [1895] made 7½ miles per hour over roads far too bad to permit any such speed for horse flesh, indicates that the speed of the present motor vehicle is already up to the legal limit allowed in cities, and up to or nearly as high a limit as safety will permit, even in the country."[3]

A journalist inquired at New York City police headquarters and at the office of the New York City Park Board early in 1896 to ascertain the regulations then in force covering the use of vehicles in New York City. At the police building, he was referred to the section of police laws relating to the speed of vehicles. "Any person who shall drive any horse through any street, lane, alley or public place within the City of New York, with greater speed than at the rate of five miles an hour, shall be deemed guilty of disorderly conduct, and upon conviction thereof by any magistrate, either upon confession of the party or competent testimony, may be fined for such offense any sum not exceeding $10; and, in default of payment of such fine, may be committed to a prison by such magistrate until the same is paid; but such imprisonment shall not exceed ten days."

The ordinances of the Park Board limited the speed of vehicles on the park drives to seven miles per hour. The four-in-hands of private owners were permitted to use the drives with either carriage or sleighs, but more than four horses were not allowed without a special permit. At that time, "No regulations have as yet been made with reference to motor carriages, or any vehicle propelled by other than animal power."[4]

Also in the spring of 1896 Indianapolis patent attorneys Thurman and Silvius had been constructing a "motor wagon" for F.M. Cook of Mt. Gilead, Ohio, a client. Wishing to test it, the firm applied in writing to the police department for permission to use a certain street for that purpose. They agreed to take every precaution and not to exceed a speed of 18 miles an hour. They did not ask for a perpetual license to be granted but only for permission given for one hour of a day to be specified at a later date. The clerk of the police board answered the company's letter and suggested that they call upon the Superintendent of Police to "see him in person."

The attorneys then wrote a second letter to the president of the board stating they could not see any reason for hesitation in granting permission when bicyclists frequently traveled at 18 miles per hour within the city limits. The Superintendent took offense and had his legal department write a letter back demanding an explanation for the language of the letter, which he construed to be an attempt at blackmail. The outcome of this disagreement was not reported but it was speculated that Thurman and Silvius would likely find it necessary to seek a place outside of the city to test their client's motor vehicle.[5]

The authorities of the town of Greenwich, Connecticut, took a stand against the automobile in the summer of 1896. According to a reporter, "Several carriages which passed through there lately frightened the staid old country plugs of Greenwich to such an extent that the prosecuting attorney interfered and forbade the operators from again venturing within the town limits."[6]

Charles Duryea discussed "bogies" associated with motor vehicles in a lengthy article in the summer of 1896. He observed the steam engine was reviled and criticized at the time of its invention, and now it was the same with the motor vehicle. The points raised by critics of the auto had no more validity than those of earlier times about earlier inventions. Regarding the question of noise, he pointed to the example of the noiseless bicycle. Since the bike was required in some jurisdictions to make noise by having a bell, Duryea drew the conclusion that society actually liked noise. Other bogies included vibration and odor.

Frightening horses was another reason for objecting to motor vehicles in the minds of some. But, "they know that such things as a piece of paper, a stray animal, a pile of rocks, a baby buggy, or a thousand and one other things, are often responsible for scared horses and runaway accidents." He declared that since none of those items caused a motor vehicle to be frightened, "we can see that the safety of the public is increased by the number of motor vehicles, that come into common use, rather than otherwise. If any one doubts this statement let him imagine all vehicles driven by motors, and he will thus see that accidents from frightening horses disappear entirely."[7]

A bill before the Massachusetts Legislature in March 1897 to license motor vehicles on the highways of that Commonwealth drew little praise from the editor of *Horseless Age.* He declared the measure "is a move in the right direction and its passage will greatly encourage the new industry all along the line." However, he added that the first draft of the proposal "is open to objection because of the needless restrictions which would make it a hindrance rather than a help to the new industry." He worried that in trying to specify how many brakes and levers a motor vehicle should have in order to be permitted on the roads "the law is getting into deep water and assuming a knowledge beyond that possessed by motor engineers of the present day."

Friends of the motor vehicle who were given a hearing before the committee dealing with the issue succeeded in convincing them that the bill should be amended to read somewhat as follows; "Motor vehicles may be run on the streets and highways of this Commonwealth, provided they are so constructed as always to be under the control of the operator." That wording, explained the editor, would not be the exact language of the act, but something like those words.[8]

As far as the editor was concerned, "It stands to reason that neither the court, the Legislature, nor any living man can specify or if called upon to specify what means an operator may adopt to attain the desired control of a vehicle, so long as the result is attained." He argued that the paragraph in the proposal having reference to the frightening of horses was certainly open to criticism. "The horse is an uncertain and at times an unmanageable animal, taking fright most unexpectedly at sights and noises, which, in the daily work of the world he must unavoidably encounter." In the introduction of a new vehicle upon the highway great care should be exercised, not because the new vehicle has not a right upon the highway, but because other vehicles have an equal right, he said. He urged car users to profess and practice forbearance and patience, with respect to the horse. In conclusion, the editor exclaimed, "Users of motor vehicles and manufacturers thereof will be forwarding their own interests if they exercise two-fold vigilance to avoid offending users of horses. By so doing they will smooth the way for the general introduction of the vehicle which cannot be frightened and cannot runaway."[9]

On April 13 and 14 a hearing was held in Massachusetts by the Committee on Roads and Bridges, to whom the proposed bill had been referred by the Massachusetts House. A great deal of interest was said to have been displayed and much testimony was offered in support of the measure which it was proposed to simplify so as to relieve the new vehicles from unnecessary restrictions. Reportedly, all that was desired by the authors of the bill was that some sanction be given to the use of cars on the streets, in order that people who wanted to operate them could feel safe from "any annoyance from lawsuits on account of frightened horses."

George Henry Hewitt, president of the Duryea Motor Wagon Company of Springfield, Massachusetts, told the committee his company received a great many letters showing that people who would otherwise use the carriages were holding back because they wanted to see what would be the result of a possible suit on account of damage or accident from the use of the motor vehicles in the street. Hewitt said, "Even if the present law permitted the running of the vehicles, some legislative sanction of their use would relieve this uncertainty and allow the speedy development and perfection of the motor carriage."[10]

At that hearing several representatives of leading merchants testified to the undoubted economy of the motor delivery over horse delivery then in use. Mr. Quimby, superintendent of Houghton and Dutton's delivery system, said his firm was anxious to use motor delivery because a truck could be run all day for less than a cent a mile, whereas it cost 20 cents a mile to run a two-horse wagon and the horses had to be changed at least once. A Duryea gasoline-powered wagon and a Whitney steam wagon were brought up to the Massachusetts State House during the hearing. The state governor, the mayor of Boston, and the members of the committee conducting the hearing were invited to ride and judge the advantages of the new vehicles for themselves. A journalist remarked, "They were not slow in accepting the invitation, and were so well pleased with the vehicle that it can be said, with some positiveness, that the bill in its amended form will go through."[11]

The committee on ordinances in New Haven, Connecticut, met to hold hearings on several petitions. One of the petitions came from the Hygeia Ice

Company, and others, for an ordinance regarding the use of horseless carriages on the streets. It was tabled by the committee in executive session. It sought to have the speed of horseless carriages regulated within the city limits. Mr. Clapp was the owner of a car frequently seen on the streets of Hartford. He argued the use of cars was not more dangerous than the use of horses.[12]

In Sacramento, California, the city Board of Trustees met in one of their weekly sessions. It already had an ordinance "that it shall be unlawful to drive any vehicle in any park in the city." A new ordinance introduced desired to fix the rate of speed at seven miles an hour within a specific area of the city bounded by Front Street, 12th Street, G Street, and P Street. That ordinance was introduced and discussed.[13]

An incident in Rochester, New York, involving a car accident brought the subject of motor vehicles prominently before the authorities of that city. A number of citizens of the city called on the city's Executive Board and at the police headquarters to protest against the use of motor carriages, particularly those propelled by steam, unless the owner furnished the city with a bond to indemnify it for any possible actions for damages from lawsuits brought to recover for injuries caused by the operation of an automobile. After giving the matter some consideration the Board concluded that it could not interfere with the "rational" use of motor vehicles, "especially those driven by electricity." However, the Board declared the emission of smoke or steam and the dropping of hot coals were items they "thought objectionable."[14]

Lamson Brothers were dry goods dealers in Toledo, Ohio, who introduced an electric delivery wagon in their business and the city authorities were unable to find in the municipal regulations any provision under which it could be taxed. A wheel tax was levied on one and two-horse carriages and wagons and on mules and bicycles "but nothing is said about electric vehicles. Consequently the vehicle goes untaxed for the present."[15]

On June 28, 1899, Chicago Mayor Carter Harrison IV directed the city law department to draft an ordinance requiring operators of automobiles and all vehicles propelled through the public streets by electric or other mechanical devices to be licensed. The proposed ordinance was to be introduced within a week and its immediate passage was advised. It was intended to subject the applicants to rigid examination and to bring the operators of horseless carriages under the supervision of the city authorities.[16]

An editor with a San Francisco newspaper commented, in July 1899, on the rapidity with which the auto was coming into general use in the East. As evidence, he cited the number of ordinances that various cities were enacting against its use. He remarked "There was once a host of ordinances against the use of bicycles. It was said of them, as of the automobile, that they frighten horses, endanger life, constitute a public nuisance and disturb the traffic of streets and highways. The bike has won its way" and so will the auto. The bike, moreover, caused an improvement in streets and highways "and so will the new machine." Editor John McNaught concluded, "The ordinances may stand fast but the automobile moves fast, and by and by it will run over the ordinances and then for self-protection the authorities will repeal them to get them out of the way."[17]

A report noted that the automobile had been "virtually barred" in the "aristocratic" summer resort of Bar Harbor, Maine. Under the present laws, it was not legal to pass a law absolutely prohibiting their use. However, the by-laws passed made it almost impossible for a car owner to run his machine in Bar Harbor during the hours from 10 a.m. to 10 p.m. Outside of those hours, it was only possible to run a car on little lanes and alleys at a speed not greater than five miles an hour, and then only after the machine had been licensed. After passing these by-laws, which referred to any vehicle propelled by machinery, it was suggested that the regulations adopted made the running of a road roller illegal so the citizens passed another by-law to permit the use of road rollers.[18]

At the request of Mayor Carter Henry Harrison IV, the city electrician of Chicago sent a letter to the city's Department of Law outlining the points to be covered in the ordinance to regulate automobiles. A license was to be issued to the operator upon examination by a board "covering his physical condition, mental balance, a reasonable knowledge of mechanical appliances and his familiarity with the parts of the apparatus liable to become deranged." The cost of the license was not to exceed 25 cents and was to be renewed annually. Accidents caused "clearly through the carelessness of operators of those vehicles would be sufficient reason for license revocation."

Operators of vehicles not licensed were to be punished by a fine of not less than $5 and not more than $25 for each offense. The speed of vehicles was not to exceed eight miles an hour. Vehicles were to be provided with a four-inch mechanically operated bell and approved brakes were to be provided for stopping vehicles. The license examining board was to consist of the commissioner of public works, the commission of health, the city engineer or the city electrician, and a secretary who was to keep records of the office and make provisions for examinations to be held twice each month. That examining board was to be given the authority to revoke licenses for violation of the ordinance on proof of carelessness or inability of the operators.[19]

Boston Mayor Josiah Quincy vetoed an ordinance adopted by the city's Board of Aldermen by which it was sought to regulate the use of automobiles in Boston. The proposed ordinance read as follows, "No person shall in any street use any vehicle other than a railroad or railroad vehicle, or a vehicle of the fire department, or a vehicle drawn or pushed by an animal, or a vehicle of a construction approved by the board of aldermen as not endangering the life or property of others." It passed by a vote of seven to five. In explaining his veto Quincy stated, "I cannot approve the passage at the present time of any regulation which seeks to impose restrictions upon the use of our streets by automobile so-called, because, in the first place, it seems to me that this important subject should be, and doubtless will be, further dealt with by State legislation, and, secondly, that in any case the present preliminary stage of development of automobiles it would be unwise for the board of aldermen to exercise its powers."[20]

When a petition was before the San Francisco Board of Supervisors from a dairyman requesting permission to run a milk wagon with a gasoline motor in the city, a local editor stated it was time for the question of rules and regulations for the coming automobile was thus fairly before the authorities of his city as it had been for some time before authorities in the East. The editor believed the issue could no longer be postponed. "In every large city the authorities are considering how to arrange rules for their use in such a way as to protect the public from danger and at the same time safeguard the rights of progressive people who desire to profit by the advantages of the new machine." He cited the *New York Tribune* in discussing the problem as it appeared there. Cars were steadily increasing and could be seen everywhere on the streets and in the parks.

The New York paper said, "Without attempting to pass upon the merits of any particular plan, it may be said unhesitatingly that some special rules for the regulation of the use of such vehicles would be entirely legitimate and may well be necessary. To make such rules would not be to discriminate against them, but merely to recognize the fact that they are different from horse vehicles and must be treated differently." The California newsman declared that not only were autos different from other vehicles but they differed widely from one another. "One type of the machine might be safety permitted, while another would be a cause of danger or a nuisance."[21]

That editor in San Francisco returned in print three days later to clarify the issue on which he was taking a position. He explained, "Every sort of vehicle used upon the streets of cities is subject to regulation. There are certain rules for street cars, for bicycles, for wagons, and for carriages, and some regulation must be provided for the automobile. *The Call* has advocated no particular rules.... So far from seeking to prevent the use of motor carriages on the streets, *The Call* would be the first to combat any attempt to enact ordinances that would handicap them."[22]

When the *Horseless Age* commented on the legal status of the motor vehicle in September 1899 it declared it to be "eminently sound.... The disabilities under which the motor vehicle now rests are due to prejudice and custom, and must rapidly be removed as enlightened judicial opinion interprets the laws already on the statute books, for according to those laws the motor vehicle has as good a right to the highways as any horse conveyance. In the coming days when the superiority of the motor is generally recognized, the onus of prejudice will rest upon the horse, and justly, for reasons often enumerated in these columns."[23]

A question arose in 1899 that troubled the industry for a short time, in a number of locations. That problem was the storage of gasoline, not just in cans stored in sheds but the gasoline in automobiles as they stood somewhere overnight. The *Horseless Age* editor wondered what would be the attitude of the fire underwriters toward the storage of gasoline for use in gasoline-powered vehicles. The liability to fire would be enhanced if large quantities of the hazardous liquid were permitted to be stored in the "stables of private owners of automobiles." People who owned horses had some type of stable on their property to house their horses. These outbuildings quickly became garages. Low-income people would not have owned horses in large cities such as New York and Chicago. They would have rented horses and horse-and-buggy rigs from livery stables, many of which converted to garages for autos.

Illustration shows an automobile driver who broke the traffic laws and has been placed in jail with other criminals, 1902. The caption says jail is the only remedy. Fines are a farce when dealing with the auto law breaker.

Continuing his musing the editor worried that the quantity of gasoline allowed in any of those stables would likely be fixed at a few gallons and thus, thought the editor, would be limited to the few gallons stored in the car tank itself. At the time there were few gas stations around and the idea of storing gasoline in cans in your garage to have enough on hand was realistic. The editor felt the main source of supply should be a tank outside, sunk in the earth, or otherwise protected, secured, and drawn from as occasion required. In buildings where children might be playing the editor suggested the screw caps of gasoline tanks should be locked in some fashion.[24]

A few days before the end of 1899 it was reported that the Bureau of Combustibles in New York was turning its attention to the storage of gasoline by motor vehicle owners. The head of that bureau stated in an interview that car owners were then violating the law in reference to the storage of this combustible and would hereafter be held to a stricter account for such violations. He argued that storage below the ground level was safest and "should be required in every case where the amount exceeds the contents of an ordinary vehicle tank." Even then possible trouble existed with regard to fire insurance protection for buildings where an auto was stored. In the case of a fire would the issuer payout, or could he avoid payment by pointing to unsafe or unlawful storage of gasoline?[25]

George Murray, chief of the New York Bureau of Combustibles, explained he believed it to be the duty of the police to be cognizant of the violation of the law by automobilists. He said the statute was emphatic and plain. And it was. The relevant law on storing gasoline made it clear the automobilist, whether owning the auto or not, and parking it someplace was always violating that part of the law.[26]

There was a more fatalistic acceptance of legislation and licensing of the automobile but the lobby still enthusiastically accepted and encouraged speed while vigorously opposing other rules such as licensing. It would take high-profile tragedies in 1902 and 1903 to start to turn the tide.

Chapter 10

Laws, Rules, and Regulations, 1900–1901

The trade journal *Horseless Age* called one of its issues the "Explosive Motor." That referred to the type of horseless carriage wherein an explosion took place in the cylinder of a gasoline engine. Some reportedly objected to such an inflammable title. The publication explained: "Those who object to our title take the ground that it is likely to mislead the public and inspire them with further dread of a machine which generates its power in so violent a manner and which on this account has been falsely described as 'dangerous' by rival interests."[1]

In January 1900 at a meeting of the Automobile Club of America, it was decided to take action for the protection of automobilists who in storing gasoline for their vehicles might come in conflict with the New York authorities. The club planned to retain lawyers to defend any automobilist arrested for violating the gasoline-storage law.[2]

The question arose as to whether gasoline could be lawfully carried in the tanks of autos on steam passenger ferries under Section 4,472 of the Revised Statutes. That section provided that no benzene or coal oil "or other like explosive burning fluids, or like dangerous articles, shall be carried as freight, or used as stores, on any steamer carrying passengers." The United States Treasury Department had jurisdiction on the matter and ruled against carrying gasoline-powered automobiles on the ferries. Immediately the Automobile Club of America petitioned the Treasury Department for a more liberal interpretation of the law, noting the law was adverse to the group's membership. The club argued that gasoline carried in the tanks of automobiles was not "freight" in the sense that was meant in the statute.[3]

Later the United States Senator Thomas C. Platt (NY) introduced a bill that sought to remove an awkward statute restriction under which owners of gasoline and naphtha-powered autos were barred from taking such vehicles aboard steamers or ferryboats. Because of the statute, the ferry boats running between Jersey City, New Jersey, and New York refused to transport autos run by other than electricity. Platt's bill allowed steamboats to carry the machines propelled by means of "explosive fuel," like naphtha and gasoline, provided there was no fire in them while they were on board.[4]

President McKinley and others posing in an open automobile with mountains and rustic structure in background, 1897.

In February 1901 Platt's bill passed both houses of Congress and was sent to the President for his signature. President William McKinley signed the Platt bill into law. That legally permitted the carrying on ferries of automobiles using gasoline as fuel. Under the law, captains of ferry boats had to right to refuse to carry such vehicles if they chose, but it was not likely that they would exercise it if the second provision of that law was obeyed. That provision mandated that the fires of steam autos had to be extinguished while the vehicle was being ferried on such a boat.[5]

For two years after the passage of the Platt law permitting ferry companies to carry automobiles using gasoline, at the option of the captain, the Hoboken Ferry Company refused to exercise that option. The company traveled between Hoboken, New Jersey, and New York but barred all gasoline-powered cars from its boats. Then the company was purchased by the Lackawanna Railroad Company and one of the first acts of the new management was to accept gasoline cars on its boats. A reporter concluded that the decision "is of interest as indicating that the prejudice against automobiles as dangerous machines is on the wane."[6]

Reportedly, the question as to whether the operator of a steam automobile should be required to obtain a steam engineer's license before being allowed to operate a steamer on the streets of Washington, D.C., had been agitating District of Columbia authorities for some time. G. Edmonston wrote to the District of Columbia Commissioners requesting permission to use a locomobile steamer. He said the vehicle was the same as an "ordinary automobile" but steam power was used. Edmonston also inquired whether he would be required to take out an engineer's license. The letter from Edmonston along with his request was referred to the board of examiners of steam engineers and a report was received from them soon after stating that a license would be required.

The Engineer Commissioner then referred the matter to the Superintendent of the Water Department who responded he had examined one of the steamers and suggested that inasmuch as the mechanism was "very simple" the operator should not be required to take out an engineer's license. Commissioner Wight reviewed the papers when they were returned to the Commissioners for action and decided that permission to run the machine on the streets should be granted but that Edmonston would be required to obtain an engineer's license if he desired to run the automobile himself.[7]

A reporter with a Chicago newspaper remarked, "Failure of the city authorities to enforce the automobile ordinance is fast becoming a source of popular complaint. The latest to protest against the recklessness of horseless carriage drivers is Commissioner McGann who, while driving on Michigan Avenue Sunday, narrowly escaped being run down by one of the new vehicles with C.K.G. Billings on the driver's box." Those facts plus the circumstances under which the ordinance became a dead letter made a good story, thought the journalist. The ordinance was fathered by the administration and was received by the public and the promoters of the automobile as "a wise and proper provision." Mayor Carter Harrison approved it, and the measure was drafted by the law department with the advice of the city electrician, Commissioner McGann, and the chief of police. The measure was then readily passed by the Chicago City Council.[8]

While the measure was pending before Mayor Harrison, C.K.G. Billings called upon the mayor in regard to the city's overdue gas bills. Billings happened to see the ordinance on the mayor's desk and complained when he realized he had to get a license to run an automobile. Billings complained forcefully and dared the city to make him appear before a licensing board to be examined, before leaving Harrison's office. Later that date City Electrician Ellicott called upon the mayor for instructions with regard to enforcement of the automobile ordinance. Harrison exclaimed, "Well, I don't think the law will hold. You can't make a citizen pay a license to ride in his own carriage." According to the reporter "that ended the matter. The ordinance became law without the mayor's signature, but Mr. Ellicott dropped it like a hot coal." Commissioner McGann alone insisted the law was good and should be enforced. Automobile lobbyists favored the ordinance, reportedly, because it would raise competency levels and thus reduce accidents. As it was, unlicensed, every accident had the potential to raise the hostility level against the new machines.[9]

A report from a Philadelphia newspaper that was reprinted in a Kansas City publication cited the arrival of the automobile age and that horseless carriages were no longer a novelty in any of the large cities in America. Pointing to France, which the article believed was somewhat ahead of the United States in the automobile age, the article declared. "One thing we can do with perfect propriety is to adopt some of the French laws regulating the operation of automobiles in parks and on public highways. Among other things these laws provide that these vehicles must be so constructed as not to allow any matter to escape which might cause explosions or unpleasant smells.... All vehicles must be lighted at night, must be reversible and capable of being brought to a standstill within a given distance." With the coming of the automobile age American municipalities, the article argued, could "profit greatly by studying the French laws before adopting rules for the regulation of horseless carriages."[10]

A law enacted in Chicago mandated that automobiles had to be equipped with fenders. All manner of autos were included in the regulation. All fenders had to be of the "basket" pattern and made of steel. Under the ordinance, it would be unlawful to operate automobiles without fenders after April 1, 1900. The penalty for violating that law was a fine of not less than $25 and not more than $100 for each offense.[11]

The directors of Forest Hills Cemetery in Boston barred all autos from the property. They placed a sign at the entrance that read, "Automobiles are not allowed in this cemetery." Thereafter only horse-drawn carriages were to be allowed entrance. The directors had followed in the action taken by the Boston Park Commission, much of whose domain lay almost contiguous to the cemetery, and the reason given by the cemetery was substantially the same as that of the Park Board. "They are afraid automobiles will frighten horses." Secretary Potter of the cemetery corporation explained by saying, "We have a large number of lots here which we are bound to keep in order perpetually, making good any damage that may be caused.... If a runaway should occur, you can see that a great deal of damage might be caused ... we do not care to take any risks." It was added that when the horses became accustomed to automobiles the ban would be removed.[12]

Brookline, Massachusetts, described as the wealthiest town near Boston, was reported to "have been a mecca for automobilists every since they began to be at all common." Rules adopted by the Selectmen of Brookline included that cars were to have a speed limit of 10 miles per hour within the city limits. Every auto in town "shall bear the number of its license in a conspicuous place in the rear of the carriage in figures of Arabic characters, not less than 2 inches in height." Every person in charge of an auto waiting for passengers in any city street, square, or public place in Brookline "shall obey the direction of any police officer respecting the place of standing, and the route to be taken when going to or leaving such place." The owner and driver of an automobile used in violation of any of the foregoing regulations would be subject to a fine of up to $20.[13]

At Albany, a bill introduced by New York State Assemblyman James K. Apgar of Westchester County would have made it unlawful to operate an auto without obtaining a license from an examining board of one person appointed by the County Board of Supervisors. In cities of "the first class," the Commissioners of Boiler Inspections would constitute the examining board. The fee for the examination was fixed at $1, and a fee of $2 was to be charged for a license that was to expire at the end of one year. The bill further provided that the Examining Board was authorized to revoke or suspend a license for a period not exceeding six months "where there is satisfactory proof of drunkenness, incompetency or reckless driving on the part of the operator." Any person violating the act was to be adjudged guilty of a misdemeanor and fined not less than 10 dollars and not more than 400 dollars.[14]

Dr. J.H. Linsley of Burlington, Vermont, owned a steamer and made a comment on the red flag law then in effect in Vermont. He wrote that he knew of no instance in which the red flag law had been enforced in Vermont and that it would be difficult to get a state's attorney to entertain an action against the driver of a steamer unless the driver was unusually careless.[15]

Dr. T. Royal Cook of Ballston Spa, New York, brought a lawsuit against Louis W. Moore of Watertown, New York, for damages caused by Cook's horse running away at the sight of a steam carriage driven by Moore. Justice Russell of the Saratoga County, New York, court held that a steam carriage was subject to the old law requiring the driver or engineer of a road locomotive to send out a flagman one-eighth of a mile ahead to warn travelers of its approach. That is, Russell ruled the red flag law was in force. In the case of Jonathan B. West of Rochester, New York, a different decision was reached. Judge Sutherland held on appeal that the steam carriage had the same rights on the highway as a horse-drawn conveyance. That is, Sutherland ruled the red flag law was not in force.[16]

A reporter in Washington, D.C., commented that the advent of the automobile had found the statutes in many of the states in an altogether unwelcome condition. One such awkward interpretation of such laws had just been rendered by a judge of the State Supreme Court of New York State, who held the law relating to road engines those "clanging, heavy panting machines for road rolling or for running threshers and the like, applies to all forms of automatic vehicles." One of the provisions of the statute was that a runner had to precede each such engine by at least an eighth of a mile bearing a red flag in order to warn approaching horsemen and drivers of the possibility of a runaway. That decision grew out of a New York case for damages initiated by the owner of a horse that became frightened at the approach of an automobile and smashed things generally. This commentator expected the red flag law would soon disappear, at least with respect to automobiles.[17]

The origins of the red flag law in New York State went back to 1866. There was no law in the state of New York limiting the speed of steamers or other horseless carriages to four miles an hour. The only law bearing on the subject was to be found in the laws of 1866, Chapter 269, Section 1. It read as follows, "Vehicles Propelled by Steam on Highways—It shall not be lawful for any owners, or the servant or agent of any owner or owners of a carriage, vehicle or engine propelled by steam to allow, permit or use the same to pass over, through or upon any public highway, road or street, unless such owner or owners, or agent or servant shall send before the same a person of mature age at least one-eighth of a mile in advance to notify and warn persons traveling or using said highway, road or street, with horses or other domestic animals, of the approach of such carriage, vehicle or engine, and at night said person to carry a red light, except in incorporated cities and villages."[18]

New York State Governor Benjamin Odell signed the amended highway bill of the Automobile Club of America in early 1901, putting the measure into force throughout New York State. One amendment was to include the old Red Flag Law from 1866 and to incorporate it fully into the new law with one sentence added. "This section shall not apply to any carriage or motor vehicle, propelled by steam, developing less than 25 horse power, other than a steam traction engine."[19]

Lawmakers in Grand Rapids, Michigan, drafted car regulating measures within city limits in November 1900. Under the terms of the measure, all persons handling autos had to be licensed by the mayor, who had the discretionary power to grant, withhold, or revoke licenses. The license fee was one dollar for a license that had a term of one year. Speed in the business center of Grand Rapids was limited to seven miles an hour and 15 miles an hour elsewhere in the city. All cars had to be equipped with bells or gongs that were not less than two inches in diameter and not more than four inches. Violations of any of the rules of the community led to a fine of 25 dollars.[20]

The city council of Rochester, New York, passed an ordinance that mandated cars to carry two lamps and a gong or a bell. The speed limit in Rochester was fixed at a maximum of six miles per hour in a defined section and a maximum speed of eight miles an hour in all other areas. Vehicles were required to keep to the right side of the street, had to pass on the left, and had to light those lamps no later than one hour after sundown.[21]

Around the same time, the authorities of Madison, New Jersey, passed an ordinance limiting the speed of autos within city limits to eight miles an hour and providing that every vehicle must have a lamp of sufficient illuminating power to be plainly seen from a distance of 100 yards. Those lamps were to be lit between one hour of sunset and sunrise. Bells or gongs also had to be carried. The bell was to be rung 50 feet from every street corner and had to be of such volume as to be heard from a distance of 100 feet. A maximum fine of $25 or imprisonment for up to 30 days was provided for a violation of the provisions of the ordinance. The minimum penalty was a $10 fine or five days in jail.[22]

Cincinnati authorities passed an ordinance introduced some weeks earlier to regulate the operation of automobiles on the city streets. It provided no auto was to be operated on the streets between sundown and daylight without a lamp of sufficient power to cast its rays 200 feet or more and without an alarm or bell or whistle, that had to be sounded at all street intersections. Speed was restricted to eight miles per hour "and no two machines may run abreast without special permission." Violations of the ordinance led to a fine of $5 for each offense.[23]

The *Horseless Age* trade publication came out with an editorial about fenders for cars, in the wake of the New York City Council's having enacted an ordinance making the addition of fenders to automobiles obligatory. The editor considered the question of fenders to be complex, with no conclusion for or against fenders being known. He was clearly against fenders in the case of pleasure carriages. "Not only are these vehicles at the moment permitted in city streets extremely manageable, but the use of fenders would so increase the space they require to move in as to constitute a grave objection, it would render the vehicles unsightly ... in general the enjoyment and use of the automobile would be seriously impaired by the adoption of such an ordinance." The editor concluded, "Let the city authorities content themselves for the present with a strict enforcement of the speed regulations, and see that no morally irresponsible persons are permitted to operate automobiles, and there would be no need of any further encroachment upon the liberties of motor vehicle users."[24]

Scranton, Pennsylvania, Director of Public Safety F.L. Wormser issued an order to Superintendent of Police Robling to strictly enforce the ordinance regulating the running of bicycles and horseless carriages on the streets of Scranton. The ordinance provided that every rider of a bicycle or horseless carriage should ring a bell when approaching the intersections of streets, turning corners, or passing any other bicycle, automobile, or vehicle. Riding bikes or driving cars at a speed greater than eight miles per hour was forbidden. The penalty for violation of any provision of the ordinance was a fine of not less than $2, nor more than $10 for each offense.[25]

Under a bill in St. Louis, horseless carriages were limited to a speed of eight miles an hour in the city and six miles an hour in the parks. The penalty for violating the ordinance was a fine that could range from $5 up to $500. Another bill proposed the auto license fee should be $20 per year.[26]

The Board of Supervisors of San Mateo County in California were expected to pass a strict ordinance at their next meeting regulating the running of automobiles on the county roads. Superintendent Coleman of San Mateo at a board meeting said the machines were becoming a hazardous recreation. He desired a limit to the speed of a car on mountain roads to be set so slow as to make the ride unattractive. After consideration, the board finally determined that the following regulations should be incorporated into an ordinance. Autos were to be operated only by those who possessed a certificate attesting to their competency. The exam for such competency was to be made by a board of examiners. On approaching a team of horses the car must turn to the side of the road and come to a stop. No noise (such as allowing steam to escape or the clanging of gongs) was to be permitted while the team was passing. A speed limit, probably of six miles per hour, was to be imposed.[27]

In February 1901 the District of Columbia Commissioners sent letters to the mayors of several cities in America asking for information relative to the police regulations in force affecting the operation of motor vehicles. Regarding those replies the Commissioners concluded, "it is shown that very little has been done officially in the cities of the country to place regulations upon the speed of this class of carriages." From New York City the mayor wrote that the matter had been referred to the New York Police Department and that it was still under consideration. In Philadelphia, no official action had been taken relative to cars in Philadelphia. The chairman of the Board of Police in Boston stated the introduction of those vehicles into the streets had not given much trouble. Horses got accustomed to the new vehicles. The only note of concern was the speed which was sometimes too great. Motor vehicles in Boston were still then under the same regulations as carriages drawn by horses.

From Indianapolis, the mayor said the use of such vehicles had not been so general as to attract attention from the legislators. The licensing of horseless carriages in Indianapolis was $3 per annum. Cincinnati had a special ordinance, number 611, that specified all motor vehicles must carry a lighted lantern after sunset and before sunrise. Speed was limited to eight miles an hour and no two cars could travel abreast. Cars in Detroit were not so common as to call the attention of the public to the need for legislation. In Buffalo, New York, no official action had been taken and autos were under the same regulations as horse-drawn carriages and bicycles.[28]

Despite the above documentation that little in the way of regulations had been imposed on the industry, the editor of the *Horseless Age* whined, "The long expected era of motor vehicle legislation is at hand.... In most cases these laws are ill judged, conceived in terror of the automobile as a sort of modern juggernaut that is going to ride over the rights of all...."[29]

The first auto legislation from the solons of South Carolina was found in the following act to prohibit careless and reckless driving on the public roads of the state. The law stated, "it shall be unlawful for any person to ride or drive any horse or mule or bicycle or locomobile or automobile upon any street or alley in any city or town or highway of this State in a willfully careless or reckless manner." Upon conviction, any violator was punished by a fine not exceeding $100 or imprisoned for a term not exceeding 30 days.[30]

George F. Chamberlin of the Automobile Club of America received a telegram from Albany, New York, that promised good news for all owners and drivers of automobiles. A bill passed the New York State Assembly and was expected to easily pass the state senate. The intent of the bill was to give autos the same privileges accorded to other vehicles: rights to drive over all roads, highways, park drives, and so forth (but barred from specific cycle, equestrian or pedestrian paths). The bill passed in the Assembly by four votes. Officials of the Park Department opposed the bill. The measure also provided that city and town officials in New York State could not pass ordinances restricting the speed of autos to less than eight miles per hour in cities and towns or less than 15 miles per hour in the county districts.[31]

A month later New York Governor Benjamin Odell signed the highway bill "of the Automobile Club of America." One section of the law required every owner of a motor vehicle to register it within 30 days after the law took effect. Registration required the name and address of the owner plus a brief description of the vehicle. The cost of registration was a $1 fee.[32]

A warning was sounded by the *Horseless Age* with regard to Massachusetts. That state was "threatened with restrictive automobile legislation. A bill is before the Legislature authorizing cities and towns to regulate the speed of autos within their jurisdiction. It was worded in such a way that vehicles propelled by horses or persons [bicycles] were not included." The trade publication and the Automobile Club of America were described as being "extremely upset." The editor asserted, "Adverse legislation of this kind has been successfully warded off in New York State and a bill substituted which is eminently fair to all interests concerned." He added, "We have no doubt that this bill ... can be adopted as a model in State automobile legislation the country over, and earnestly request out readers, wherever they may be, to exert their influence to that end."

Continuing in his hysteria the editor thundered, "In Massachusetts, in particular, the situation appears to be grave, calling for immediate and determined action on the part of both of the Boston automobile clubs. To let the occasion slip and saddle the sport and the industry of the Bay State with such onerous conditions would be inexcusable in the light of New York State's excellent example."[33]

The "dangerous conditions" of the streets of Washington, D.C., as described by a reporter with a local newspaper, received the serious consideration of Major Richard H. Sylvester, the DC Chief of Police. It was expected that several additions to the police regulations would shortly be forwarded to the Commissioners for approval. A corps of bicycle cops were recently detailed to patrol the main thoroughfares and arrest those persons found driving their vehicles at an unlawful rate of speed. But few arrests were made and those who had been taken into court escaped with "light fines." Chief Sylvester remarked, "The most serious offenders against the speed regulation are the operators of automobiles and other self-propelling vehicles."

When bicycles were introduced to the population the people were awakened to the new dangers. Regulations were made and enforced and soon the danger was minimized. But, observed the journalist, "Since the introduction of the self-propelling vehicle practically nothing has been done to relieve the dangerous conditions upon the streets and regulate the operation of the vehicles. It is not an uncommon sight to see these vehicles spinning over the smooth asphalt at from twenty to thirty miles an hour, shooting around corners with a suddenness that drives terror to the hearts of even those who are used to heavy travel and crowded roadways."[34]

The Indiana Supreme Court rendered a decision in April 1901 reversing a judgment for damages recovered by Claude Bennett against Edward Bogue. The court held that a city or town had no power by ordinance to exclude from its streets autos, bicycles, motorcycles, or other vehicles operated by something other than a horse on the basis of their being new or novel. The fact they interfered with drivers of animals and that injury occurred by reason of fright to such animals made no difference.

The plaintiff was a boy of 12 who was riding a bike that collided with a steamer that Bogue was driving through the streets of Kokomo, Indiana. One of the facts relied on to show negligence on the part of Bogue that caused the resultant injury was that he was violating a city ordinance. That ordinance prohibited the running of steam vehicles through the streets of Kokomo. Judge Monks, who wrote the opinion, declared, "Horses may be and often are frightened by the newly adopted locomotion, but it would be as reasonable to treat the horse as a public nuisance for its tendency to shy and be frightened by unaccustomed objects as to regard the vehicle propelled by new methods of locomotion as a public nuisance for its tendency to frighten horses."

In the case of injury, the question was down to whether there was negligence imputed to someone. Monks stated city authorities had no authority over the street to prohibit the running of automobiles on all of its streets. "Such an ordinance is not a reasonable exercise of the power of cities over their streets, and is therefore invalid." Monks did agree that authorities could regulate public travel on streets and prohibit certain classes of vehicles from using certain streets, such as establishing bicycle paths and pedestrian zones.[35]

John T. McDonough, New York State Secretary of State, in accordance with Section 166 of the Highway Act began to register autos in 1901. Each owner had to register his vehicle giving his name and address, a brief description of the machine, and pay the $1 fee. In return, the owner received a certificate of registration signed by McDonough. According to a journalist, "One of the objects of the law was to put a stop to the harassing of the owners of automobiles with local regulations. The law says that the owners of automobiles 'shall not be required to obtain any license or permit pursuant to the provisions of any local or municipal resolution or ordinance.'"

As of September 3, 1901, 715 persons had paid the fee to have their vehicles registered. Inhabitants of other states about to make a tour with an auto in New York State sent to Albany and procured the Secretary of State's certificate. In the article 18 people were listed who had registered automobiles. They included John Jacob Astor (registered three cars), Albert C. Bostwick (registered seven autos), Henry Clews, Frank Jay Gould, Edwin Gould, George J. Gould, Charles R. Otis, George Foster Peabody, William Rockefeller, J.R. Roosevelt, and Alfred G. Vanderbilt.[36]

An editorial in a New York City newspaper declared that auto accidents had become too numerous in that city. The auto had come to stay and there was no doubt about that. Nonetheless, regulations of cars were needed and the vehicles had to be kept within the ordinary speed limit. It was just a general comment but part of a growing chorus demanding more control be exercised by the authorities over the running of horseless carriages. The editorial stated, "The proper regulation of automobile driving is, we believe, similarly to be effected. Let the majority of motormen, who are law abiding and courteous, make it plain that they disapprove the abuses which are now so often practical, and that the offending motormen will lose caste in the automobile world, and the evil will speedily be corrected."[37]

An editorial on the same subject in the same newspaper appeared six weeks after the first one. The editor again mentioned the increasing number of auto accidents and reckless driving in general. "The abuse of their privileges by the reckless automobile racers has convinced almost every community which they frequent, both at home and abroad, of the necessity of imposing stricter limits upon their speed, providing distinct regulations for their conduct and requiring proof of competence to manage the machines. We may expect in due time to see the persons who think it smart to dash along roads at the rate of fifty miles an hour, frightening horses and running over pedestrians, reduced to order by wholesome discipline."

Wistfully the editor mentioned France where cars had to carry license plates on the front and rear. Those plates had to be illuminated at night and have "large figures" on them. It might solve one of the problems in New York, namely the escape of fleeing drivers who could not be identified. The auto must be regulated insisted the editor; "It cannot be allowed to have the liberty permitted to a horse and wagon under laws made for horse and wagon conditions.... They should in all cases be required to have expert managers, and be equipped with appliances fully adequate to the control under all circumstances of the energy which they wield."[38]

Increasing accidents and deaths led to a greater push for legislation and a change in attitude as the lobby industry accepted the inevitable, to a degree.

Chapter 11

Laws, Rules, and Regulations, 1902–1903

At the beginning of 1902 new auto regulations appeared to be in the works. A bill was then in contemplation making speeding above the limits prescribed by the current New York State law a misdemeanor punishable by imprisonment. It was introduced by Senator Cocks of Nassau County, Long Island. The *Horseless Age* noted that was not by any means the only anti-auto legislation proposed and the situation appeared so "alarming" that Albert R. Shattuck, president of the Automobile Club of America, and several members of the Law Committee of the ACA went to Albany to lobby against the measure. George F. Chamberlain, chairman of that Law Committee was quoted as saying there was a "perfect flood of anti-automobile bills pending. He emphasized the necessity of co-operation from the National Association of Automobile Manufacturers and the clubs of Buffalo, Syracuse and Long Island in fighting these bills."

In the previous winter's fight at Albany "against hostile legislation during the discussion of the present highway law the National Association of Automobile Manufacturers took an active part and was represented by counsel at the hearings." NAAM president S.T. Davis, Jr., was asked what action his group proposed to take in the emergency. He said the situation would receive the attention of the organization's executive committee at its next meeting.[1]

Some six weeks later, the trade publication called it gratifying that the Robinson bill had increased the speed limits in city and county to 10 and 20 miles per hour respectively. But the efforts of "the automobile interests" to strike out altogether the "misdemeanor" clause in the Cocks bill had been futile, to that time. Punishment for exceeding the speed limit in the Robinson bill "seems unreasonably high," the journal opined, expressing hope of getting it reduced.[2]

When the hearing on the Cocks bill took place before the Codes Committee of the New York State Senate, Shattuck, as president of the ACA, appeared. He gave what a pro-auto reporter called a "very able address, in which he opposed the measure as too drastic. He said that he and his confreres objected to the automobile public being classed as criminals." Chamberlin of the ACA objected to the speed limit of 15 on county roads, citing recent brake tests carried out in Great Britain. Senators Cocks, Henry Hill and Patrick Trainor inquired why the

ACA had not taken proceedings against some of the more prominent violators of the speed law. Chamberlin retorted by asking why the authorities had not acted under the present code. Under the Cocks bill a speeding violation was a misdemeanor. That meant a fine of not more than $500 or a commitment to jail of not more than one year, or both.[3]

The Cocks "automobile speed bill" passed in the New York Senate. It proposed a speed limit of eight miles an hour for city and town limits and 20 miles per hour elsewhere in the state. The penalty for a first offense was to be a fine of $50. For the second and subsequent offense, the penalty was to be a fine or imprisonment not to exceed $100 or six months in jail or both. The penalty was a proposed amendment to his bill that Cocks opposed and cited the extreme difficulty authorities had in catching speeders. It was still the day of the open car and drivers wore green goggles, peaked caps, and masks and were close to impossible to identify. Catching a speeder was often a matter of luck, such as one being held up by a long, passing train. The penalty amendment came from Senator Edgar Brackett and passed by a vote of 24 to 19. Senator William McKinney argued the amendment "simply softened the rigors of the law for the benefit of a privileged class."[4]

The Cocks bill received New York governor Benjamin Odell's signature on March 28, 1902, thus becoming law. That law provided a speed limit of eight miles an hour in cities and incorporated villages. It included the words "except where a greater rate of speed is permitted by the ordinance of a city."[5]

The House of Representatives in Iowa passed a bill in February 1902 to regulate the running of automobiles on the highways and streets of Iowa. The bill required autos to have brakes, lights, and other appliances, and on a signal from a driver of a horse team to the auto it had to come to a full stop, so as not to scare the horses. Speed was regulated to eight miles an hour on streets of cities and towns and 15 miles an hour in the country. On bridges, the maximum speed was five miles an hour. As well, the bill required that licenses be secured by people who ran autos. Some members of the House, unhappy with the bill, offered a total of 22 amendments, all rejected. The bill passed with 88 votes in favor and 12 "not voting."[6]

A speed bill was introduced into the Massachusetts Legislature, fathered by Representative Collins of Great Barrington. Under that bill, the speed was limited to 10 miles an hour within the limits of any city or fire district, and 15 miles per hour outside such limits. Also the selectmen of any town could limit speed further in business districts or thickly settled areas of their town, provided they posted notices to that effect.[7]

Not every state got on the bandwagon to limit the speed of automobiles. A bill was voted down in the New Jersey Senate at Trenton on February 25, 1902. The proposal would have limited the speed of automobiles.[8]

In Washington, the District of Columbia Commissioners gave a public hearing to a representative of the National Capital Automobile Club. The club had let it be known it wanted to appear before the board to discuss the police regulations relating to motor vehicles. Charles E. Foster was that representative. Foster said the club was in general agreement with the regulations. He agreed there should be a speed limit and also agreed there should be some means of identifying the operator of any machine who violated the regulations. Foster said that what his club opposed was that the regulations should apply to all vehicles, not just motor vehicles. The club denied the right of the Commissioners to single out one class of vehicle for regulations that did not apply to all the others. He added that his club had sought legal advice and was led to believe this proposed law would not stand up in court and would be thrown out as a discriminatory law.[9]

The idea of a national license for cars had been briefly mentioned. This time the idea put forward in the trade journal *Horseless Age* was for national automobile legislation. "It would certainly be a great incentive to automobile touring if laws could be passed by the National Government, regulating the speed of automobiles for the whole country, and providing for the issue of operators' permits good in any part of the country. The need for such legislation is especially felt by automobilists in the Eastern states, where touring and automobilism generally are most developed." It was annoying if a driver planned to pass through several states on a touring trip but "before a trip of this kind can be entered upon the automobile laws of all the states must be studied and a permit obtained in each for driving an automobile."

The journal complained further, "Aside from the speed limits and rules for obtaining driving permits, the laws usually make provision for identification plates, give rules for carrying lamps, etc., and these, in some instances, are widely different and cannot be satisfied by the same apparatus." It noted automobile regulations in force over the entire country had been passed in the parliaments of England and France and that greatly simplified things. A hopeful sign for the writer was that the AAA had included national legislation in its program of things to get done. Such restrictions and obstacles were to be removed if auto touring was to dramatically increase, as this writer believed it would over the coming few years.[10]

A new Rhode Island automobile law set a speed limit of eight miles an hour within the "compact" parts of cities and towns and 10 miles per hour outside the compact parts. Speed was to be reduced at intersections only until the auto was through the intersection. Each owner was to "conspicuously" display the initials of his name in a suitable place on his motor vehicle in block letters not less than two inches high "in order that the owner of any such machine may be readily ascertained." A car had to have a bell or horn "but shall not so cause said bell or horn to cause unnecessary noise or disturbance." A muffler had to be attached in the case of any vehicle that used an "explosive engine." Violation of the regulations for a first offense was a $10 fine or 10 days in jail. For a second and subsequent offense, the penalty was $20 or 20 days in jail.[11]

Mayor James M. Seymour of Newark, New Jersey, returned to the Board of Works the ordinance recently passed to regulate the speed of automobiles. "He vetoed it because it provided heavier penalties for fast automobiles than the original ordinance forbidding the fast running of trolley cars and horse-drawn vehicles," explained a reporter. He thought the fine should be the same as that imposed on the other classes of vehicles, arguing the higher penalty was discrimination.[12] The city fathers of Binghamton, New York, who were trying to enforce their seven miles per hour speed limit found the ordinance to conflict with the New York State speed law and had to amend their ordinance.[13]

Henry G. Morris, president of the Philadelphia Automobile Club, and his vice president John S. Muckle were appointed members of a committee. They and the representatives of the Road Drivers' Association and the Wheelmen's Society were to confer with a city council committee and prepare a suitable ordinance "to regulate all forms of transportation within the city of Philadelphia."[14]

In charging the Grand Jury of Bucks County, Pennsylvania, for the September 1902 term, the court called attention to the "new form of nuisance that was menacing the public," referring to automobiles. "It is a common thing to read of deaths caused by the engines being run by reckless men, who, by reason of their great wealth, think they owe nothing to the safety of the community. What farmer or farmer's wife feels safe to hitch up and drive upon the public highway by reason of these engines?" asked the judge. He was reminding the jury that the safety of the public on the streets was a consideration for them and instructing them that the drivers who ran engines at reckless speed could be arrested and indicted "notwithstanding their social or financial standing." The judge hoped this "plain violation of the law" would draw the attention of police and that any violation would be brought before the court where prompt justice would be meted out.[15]

With pressure mounting for more legislation regarding the automobile, the *Horseless Age* published an editorial summarizing the benefits of the car. It declared the new machine to be safer, cheaper, healthier, and a "more expeditious and comfortable mode of travel," compared to the horse. The editor thought the car had come nowhere close to its potential and that it was still mainly a pleasure vehicle. A car was especially advantageous for touring, as a carriage with a good team of horses could travel only 30 to 40 miles in a day. With an automobile, twice that distance could be covered in less actual running time. With the horse gone, there was no manure or dust on city streets. Sanitary conditions improved "and the noise and traffic lessened, owing to the greater speed and shorter length of the vehicles, there will be room for more traffic with less crowding." His optimistic confidence was nowhere more misplaced than when he added "owing to the greatly superior control of motor vehicles, the streets will be safer for pedestrians."[16]

Herman Unger of Newark, New Jersey, was stopped for fast driving at Scotch Plains, New Jersey. He carried his case to the Supreme Court. His lawyers claimed the speeding law was unconstitutional because it fixed a different rate of speed for automobiles from that of other vehicles.[17]

Auto regulations in Kansas City, Missouri, required a maximum speed of eight miles an hour in downtown business districts and 10 miles an hour in other areas of the city. Side-lighted lamps that were visible at a distance of 100 feet had to be provided on the vehicle. Identifying numbers of the machine had to be painted in red and legible figures at least one inch long upon the front and side of each lamp. Owners of cars had to register with the license inspector. On the rear of each automobile there had to be painted in white on a black background legible figures at least eight inches in height. The driver had to be duly licensed, which involved undergoing an examination before the board of engineers as to his capacity and skill. A fee of $3 was charged for each license with a $1 renewal fee. Drivers had to reduce speed and, if necessary, come to a stop when horses showed evidence of fright. At crossings, speed was to be reduced from the stated rate of eight or ten miles per hour. Violation of the ordinance was a misdemeanor and upon conviction, the fine imposed was to be not less than $1, nor more than $500.[18]

A major piece on automobile legislation was published in *Horseless Age* on November 5, 1902, and ran to eight pages in length. It began, "The whole subject of automobile legislation in the United States may be said to resolve itself into the questions of proper speed limits, license and how to secure the greatest possible uniformity of regulation throughout the land." Continuing on, the piece said, "At one time it was held that no special legislation was necessary to regulate the new form of locomotion, but this view, if still held by some has certainly lost ground during the last year." Several states such as New York, Connecticut, and Massachusetts had already passed laws regulating traffic. In states in which there were as yet no such laws, numerous local ordinances had been passed. He cited Chamberlin of the ACA Law Committee, pointing out that no limit could be prescribed for any specified district which was safe for all conditions. If limits were fixed low enough to be safe for the worst conditions, they would be too restrictive to render auto traffic practicable.

For example, it was so difficult to establish speed limits because there were too many districts, and so forth. "This fact is recognized by all State laws, since they contain a clause stipulating that the vehicles shall not be driven at any greater rate of speed than is safe and proper, having regard for the conditions of traffic upon the road or words to that effect." What was not mentioned was that while such conditions were stipulated in some regulations, most added a rider to specify "but under no circumstance more than 10 miles an hour." Commenting on the vague clause the editor declared, "The question arises, is not this rule sufficient, and is not any definite speed limit which does not take account of the condition of traffic upon the road superfluous and injurious to the interest of automobilists?" He did not agree with the idea that a speed limit was desirable, even for open country.[19]

Regarding licenses, the article noted that Chicago was the first to adopt licensing of drivers. Recently Cleveland, Ohio, and some smaller communities followed suit. "There is little or no objection to licensing if the laws are formulated so as to insure the greatest convenience in obtaining the license and to prevent abuses of a political nature." The editor admitted that a Federal license law seemed incompatible with the United States' system of government. The least that could be hoped for was state license laws and an agreement between neighboring, if not all, states, recognizing licenses issued by the other states. Speed laws in New York State were compared with those in Massachusetts. In the former, speeds were eight miles and 20 miles an hour (city and county) while in the latter jurisdiction, the comparable speeds were 10 miles an hour and 15 miles an hour. The New York State law gave local authorities the discretion of increasing speed limits in towns if they wished. In Massachusetts, the law gave local authorities the discretion to decrease the limit. The *Horseless Age* editor preferred the New York State model.[20]

The piece aired the views of officials of some automobile clubs and organizations. One was Winthrop Eugene Scarritt, president of the AAA. Referring to existing New York State law Scarritt thought it "to be fair" although he would prefer a speed of 10 miles an hour in cities. He regarded all legislation as a compromise and declared, "We automobilists have to be considerate of the feelings of other users of the highways for, while we may be driving in the city at a rate that is perfectly safe, and at which we have and know we have our machines under absolute control, yet that speed may appear to spectators to be unreasonable and dangerous. We must take into consideration the feelings of those not accustomed to automobiling and who regard it as a dangerous mode of travel, and be willing to sacrifice something in the way of speed to propitiate the general public during this probationary and educational period through which the automobile is passing."

Scarritt objected to the jail penalty and thought it should not be on the books, saying it enabled magistrates to jail a person for running at a speed of, say, 8.5 miles per hour. He felt impounding the car itself for periods of 10, 30, or 90 days would be equally effective as a punishment "and at the same time would avoid the disgrace which always attaches to a term in jail." Also, he declared himself in favor of a national licensing system and if not possible then a state system. About laws requiring cars to carry lights, Scarritt grumbled, "it is very necessary that horse-drawn vehicles should be similarly equipped." He based that not on any objective facts but only on his "own experience." For flagrant violators of auto laws, he argued the license should be suspended "for a proper length of time," rather than a jail penalty.[21]

George Chamberlin, chairman of the Law Committee of the Automobile Club of America, expressed a view that "no special legislation whatever is necessary." It was provided that everyone could rely on no person driving at a greater speed than was recommended and proper.[22]

Albert R. Shattuck was president of the Automobile Club of America. He felt it advisable to have a federal license for car drivers. But he added that attorneys for his club had advised him that such a law would be unconstitutional because it would violate states' rights "and all effort to procure a Federal or national license has been abandoned by the club." At a recent meeting of the ACA, a committee was appointed to confer with a National Association of Automobile Manufacturers committee to consider the licensing of drivers and the passing of such laws. After some meetings, a joint committee of the two organizations decided they would together try to procure legislation on the following points: a state should license operators after they passed an examination showing their skills, and the state should supervise in some manner the construction of all autos used in the state, for safety's sake.

They also wanted to get all states to pass a similar law with reciprocal recognition by other states. Shattuck said, "There is no question in my mind that some better control of operators of automobiles is necessary than that which now exists. Too many young men think they are born with a knowledge of how to operate an automobile, that it requires no teaching and no experience. They buy one and start out with it. The result is disastrous not only to them and their passengers, but to the public at large, and the public feel that they should be protected from people of this kind." He added, "Then, too, some manufacturers are foolishly building automobiles without proper devices and a proper strength of parts to insure safety to their occupants and to others on the highways. This is something which should be prevented by the State."[23]

A.R. Shattuck, 1900.

Ellicott Evans was president of the Buffalo,

New York, Automobile Club. He explained the people in Buffalo were under a very old ordinance that allowed a maximum speed of only five miles an hour on Main Street and eight miles an hour on the rest of the streets. All summer his group agitated for maximum speeds of eight in the downtown area and 15 elsewhere. Regarding the licensing of drivers, Evans remarked the question had never arisen in Buffalo "as automobile owners ... are given instructions before the machines are turned over to them, which does away with a great deal of reckless operating."[24]

Dr. W.H. Bergtold was secretary of the Colorado Automobile Club. He claimed his club members were almost unanimously against licensing or numbering the cars but agreed that if identification marks be required on the carriages they should take the form of the owners' initials, and not numbers. During the summer the City Park Commissioners in Denver put into effect a rule excluding autos from City Park after sunset. The club took action and through its legal rights committee took the first step asking for an injunction in the matter, but before that injunction could be executed "the obnoxious rule was withdrawn." The existing ordinance in Denver concerning the speed of ordinary vehicles limited them to eight miles an hour and at street intersections to four miles per hour. There was no special ordinance regulating automobiles in Denver.[25]

James M. Padgett was president of the Topeka, Kansas, Automobile Club. He said the thought of placing a special tax or license fee on autos "struck us as one of the most ridiculous propositions ever advanced." Why impose one? he wondered. "An automobile does not bring filth upon the streets; it causes no wear upon the pavements like a vehicle drawn by a horse with feet shod with steel, cutting away little particles of the asphalt and brick passing until soon it has to be replaced. The owner of an automobile should receive an annuity from the city instead of having to pay a fine or special tax."[26]

This lengthy article featured only one voice that it described as an opponent of automobiles. That was Horace E. Parker, secretary of the Committee of Fifty. That group deplored the present tendency of so many automobilists to drive at an unreasonably fast rate of speed, thereby endangering the lives and limbs of other persons, and their motive was to support such legislation as would effectually stop fast driving. The Committee of Fifty provided data showing the relative speed at which autos and horse-drawn vehicles traveled. The data were compiled at different New York City points on October 21–22, 1902. Those compiling the data used stop watches.

At one check point, eight autos and 45 horse-drawn vehicles were measured. All the cars were over the speed limit of eight miles per hour. The slowest was timed at 8.57 miles an hour and the fastest at 13.85 miles per hour. All the horses were within the speed limit except five. The fastest was timed at 12.85 miles an hour. At another check point, 22 cars and 130 horses were timed. Thirteen of the cars exceeded the limit, running from 11 to 16 miles an hour. Twelve horses were timed at from 10 to 12 miles an hour. Parker stated he considered the speed indulged in by automobilists to be "outrageous." He said pedestrians should not be so dependent upon the whims of automobilists that their privilege to cross the street in safety was challenged, and the law should be made to protect them.[27]

The article listed the number of states that had automobile regulations in force when the article appeared in print. A total of 38 states were listed. Of those, 27 had some type of regulations while the other 11 states had no regulations. Cities that had regulations could be found in the following states: New Jersey, Pennsylvania, Illinois, Rhode Island, California, Michigan, Wisconsin, Missouri, Indiana, Maryland, Florida, Georgia, New Hampshire, Vermont, West Virginia, Tennessee, Minnesota, Iowa, South Carolina, and North Carolina. Cities with pending regulations were to be found in the following states: New York, North Dakota, Kansas, Nebraska, Louisiana, Colorado, Idaho, Kentucky, Oregon, Washington, Utah, and Wyoming.[28]

Around the same time as the *Horseless Age* article appeared, one on the same topic appeared in a New York City newspaper. The editor declared, "Each new day adds to the number of arrests of people for running automobiles too fast on the public roads, and adds, also, to the number and petulance of complaints by automobile drivers that the law is absurdly strict or is enforced in too puritanical a spirit. Thoughtful men will, we believe, generally approve the arrests, and will regard the complaints of the 'scorchers' [speeders] as unfounded." The editor cited France, a leading automobile country, as a country that was much more severe in terms of auto regulations. There was a national decree prescribed at length and in detail how autos had to be constructed and equipped with brakes, bell, horn, lamps, and so on, and how they had to be operated and how licenses (national) to run them had to be obtained.

Nowhere, except by special permit, might the speed exceed 30 kilometers per hour (18.75 miles per hour), while in cities, towns, and villages it was 20 kilometers (12.5). No special permit was granted in thickly settled areas. Thus, it was not possible to have a road race on the equivalent of the roads of Staten Island, New York. Local municipalities in France were empowered to make even stricter rules. In Berlin, Germany, an auto must not have excessive noise or emit smoke, steam, or odors. That is, only a small number of cars in use in America would be permitted on the streets of Berlin at all. The speed limit there was a maximum of 10 miles per hour.

In Austria, the speed limit was also 10 miles per hour. On busy city streets, it was not to exceed the speed of a person walking, about four miles an hour. In Holland, the speed limit was 12.5 miles an hour in the open country and 4.9 miles an hour elsewhere. The editor of the New York newspaper argued that American auto laws were very liberal compared with the rules in Europe. In Austria, if rules were violated and any person injured the penalty varied from one month to two years imprisonment; if death occurred that penalty could be three years of imprisonment. He concluded, "It will be found, we think, that our laws are liberal almost to laxity, and that our penalties are lax indeed."[29]

A third article from the same time looked at automobiles abroad. The U.S. State Department received from American consuls in Europe reports on the subject of the regulation of automobiles in foreign countries. Those reports were obtained mainly at the request of the District of Columbia Commissioners, to whom the material was forwarded. Those Commissioners looked at more stringent regulations in DC and wanted foreign data for comparison purposes. The general law on the subject of steam engines had been held to apply in DC to automobiles so propelled. As a result, all operators of steamers in DC were licensed, but nothing was in force for vehicles under other motive powers.

Rules in Europe were said to be stringent. Despite local car owners strenuously objecting to the idea of being compelled to register their vehicles and for each to display on his machine the number of his permit, "Yet the requirement is one of the first and foremost contained in the laws of all the foreign countries from which reports have been received." In many instances, it was stipulated that not only must a number be displayed in large figures, but that there should be attached to the machine "a larger-sized plate bearing the name and address of the owner in ineffaceable letters."

In several European nations, the manufacture of automobiles was strictly regulated. In practically all the nations examined, no permit to operate an auto was issued to a person under 18 years of age. In Vienna, Austria, only cars that had been inspected and approved regarding mechanics and safety could be driven on the streets. The rate of speed allowed in popular areas "must not be greater than that of a horse at a good trot." In Belgium, the speed allowed was that of a horse at an "ordinary trot." In the United Kingdom, the maximum speed was 12 miles an hour, but less in cities.[30]

Reportedly the Streets and Walks Committee of the Topeka, Kansas, City Council and the automobile owners of the city had agreed upon the terms for the proposed ordinance. On the busiest streets, the maximum speed would be eight miles an hour, and 16 miles an hour on the other streets. Autos were required to carry "alarm gongs" although nothing was said about headlights "but an automobile pretty nearly has to have these anyway."[31]

In Dubuque, Iowa, an automobile ordinance was in contemplation for the city. There were only three or four machines in the city, in November 1902, but there were expected to be several more in the coming year.[32] St. Louis, Missouri, adopted an identification system for cars, a vehicle license tax of $10 per year, and a speed limit of eight miles an hour on the streets and six miles per hour in the parks. According to a local journalist, "Public safety requires limitations to speed, police regulations require facility of identification and equity demands assessment of a license tax. In all respects the provisions seem to be necessary from a public standpoint."[33]

In Peoria, Illinois, an ordinance was introduced by Alderman Proctor and subsequently passed. The maximum speed in the downtown area was set at eight miles an hour. Outside of that area but within the city limits the speed was set at 15 miles an hour. Each machine had to have a number consisting of aluminum figures four inches high and 2.5 inches wide. That number was furnished by the city clerk. Each driver had to pay a license fee of $10 a year. It was also noted that the case of car owner Louis Lichtig of Toledo, Ohio, would likely be taken up by the Toledo Auto Club and fought by them through the courts.[34]

Always in a state of frantic worry, the *Horseless Age* ranted once again, early in 1903, because "a lot of very objectionable automobile legislation is about to be attempted in the New Jersey Legislature and that measure has caused a considerable stir in the automobile circles of that State." Assemblyman Henry Scovel of Camden, New Jersey, introduced a bill providing that a board of examiners consisting of five members be named by the governor of the state to examine automobilists as to their fitness to operate horseless carriages. The measure also proposed that an annual license fee of $5 be established; that the speed limit be 15 miles per hour; that anyone found guilty of operating a machine without a license could be arrested and fined $50, or jailed for 30 days, or both. It provided that if a speed limit of 15 miles an hour was rigidly enforced it would "greatly limit the benefits to be derived from the use of automobiles." The trade journal cited the New York State speed of 20 miles an hour: "Even more objectionable than the speed limit is the method of licensing proposed which takes the form of a method of special taxation."

Scovel noted that in New York, licenses granted by the state remained valid indefinitely. In conclusion, Scovel complained, "The attempt now made in New Jersey to burden the automobilists with special taxes and to subject them to various annoyances demands concerted opposition. It is to be hoped that the various automobile clubs in the State will join hands in fighting the measure and we believe the subject is one of sufficient importance to call to the attention of the A.A.A."[35]

After a number of modifications, the Scovel measure passed the New Jersey Legislature on March 19 and then awaited only the governor's signature before becoming law. The major concession won by the automobilists was that physicians who used them for house calls, then numbering about 40 in the state, would not be stopped for speeding. Perhaps more importantly, the bill no longer called for the arrest and possible jailing of violators of the speed limit.[36]

More hackles were raised at that time on the back of the *Horseless Age*. This time the state was Pennsylvania. "Of all the obnoxious automobile legislation which has been proposed or enacted the present winter, the bill just introduced in the Pennsylvania Legislature may well be regarded as the limit. It seems to have been drawn up on the supposition that automobiles on the highways constitute an inherent danger to the public ... and that an elaborate system of examining, licensing and bonding is required to prevent serious calamities." Reciting his objections, the journalist said, "The speed limit of 12 miles an hour in the country is much too low. The requirement of licenses for the operation of all kinds of vehicles is unjustified; electric and simple gasoline machines are commonly operated by women and children thus proving that no special mechanical knowledge is required for operating such simple vehicles. The annual license fee is an injustice, as other users of the road are not required to pay any such fees, and the automobile has a tendency to improve the roads instead of destroying them like horses and horse vehicles."[37]

The Indiana Legislature passed an auto regulation law "at the instance of the Indiana Auto Club." The law did not provide any definite speed limit "and the club congratulated itself on seeing so liberal a measure adopted." Then they realized that with no limit specified by the state, each municipality could set its limit. This reporter favored statewide speed limits if there had to be any limits at all. There was then a rush of states to pass legislation, and in the spring of 1903 the following had such legislation pending: New York, Connecticut, Massachusetts, New Hampshire, Maine, New Jersey, Pennsylvania, and Wisconsin.[38]

A newspaper in the nation's capital urged the District of Columbia Commissioners to secure automobile regulations. "The prime requirement is an ordinance which will cause repetitions of the offense of over speeding to become not only costly but dangerous to the status of the machine." The reporter wanted to see the machines given a number for identification purposes. The licenses should run with the machines and not be confined to the individuals who may serve as drivers. He suggested a fine for speeding of $25 for a first offense, $35 for a second offense, $50 for a third offense, and ruled off the roads in Washington forever, on a fourth offense. "Until some such drastic and yet altogether reasonable ordinance is adopted, the streets will remain unsafe for pedestrians and even for the users of horse vehicles."[39]

Under such pressure, the DC Commissioners decided to grant a public hearing on the subject of proposed regulations regarding the operation of cars in Washington and the District. The public had reportedly sent the Commissioners a large number of letters on the issue. Commissioner West "has been fairly besieged with callers, most of whom are loud in their approval of his course in desiring the further regulation of the horseless vehicles." Wayne MacVeagh, former attorney general, was in Philadelphia during their crusade against speeders and became acquainted with the benefits of licensing and numbering cars. The reporter thought it was all but assured the Commissioners would insist upon the licensing and numbering of all autos.[40]

An editorial from a Washington newspaper declared, "We cannot but think that the National Capital Automobile Club is badly advised in opposing the enactment of any speeding or tagging regulations of the District Commissioners." Club Secretary Erskine M. Sunderland condemned the proposed numbering ordinance as an "indignity" to which no automobile owner or driver "will submit." The club, he said, would fight any such "humiliating restriction to a finish" even to taking it to the United States Supreme Court. Sunderland also told West that "no regulations regarding automobile operation in this city are necessary." The editor argued it was useless to assume, as Sunderland seemed to, that the Commissioners "will not be sustained by public sentiment in enacting a sensible and moderate automobile code."[41]

The hearing in Washington on April 14 was well attended. A man named MacFarland, president of the Board of Commissioners, stated that two years earlier the Commissioners had produced the draft of a paragraph covering car operation, which was introduced as part of a bill regulating the operation of street railways in DC. That bill was not adopted and the proposed law on autos was not pursued. The new draft measure being considered mandated that operators were to be examined as to competence by the Board of Examiners of steam engines. All licenses were to be numbered and the number displayed on the rear of the vehicle.

Club Secretary Sunderland made the first remarks at that hearing. He explained that newspapers had placed it in the wrong light and that he and his club did not oppose all regulations. It felt the present law in DC was sufficient to deal with any questions arising out of the operation of horseless vehicles. Sunderland then objected to pretty much every feature of the proposal, including identification. In response to questions from Commissioners, Sunderland said there were between 200 and 300 members of the National Capital Automobile Club. Dr. H.M. Hasbrouck said he objected, as the owner of private property, to having that property numbered. "Our automobiles are costly, choice affairs. How many of our citizens would consent to having their $3,000 barouches or other types of carriages numbered?"

When the Commissioners asked Hasbrouck if no numbering system was used on autos, how would the police capture the speeders, he admitted he had no idea. He asked his colleagues to answer. To which Dr. W.B. French arose and stated, "Let the policeman get on a trolley car and overtake the automobile." That answer reportedly got "much applause" from the automobilists in the room. When Hasbrouck was pressed for a "serious" answer he said he did not know how to do it. French later added the present agitation over automobiles was the result of "newspaper hysterics." D.W. Lambert of the legal firm Lambert and Baker, employed by the club, was in attendance. He spoke for a few minutes on the legal points involved and said he doubted the power of the Commissioners to revoke an automobile license, as proposed in some circumstances in the measure proposed, and thus "deprive a man of the use of his property."[42]

A local reporter observed, mockingly, that he was pleased the National Capital Automobile Club was not holding that the tagging of autos to be "an indignity." Even in Sunderland's club, it appeared "this common sense conclusion finds some acceptance." He noted that the objection to licensing and numbering autos had been, in fact, "most frivolous." In conclusion, the newsman stated, "The public is entitled to that measure of protection against careless and reckless chauffeurs which the possibility of certain identification gives. Only owners and drivers who seek to escape responsibility will seriously protest against a tagging ordinance. Those who fully realize their obligations to the community will gladly cooperate in preparing and enforcing both anti-speeding and tagging laws."[43]

Commissioner Henry L. West completed the draft of the new auto regulations later in April. Those regulations required all autos to be registered and have a number "conspicuously painted" upon them. No license revocation was in the new rules, just fines that increased with each offense and even possible imprisonment. An examination for competency would still be held but not done by steam engineers. A new examining board would be created, the members of which would be drafted from District of Columbia services.

The proposed board would be composed of two steam engineers, two experts in gasoline and naphtha engines, and one electrician. Under those regulations autos running north and south would have the right of way over cars running east and west. There would be no numbers of a vehicle's lamps. There was no change in speed limits. Maximum speed remained at 12 miles per hour with a reduction to six miles while crossing streets. No fee was required for a license. A newsman remarked, "All the chief objections, except the numbering of the carriages, have been omitted from the revised rules."[44]

An organization of automobilists known as the National Capital Automobilist Association was formed in May 1903 by more than 50 people. They proposed to fight the new automobile regulations even to the Supreme Court. A fund of nearly $600 was raised, to that end. A committee was struck to retain lawyers. The meeting was held at the home of Dr. William B. French. The sense of the meeting was that the regulation permitting police officers to stop all autos and demand to see the licenses "would expose the wives and daughters of the automobilists to annoyance and impertinence." French stated he accepted speed limits "but we do object to having our carriages disfigured by huge signs and numbers." Two people at that meeting had names that became, and remain, famous in automobiles, S.S. Olds and Horace A. Dodge. When asked to comment on that development Commissioner West said he was not in the least disturbed by the new group. He remained convinced of the fairness of the regulations and he was convinced they would stand a court test.[45]

Legal proceedings were instituted in a court in Washington in June 1903 by Carl J. Lockwood. He represented the automobilists opposed to the new auto rules that were to take effect in Washington on June 7. The suit to enjoin the rules from coming into effect was against the District of Columbia and the DC Commissioners. The law firm handling the case was headed by Wilton J. Lambert and D.W. Baker. Lockwood sold cars for the Stanley Motor Carriage Company. He said that if it were not for the proposed regulations he could earn upward of $200 a month. In his complaint, among other things he grumbled that numbering vehicles would not only not serve any good purpose it would tend to prevent the owners from loaning or renting their machine and thus deprived the owner of the full use of their property.[46]

When Lockwood explained to the court his reasons, he remarked he did not object to the speed limit of 12 miles an hour but he still objected to the numbering of vehicles. No other type of vehicle was forced to carry numbers. At length, he complained about the carrying of lights on machines run on gasoline. He called it dangerous and having the potential for explosions. Meanwhile, Erskine M. Sunderland was fined $20 by Judge Kimball in Police Court for speeding. He immediately announced he would take an appeal to the Court of Appeals for the District.[47]

Those Washington, D.C., regulations took effect on June 8. People had 30 days to take out permits and register their machines. For gasoline and electric machines, the examination would be "purely mental," it was believed, to satisfy the examiners as to the knowledge of the operators on the care of the machine and the fuel used. A new suit was then filed by the Lockwood group as it again sought to have the courts enjoin the Commissioners from implementing those car regulations.[48]

More court sessions followed regarding the Lockwood group's efforts to block the DC auto law. One case was dismissed. Submitted to the court by the Commissioners was a list of incidents involving cars, plus a separate list of the police records for auto violations of some of the people who testified on behalf of Lockwood. On July 15, 1903, Justice Gould upheld the auto regulations. Unless an appeal was taken, the DC Commissioners announced they would immediately begin to enforce the provisions of the regulations, which had been placed on hold pending a court decision.[49]

A course of study was inaugurated at Washington, D.C., police headquarters in August 1903. It was designed to instruct the newly appointed members of the force and the members of the bicycle squad on the best method in which to enforce the regulations of the new code governing the use of cars. Those regulations had finally gone into effect on August 29. Chief Sylvester planned to have all 60 members of the bicycle squad before him so they could expound fully on the new auto regulations. When they had a grasp of the material, "they will be sent forth with instructions to arrest and prosecute every violator, but in no case to persecute the automobilist."[50]

Commissioner West submitted a report on the first three months of enforcing the regulations. During that period the police made 53 arrests, of which 40 were for "fast running" as speeding was often called. The maximum fine of $40 was never imposed. In seven cases the fine was $20; in ten cases it was $10. All other offenders were fined amounts ranging from $1 to $5. One case was dismissed.[51]

In response to West's report that the maximum fine was not imposed, a local newspaper responded. The paper agreed with the idea that the maximum fine should be imposed when it appeared the driver had deliberately and knowingly exceeded the speed limit. In those 40 or so arrests there was a record of only two people having been arrested more than once. At the same time, the bicycle policemen declared they had repeatedly arrested the same person but those detained had given false names, thus avoiding being serial offenders. Under the present system, the name was entered and not the number of the machine. The newspaper chided the police department for its shoddy record-keeping. "Certainly the present haphazard method of punishment and record-keeping should be corrected."[52]

A Minneapolis newspaper wrote of the efforts to regulate automobiles there. The paper had repeatedly come out in favor of all cars' carrying large number plates in the front and rear. The paper wanted to see "good-sized" figures and a requirement that night lights be carried by automobiles.[53]

A law regulating cars was enacted in April 1903. Minneapolis Automobile Club members stated the club was "well satisfied" with the new state law. "The provisions in regard to speed are regarded as especially liberal." Those club members were then working for the passage of the ordinance pending before the city council. State law permitted a speed of 25 miles an hour "outside the thickly settled or business portions" of cities. The city ordinance for Minneapolis permitted a speed of 15 miles an hour outside a radius of 1.5 miles from city hall. The proposed ordinance provided for a city license and the numbering of autos, as did the state law. It stated that the state license was not necessary where there was a municipal ordinance that covered the ground.[54]

An editorial in a New York City newspaper thought that automobilists who followed the efforts of legislatures in many states would heave a sigh of relief when those legislatures adjourned for the summer. Because, in the opinion of the motorists, "several of these law-making bodies have shown not only extraordinary inability to deal with the automobile situation, but have also exhibited a desire to deny to the drivers of the self-moving vehicles the rights and privileges commonly enjoyed by the horsemen." Some of the laws in force were described as "Czar-like." However, the editor thought, on balance, most of the laws regulating automobiles were "satisfactory."[55]

The Board of Governors of the ACA held a meeting to consider the Doughty-Bailey bill, which was then before New York Governor Benjamin Odell awaiting his signature. The article explained all the automobilists of the entire state were against the measure and there was then being formed a movement of all persons interested in automobiles, aside from officials of the club, to go before the governor and protest. The goal was to kill the measure. It was admitted that ACA approved the bill while it was being passed through the legislature. That was because the club thought it to be the best obtainable at the time and expected that in the following year, an effort would have been made to "have the objectionable features eliminated and replaced by more liberal provisions." ACA members were then circulating a petition. President Budlong of NAAM had been in contact with the governor and had received from him assurances that the bill would not be signed until NAAM was heard from in protest. A committee from NAAM would call upon Odell after his return from St. Louis. Another protest Governor Odell received came from the New York State Association of Automobile Clubs.[56]

When New York State Senator Edwin Bailey, Jr., introduced his bill in the middle of March 1903 to regulate autos, opinions varied. Some felt that in some respects the bill "tries to meet the wishes of the Automobile Club of America," as it embodied some of the suggestions made by A.R. Shattuck of the ACA. One of the important sections was that all chauffeurs operating a machine of more than one horsepower had to be licensed and pass an examination as to their competency. There was to be a $5 charge for each license issued. All cars had to be registered with the New York Secretary of State. Bailey predicted that the ACA would accept the bill and that a conference would be held resulting in a bill that would satisfy both parties.[57]

In May the ACA announced it would not oppose the signing of the Doughty-Bailey bill by Governor Odell. The decision was reached unanimously by club members at a special meeting attended by a "large number" of club members. Nonetheless, at the meeting, the bill was "universally condemned." Among those who took part in the discussion was William C. Whitney, who spoke against the measure and declared the operation of the bill would make all drivers of automobiles "criminals." He, for one, said he would not own one.

Edwin Bailey, Jr., 1902.

The club resolved not to have a representative at the hearing on the Bailey proposal, despite its strong opposition to the measure, which it termed "prejudicial" to the interests of New York State motorists, because "the public prejudice against the automobiles being so apparent that any opposition to a measure of the Automobile Club would ensure its positive passage."[58]

The *Horseless Age* continued to vent its fury on auto

regulations and, of course, had something to say on the pending measure in New York State. "During the last fortnight automobile circles throughout the State of New York have been in a state of intense agitation. An obnoxious automobile bill has passed both houses of the Legislature and was at the point of becoming law. The problem was to array against the bill all possible resisting forces and prevent its becoming a law by securing the Governor's veto, and also locale the responsibility for the objectionable measure." The trade journal thought many were to share the indirect blame. One was the ACA because the president of that organization had approved the bill, or at least consented to it in the form in which it passed the Senate. There were rumors about dissension in the ACA, a formal repudiation of his action, or even the formation of a rival automobile group. But all such talk ended when, after a meeting, the ACA decided not to send a protesting delegation to Albany and passed a vote of confidence in the president and the Law Committee.[59]

When that proposed New York State legislation was introduced in both houses of the Legislature during the second week of March 1903, it was done at the instance of counsel for the Long Island Protective Association. The bill amended the existing automotive law, known as the Cocks law. Those bills contained "very drastic restrictions." Among the most objectionable were that persons walking or driving domestic animals upon the highway had to be passed at speeds no greater than eight miles an hour. President Shattuck of the ACA and Judge James C. Church of the ACA Law Committee went at once to Albany, and "in conference" with the sponsors of the bill secured what they considered to be "a number of valuable concessions."

Both sides agreed on the amended text. When that was published attention was called to some of the "very objectionable clauses" and active steps were at once taken toward the organization of the New York State Association of Automobile Clubs to oppose the passage of the bill. A number of New York publications began to attack Shattuck. The bill nonetheless passed the Senate on April 17 and on April 24 the Board of Governors of the ACA decided to uphold their president and not protest the bill as a club, but to oppose the measure as individuals. That led to the May meeting of the group, its vote of confidence, and so forth. Before he signed the bill, Governor Odell was still being lobbied by delegates from the New York State Association of Automobile Clubs, NAAM, and the New York Automobile Trade Association. The reporter from *Horseless Age* took some hope, though, even if Odell signed. He hoped those protests "will tend to temper the administration of the law and will pave the way for more lenient legislation next winter, provided, of course, automaniacs heed the public protests against furious driving and show more consideration in future for the common rights of the road."[60]

At the public hearing on the New York State Bailey bill, about 75 people were present. "Those who protested against the measure were represented by able counsel and fought well, while the supporters of the measure were as well represented by Congressman I. Townsend Scudder." Makers of autos were represented by three people. One person was from the New York Trade Association and one from the American League. As well, there were five more people who appeared for automobile organizations in every part of the state. One speaker noted some $100 million was invested in the auto industry. The industry gave employment to 150,000 men of which 10,000 were in New York State. The output of the industry in 1903 was put at $26 million. And, said an opponent of the Bailey bill, "If this bill becomes a law the market this State affords now—and it is enormous—will be practically taken away from the trade…." If the New York State example was followed by other states the "devastation" would spread.

One speaker fretted, "Will this State kill the automobile industry? That this state of affairs will be brought no one can doubt, because no man could feel that he could run an automobile and keep out of jail." That was from De Lancey Nicoll, who represented auto manufacturers. John Shatterfield, representing an auto club, said he had experience here and abroad and here regulations were most drastic. In France, he said, "one is given the right to use judgment, and to ride as long as he preserves reason." This bill put the speed limit at eight miles an hour in cities and towns, 15 miles per hour in "thinly settled" sections, and 20 miles an hour in open country.[61]

That Bailey bill was signed into law on May 15, 1903, by Governor Benjamin Odell. With the enactment of that measure the old existing Cocks law was repealed. It was said that Odell decided to sign the bill "in the interest of the general public, not of automobile owners." The old law required all cars to register with the New York Secretary of State but provided no penalty for failure to comply. "The result being that after a short time when this defect became generally known, restrictions practically ceased. The rules regarding initials were also too indefinite, many owners having their initials painted in fine black lines on dark red ground, so that they could not be read 10 feet off." Those defects were eliminated in the Bailey law, and the *Horseless Age* editor gratifyingly admitted the new law therefore was "in some respects an improvement over the Cocks law."[62]

From the office of the New York Secretary of State at Albany, it was reported that 4,400 names of automobile users had already been registered in compliance with the Bailey law, ten days after that law went into effect. New names were coming into the office at the rate of 150 per day.[63]

In August 1903 three New York justices declared unconstitutional an important section of the Bailey law. The court held it discriminated between classes of automobilists. The section of Bailey that required car owners to register with the Secretary of State and display numbers on the backs of their vehicles was unconstitutional because it discriminated. That is, it should be applied to all autos and users of vehicles on public highways. "The statute, however," said the judges,

THE FIRST HOLD-UP UNDER THE NEW AUTO LAW SIGNED BY GOVERNOR ODELL.
BY A. P. YATES, SYRACUSE, N. Y.

Under a law signed by New York Governor Odell in 1903, a car was forced to stop if a person was leading or driving domestic animals and those animals became restive. The man with the animals had only to extend his arm to command the car to stop.

"exempted dealers and manufacturers from that provision which the court held as an unconstitutional and unfair discrimination against private owners."[64]

That lawsuit was brought by the ACA through its counsel W.W. Niles. The relevant section of the law read, "Every person hereafter acquiring an automobile or motor vehicle shall, within ten days after acquiring same, register with the Secretary of State, as required by this section. This section shall not apply to a person manufacturing or dealing in automobiles, except those for his own private use." The ruling of the court applied only to New York City. Motorists could drive through the city without number plates, but not in other parts of the state.[65]

As of early May 1903 more than 1,050 people in Chicago held a driving license. Up to August 15, 1,100 automobile licenses were issued by the Highway Commission in Boston, Massachusetts. Up to July 15, the total number of automobile licenses issued in Cleveland was 919, an increase of 550 over one year earlier.[66]

In Indianapolis, Mayor Charles A. Brookwalter signed an ordinance regulating the speed of automobiles. The maximum speed was six miles an hour in the rectangle in a busy part of town and 12 miles an hour outside that zone. Each auto had to be registered with the city controller and numbered. However, the car had only to display the initials of the owner.[67]

At the request of St. Paul, Minnesota, police chief O'Connor, an attempt was made to have the city council pass an ordinance that registered and numbered automobiles. However, the measure failed to pass and was sent to the city's Committee on Streets. Car owners protested against the number size in the proposal—four inches high. But it was stated that was the size used in most jurisdictions where numbering was required. O'Connor stressed that such a size was needed because of the speed of some of the machines and some means of identification was necessary to control speeding.[68]

A meeting was held in San Rafael, California, by the Board of Supervisors to determine the fate of autos, as far as Marin County was concerned. It was generally believed that an ordinance would be passed prohibiting drivers from operating their machine on the county roads "but by strong arguments and certain agreements of the California Automobile Club, it now seems that machines will be allowed to go on the boulevards, but not on the mountain grades." Some time earlier the Board passed an ordinance putting strong restrictions upon autos. That ordinance was disregarded, and several arrests followed but no convictions were obtained. The ordinance was declared void by Judge Lennon in the Superior Court.

What prompted the meeting was a petition presented to the Board setting forth the fact that cars were dangerous to public safety due to the narrow roads in Marin. It was signed by "many prominent citizens." The new, harsh ordinance was drawn up but failed to come up for a vote on the expected day. F.A. Hyde, president of the California Auto Club, was present and informed the board that it could not stop automobiling; that such action would be illegal, and if it did pass the ordinance the auto club would take the matter to court. However, he added that he wished to cooperate with the board "and if you frame an ordinance allowing automobiles on all roads except the narrow mountain grades we will endeavor to see the law enforced." The final language of the measure was deferred to an unspecified date.[69]

At the end of June 1903, it was reported that the legality of Marin County, California's, auto ordinance was to be tested in court. That came about with orders to the driver to run along forbidden roads, as well as to "scorch" [speed] along the public highways after sunset. As a result, chauffeur T.S. Rockett was arrested on a charge of violating county ordinance #127, which banned cars from running on any road in Marin County between the hours of six p.m. and five a.m. Rockett was assessed $100 bail. That ordinance was passed on June 4, 1903, by the Board of Supervisors.[70]

In St. Louis, Missouri, there were some 500 motor vehicles to be found. The St. Louis Automobile Club had 80 members but no clubhouse. Under the speed law, a car could not exceed eight miles an hour while passing a team of horses, oxen, or a pedestrian. The law did not say how fast to go when a vehicle was not passing any of those things. One of the original automobile men of St. Louis, Dr. E.M. Senseney, said, "When an automobilist runs a man down the papers give the accident a column, but the street railways continue to kill people every day and the subject is given only a few lines." Senseney added, "Automobilists are harassed, abused, blackmailed and slandered. If a horse shies at an automobile, the owner of the horse sues the automobilist for damages." He explained they were forming and organizing an "automobile legislative association" in St. Louis. That proposed group intended to have a reserve fund of $10,000. The chief purpose of the organization would be to fight damage suits brought against members of the group. At the time there were 500 machines registered in St. Louis.[71]

A worried editor with *Horseless Age* noted that in the excitement over the Bailey law in New York State "the very much more restrictive and objectionable legislation in several Western States, particularly Missouri, has apparently remained unnoticed in automobile centers." The Missouri law required cars to stop whenever they met a horse vehicle and to remain stationary until the latter had passed. It also limited speed everywhere to nine miles an hour. "This is by far the lowest limit of speed that has yet been enforced anywhere for the open country, and is far below what is reasonable and proper," the editor fumed. "It is a significant fact that this law was adopted by a body of legislators which has become notorious for the implication of its members in boodling scandals." In conclusion, the editor seethed, "Missouri may be an agriculture State and have little regard for automobile interests, but this cannot change the fundamental principles regarding the road rights of automobiles."[72]

An auto ordinance adopted by the Sumter, South Carolina, City Council on June 24, 1903, provided that no automobiles were to be run on the sidewalks. Maximum speed was five miles an hour within the city fire limits and 10 miles an hour elsewhere within the city limits. When turning corners a car's maximum speed was four miles per hour. A gong, bell, or horn had to be sounded when an auto approached any vehicle or pedestrian. All autos had to carry lamps at night. Penalty for violators of the ordinance was a fine of not less than $10 and not more than $100, or imprisonment, at the discretion of the mayor. In the case of property damage, the mayor was empowered to add to the fine imposed to include the damages sustained by the injured party.[73]

Two arrests marked the opening of a campaign in St. Paul against unnumbered vehicles. The making of arrests was effected by placing a wire seal on the wheels of automobiles found standing without license numbers. A heavy fine was the penalty for breaking such rules. And thus, apparently, the first car clamp was born.[74]

According to President Day of the Association of Licensed Automobile Manufacturers, 150 firms had been incorporated to make gasoline vehicles, as of July

1903. Some had already expired but about 100 remained in operation. Of those, 26 firms made 90 percent of the entire output of gas cars.[75]

St. Louis License Collector Clifford urged the police to enforce the law regulating automobiles. The license fee was $10 a year. The number had to be displayed conspicuously on the car in figures that were not less than three inches high. The maximum speed in St. Louis was eight miles an hour on city streets and six miles per hour in public parks. A light was mandatory on each side of the carriage. Clifford called those rules fair and reasonable and observed, "Just laws can only have the effect of making the machine more popular."[76]

Up until August 9, 1903, there were 3,400 automobilists who had registered their vehicles under New Jersey law. In court proceedings, A.C. Banker of Chicago asked for an injunction restraining the authorities from arresting him for failing to procure a license. In its answer, the Chicago Corporation counsel acknowledged that an order had been issued for Banker's arrest. He explained that Banker had to be arrested because he habitually ran his auto at illegal speeds. The Board of Supervisors of San Diego County, California, passed a new and more stringent auto ordinance. No maximum speed was established but it had to be "reasonable and proper." The ACA and other auto lobbyists loved those kinds of vague and useless statutes. Drivers had to stop when signaled to do so and had to have horns or bells. In passing domestic animals driven by a person the automobilist had to take the outside of the grade "without reference to the right or left of the road." For violating the ordinance the penalty was a fine of not less than $25, nor more than $100, and 15 to 30 days imprisonment.[77]

An editor with a St. Louis newspaper urged a measure be adopted to regulate autos in that city. "It should be a bomb-proof instrument, referring specifically to automobiles, and fixing heavy penalties for violation of its provisions." Chicago, he noted, limited the speed and did not permit the machines to carry whistles or bells, "on the theory that it is the duty of the chauffeur to keep out of the way of vehicles and pedestrians, and not vice versa."[78]

In attempting to rationalize the domination of the automobile at the expense of all others, the editor of the *Horseless Age* reached a peak of irrational, illogical arguments in a piece published on October 21, 1903. "Attention has repeatedly been called to the beneficial influences of automobile riding in cases of certain diseases. These beneficial effects are principally the result of two causes—the breathing of fresh and pure air and the continual slight vibration of the car." Automobiling, he wrote, was "an efficacious antidote to the effects of hot weather...." An auto trip "is also very restful to the nerves.... Automobile rides have been recommended by eminent medical authorities as a cure for nervousness." Needless to say, no details were provided. An automobile ride, he concluded, "in good weather has a refreshing and exhilarating influence and has been observed to restore interest in life in despondent people."[79]

F.A. Hyde was the president of the Automobile Club of California. He was the author of a full-page piece that appeared in a San Francisco newspaper. Mostly the article praised the wonderful world of automobiles. Later in the piece he moved on to talk about laws and ordinances. "As to county ordinances, I am pleased to say that they have not so far been oppressive, except in the county of Marin, which has an ordinance that practically excludes automobiles." He explained the first ordinance they passed required every car to be brought to a full stop within 300 feet of any person riding, driving, or leading a horse or other domestic animal. One of the club's members was arrested for violating that provision. His case was taken before the Superior Court and his club took up the matter. The judge concluded the ordinance was reasonable and proper. So the club took the case to the Supreme Court of California.

Since then, explained Hyde, they had left the Marin County ordinance alone. "In fact, we do not think much of Marin County, anyhow. It may do for some people who are satisfied with ancient methods of locomotion, but for automobilists the hills are too steep and the level roads too few." San Francisco had, he felt, "a very reasonable ordinance" which set a speed limit of eight miles an hour in the fire zone and 12 miles an hour outside of it. In San Mateo and Alameda counties, the speed limit was 15 miles an hour. In Santa Clara County that limit was 20 miles per hour. "For each and every ordinance that has been passed in California or elsewhere there are some few automobilists to blame. The public is not naturally opposed to automobiling. At first they were well received, but presently some of the same kind of fools and reckless persons who first created opposition to the bicycle took hold of the automobiles and acted as if they owned the whole road and everyone must get out of their way." Hyde believed that in time people would get over an unreasonable craze for speed "and when that comes, the restrictive ordinances will disappear, clubs will no longer be necessary for protection...."[80]

Appendix A: Selected Laws, 1902–1903

An Act to Permit of the Running of Motor Vehicles in this Commonwealth [Massachusetts].

Be it enacted by the Senate and House of Representatives in General Court assembled, and by the authority of same, as follows:

Section 1. Motor vehicles may be run on the streets or highways of this Commonwealth. Said vehicles being made safe by being so constructed as,

First: To be under the full control of the operator or driver at all times by means of sufficient levers to throw said vehicles out of power at will:

Second: Which is supplied with steering apparatus so efficient as to make it easy for the driver to keep the safe line over rough roads by being supplied with competent levers and stays for this purpose, so that obstructions in the highway may not throw the vehicle dangerously out of its course;

Third: Which is also furnished and equipped with two distinct separate brakes with two or more modes of operating said brakes;

Fourth: Which is provided and equipped with a suitable stay, safeguard device which shall be sufficient to hold all the levers which release the power from the wheels of the vehicle, and also those levers which apply the several brakes in place when applied for the purpose of leaving the vehicle, so that an unauthorized application of the motive power cannot cause the vehicle to run where it might be dangerous;

Fifth: And which is so constructed and its novelties so covered and hid as not to be liable to frighten horses on the highway by its novel appearance.

Section 2. That only such motor vehicles as answer to the above requirements shall be permitted to run on the highways of this Commonwealth.

Section 3. That it shall be the duty of the State police to see that the provisions of this act are complied with.

Section 4. This act shall take effect upon its passage.

[Source: *Horseless Age,* March 1897, p. 7, verbatim.]

The complex of automobile regulations grew enormously in just six years in Massachusetts.

Following is the complete text of the Massachusetts State law (House Bill No. 1.560) which went into effect on Wednesday, June 4 [1903]:

Sec 1. Registration

All automobiles and motor cycles shall be registered by the owner or person in control thereof in accordance with the provisions of this act. Application for such registration may be made, by mail or otherwise, to the Massachusetts Highway Commission or any agent thereof designated for this purpose, upon blanks prepared under its authority. The application shall, in addition to such other particulars as may be required by said commission, contain a statement of the name, place of residence and address of the applicant, with a brief description of the automobile or motor cycle, including the name of the maker, the number, if any, affixed by the maker, the character of the motor power stated in figures of horse power; and with such application shall be deposited a registration fee of $2. The said commission or its duly authorized agent shall then register, in a book to be kept for the purpose, the automobile or motor cycle described in the application, giving to such automobile or motor cycle a distinguishing number or other mark, and shall thereupon issue to the applicant a certificate of registration. Said certificate shall contain the name, place of residence and address of the applicant and the registered number or mark, shall prescribe the manner in which said registered number or mark shall be inscribed or displayed upon the automobile or motor cycle, and shall be in such form and contain such further provisions as the commission may determine. A proper record of all applications and of all certificates issued shall be kept by the commission at its main office, and shall be open to the inspection of any person during reasonable business hours. The certificate of registration shall always be carried in some easily accessible place in the automobile or motor cycle described therein.

Upon the sale of any automobile or motor cycle, its registration shall expire, and the vendor shall immediately return the certificate of registration to the highway commission, with notice of the sale, and of the name, place of residence and address of the vendee.

Sec. 2 Dealers' License

Every manufacturer of or dealer in automobiles or motor cycles may, instead of registering each automobile or motor cycle owned or controlled by him, make application upon a blank provided by said commission for a general distinguishing number or make, and said commission may, if satisfied of the facts stated in said application, grant said application and issue to the applicant a certificate of registration containing the name, place of residence and address of the applicant, the general distinguishing number or mark assigned to him, and made in such form and containing such further provisions as said commission may determine; and all automobiles and motor cycles owned or controlled by such manufacturer or dealer shall, until sold or let for hire or loaned for a period of more than five successive days, be regarded as registered under such general distinguishing number or mark. The fee for every such license shall be $10.

Sec. 3 Identification Numbers

Except as otherwise provided herein, no automobile or motor cycle shall, after the 1st day of September in the year 1903, be operated upon any public highway or private way laid out under authority of statute, unless registered as above provided, and the registered number or mark of every automobile and motor cycle operated as aforesaid shall at all times plainly be displayed thereon in Arabic numerals not less than 4 inches long, and conforming in this and other details to the requirements prescribed by the highway commission in its certificate of registration.

Sec. 4 Operators' License

Licenses for operating automobiles and motor cycles shall be issued by the Massachusetts Highway Commission or duly authorized agents thereof. Application shall be made upon blanks prepared by the commission for this purpose, and the licenses issued shall be in such form and shall contain such provisions as said commission may determine. To each licensee shall be assigned some distinguishing number or mark, and a proper record of all applications for license and of all licenses issued shall be kept by the commission at its main office, and shall be open to the inspection of any person during reasonable business hours. Each license shall state the name, place of residence and address of the licensee and the distinguishing number or mask assigned to him.

Special licenses for operating automobiles or motor cycles for hire shall be issued by the commission, but no such license shall be issued until the commission or its authorized agent shall have satisfied itself or himself that the applicant is a proper person to receive it. Such licenses shall be granted for one year only.

The fee for each license to operate shall be $2. All fees shall be deposited at the time of making the application. The commission may at any time suspend or revoke any license for any misconduct of the licensee. Before a license to operate is granted the applicant shall pass such examination as to his qualifications as may be required by the State Highway Commission.

Sec. 5 Vehicles for Hire

Except as hereinafter provided, no person shall, on or after the 1st day of September in the year 1903, operate an automobile or motor cycle upon any public highway or private way laid out under authority of statue, unless licensed so to do under the provisions of this act. No person shall operate an automobile or motor cycle for hire, unless specially licensed by the commission so to do. No person shall employ for hire as chauffeur or operator of an automobile or motor cycle any person not specially licensed as aforesaid, and every chauffeur or operator for hire shall, while so acting, display the distinguishing number or mark assigned to him, in such manner as may be prescribed by the commission.

Sec. 6 Exemption of Drivers Licensed Elsewhere

Automobiles or motor cycles owned by non-residents of this State and driven by a person residing and licensed in some other State may be operated on the roads and highways of this State, subject, however, to the speed limitations contained in Section 4, and to any local regulations permitted under Section 8, and to such further regulations as the highway commission may make. The provisions of this section shall not prevent the operating of automobiles by unlicensed persons if riding with or accompanied by a licensed chauffeur or operator.

Sec. 7 Conduct on Meeting Horses

Every person having control or charge of an automobile or motor cycle shall, whenever upon any public street or way and approaching any vehicle drawn by a horse or horses, or any horse upon which any person is riding, operate, manage and control such automobile or motor cycle in such manner as to exercise every reasonable precaution to prevent the frightening of such horse or horses, and to insure the safety and protection of any person riding or driving the same. And if such horse or horses appear to be frightened, the person in control of such automobile or motor cycle shall reduce its speed, and if requested by signal or otherwise by the rider or driver of such horse or horses, shall not proceed farther toward such animal unless such movement be necessary to avoid accident or injury, or until such animal appears to be under the control of its rider or driver, and in case of extreme fright shall reduce the motive power to a full stop.

Sec. 8 Speed Limit

No automobile or motor cycle shall be run on any public way or private way laid out under the authority or statute outside the limits of a city or the thickly settle or business part of a town or fire district at a speed exceeding 15 miles an hour, or within a city or the thickly settled or business part of a town or fire district at a speed exceeding 10 miles an hour. Upon approaching a crossing of intersecting ways, also in traversing a crossing or intersection, and in going around a corner or a curve in the highway, every person operating an automobile or motor cycle shall run it at a rate of speed less than that hereinbefore specified and at no time greater than is reasonable and proper, having regard to traffic and the use of the way and the safety of the public, and in no event exceeding 8 miles an hour.

Sec 9. Penalties

The commission may, after due hearing, suspend or revoke a certificate issued under Section 1 of this act, or the license issued to any person under Section 3 of this act, for any cause which it may deem sufficient; and any person convicted of violating any provision of this act shall be punished by a fine not exceeding $25 for a first offense, and not exceeding $50 for second and subsequent offenses. Any person convicted of operating or causing or permitting any other person to operate an automobile or motor cycle after a revocation or suspension of the certificate or license granted under this act for such vehicle shall be punished by a fine not exceeding $100, or by imprisonment for a term of ten days, or by both such fine and imprisonment.

Sec. 10 Equipment

Every automobile or motor cycle operated in this Commonwealth shall be provided with an adequate brake, with a muffler, and with a suitable bell, horn or other means of signaling, and shall, during the period from one hour after sunset to one hour before sunrise, display lights, with the registered number or mark thereon, of such size as may be prescribed by the highway commission.

Sec. 11 Locking of Cars Left in Street

Every automobile or motor cycle shall be provided with a lock, key or other device to prevent said vehicle from being set in motion, and no person shall allow any such vehicle operated by him to stand or remain unattended in any street, avenue, road, alley, highway, park, parkway or other public place without first locking, fastening or fixing the vehicle as above provided.

Sec. 12 Fees and Expenses

The fees received under the provisions of this act shall be paid monthly by the secretary of the highway commission into the treasury of the Commonwealth; and such expenses as many be necessary in carrying out the provisions of this act shall be paid out of the treasury of the Commonwealth.

Sec. 13 Definition of Terms

The terms automobile and motor cycle as used in this act shall include all vehicles propelled by power other than muscular power, excepting railroad and railway cars and motor vehicles running only upon rails or tracks, and steam road rollers.

Sec. 14 Local Option and Appeals

Nothing herein contained shall be so construed as to affect the rights of boards of park commissioners as authorized by law. Boards of aldermen of cities and the selectmen of towns may make special regulations as to the speed of automobiles and motor cycles, and as to the use of such vehicles upon particular roads or ways, including the right to exclude them altogether therefrom. Such exclusion, however, shall be subject to an appeal to the Massachusetts Highway Commission, whose decision in the case shall be final. No such special regulation shall be effective unless notice of the same is posted conspicuously at the points where any road affected thereby joins other roads.

Sec. 15 Repeal of Old Law

Chapter 315 of the acts of the year 1902 is hereby repealed.

Sec. 16 Date of Going into Effect

Except as otherwise provided herein, this act shall take effect upon its passage.

[Source: *Horseless Age*, July 1, 1903, pp. 22–23, verbatim.]

Minnesota State Law on Automobiles. Chapter 356—H. F. No. 671.

Be it enacted by the Legislature of the State of Minnesota:

Sec 1. No person, driver or operator in charge of any automobile, motor vehicle or motor cycle on any public road, highway or street within the State shall drive, operate, move, or permit the same to be driven, operated or moved at a rate of speed faster than 8 miles per hour within the thickly settle or business portion of any city or village within this State, nor outside of such thickly settled or business portion of any city or village on any public road, highway or street, at a rate of speed faster than 25 miles per hour, nor over any crossing or crosswalk within the limits of any city or village, at a rate faster than 4 miles per hour when any person is upon the same.

Sec 2. The driver or operator in charge of any automobile, motor vehicle or motor cycle on any public road, highway or street within this State when signaled by the driver of any vehicle propelled by horses, shall stop said automobile, motor vehicle, or motor cycle until the other vehicle has passed.

Sec 3. Every automobile, motor vehicle or motor cycle, when driven on any public road, highway or street within this State shall, during the hours of darkness have fixed upon some conspicuous part thereof, at least one lighted lamp suitable for the use of said automobile, motor vehicle or motor cycle, respectively.

Sec 4. Every automobile, motor vehicle or motor cycle using gasoline as motive power shall use the "muffler" so called, and the same shall not be cut out or disconnected within the limits of any city or village within this State. Every automobile, motor vehicle or motor cycle shall be provided with a bell or horn, which shall be rung or blown whenever there is danger of collision or accident. The driver or operator of every automobile, motor vehicle or motor cycle shall be governed by the usual law of the road by turning to the right in meeting vehicles, teams and persons moving or headed in an opposite direction, and by turning to the left in passing vehicles, teams and persons moving or headed in the same direction.

Sec 5. Before any automobile, motor vehicle or motor cycle shall be driven or operated upon any public road, highway or street within this State the owner thereof shall take out a license for said automobile, motor vehicle or motor cycle, which said license shall be issued by any State boiler inspector in the county where such automobile, motor vehicle or motor cycle is owned. Any person obtaining such license shall pay for the same the sum of $2 to said boiler inspector, who shall issue such license and shall record each license issued by number in consecutive order. The number of each license shall be painted in plain figures upon the back part of each machine in a conspicuous place, and said figures shall not be less than 4½ inches high and of proportionate width.

Provided, however, that nothing in this section contained shall be construed to refer to any driver or operator of any automobile, motor vehicle or motor cycle licensed by any municipality in this State, nor to any automobile, motor vehicle or motor cycle, the numbering of which is provided for by any such municipality.

Sec 6. Any boiler inspector issuing a license shall keep a correct record of all licenses issued in a book to be kept for that purpose. He shall make a correct report to the county treasurer of the county in which he resides at the end of each month of all licenses issued during the month, if any, together with one-half of all fees collected, and shall turn over to such county treasurer one-half of all such fees; the other one-half of the fees so collected he shall be allowed to retain for his services for issuing such licenses.

Sec 7. Any person violating any of the provisions if this act is guilty of a misdemeanor.

Sec 8. This act shall take effect and be in force from and after its passage.

Approved April 21, 1903.

[SOURCE: *Horseless Age*, July 29, 1903, p. 131, verbatim.]

Automobile Legislation in the United States

NEW YORK STATE

Comparatively few counties and towns in this State have adopted special legislation, relying almost generally upon the existing state law.

State Law, signed April 25, 1901 (Condensed).

The owner of a carriage, propelled by steam, shall not allow the same to pass over any public highway or street, except upon railroad tracks, unless such owners shall send before the same a person of mature age at least one-eighth of a mile in advance, or shall notify and warn persons traveling such highway or street, with horses or other domestic animals, of the approach of such carriage; and at night such person shall carry a red light, except in incorporated villages and cities. (This section shall not apply to any carriage or motor vehicle propelled by steam, developing less than 25 horse power, other than a steam traction engine.)

The commissioners or other authorities having charge of any highway, public street or park shall have no power to pass any ordinance or regulation by which any person using a bicycle or tricycle, an automobile or motor vehicle, shall be excluded or prohibited from the free use of any highway, public street, etc., at any time when the same is open to the free use of persons using other pleasure carriages, except upon a driveway, speedway or road expressly set apart by law for the exclusive use of horses and light carriages. The board of supervisors of any county may adopt ordinances regulating the speed of automobiles or motor vehicles on the highways or streets of such county, outside the limits of cities. No ordinance or regulation adopted by the authorities of any municipality in pursuance of this section or of any other law shall require an automobile or motor vehicle to travel at a lower rate of speed than 8 miles per hour within any city, town or village of the State in the built up portions thereof, nor at a slower speed than 15 miles per hour where the same are not build up. An ordinance adopted by a board of supervisors in pursuance of this section, regulating the rate of speed of automobiles on the highways or streets of such county outside of cities shall supersede any such ordinance in such county adopted by the authorities of a town or village. But nothing herein shall prevent the passage of any regulation, ordinance or rule regulating the use of bicycles or tricycles in highways, etc., or the regulation of the speed of carriages or automobiles in public parks and upon parkways and driveways in the city of New York, under the exclusive jurisdiction and control of the department of parks of said city, nor prevent any such authorities in any other city from regulating the speed of any vehicle herein described in such a manner as to limit and determine the proper rate of speed with which such vehicles may be propelled, nor in such manner as to require or prohibit the use of bells, lamps and other appurtenances, nor to prohibit the use of any vehicle upon that part of the highway known as the footpath or sidewalk.

Every owner of an automobile shall, within thirty days after the amendment to this section takes effect, file in the office of the Secretary of State a statement of his name and address, with a brief description of the character of such vehicle, and shall pay to the Secretary of State a registration fee of $1. The Secretary of State shall issue to such person a certificate, stating that he has registered in accordance with this section, and shall cause the names of such persons to be entered in alphabetical order in a book kept for such purpose. Every person hereafter acquiring an automobile or motor vehicle shall, within ten days after acquiring the same, register with the Secretary of State as required by this section.

This section shall not apply to a person manufacturing or dealing in automobiles or motor vehicles, except those for his own private use.

No person driving an automobile on any street, etc., in this State, shall drive the same at any speed greater than is reasonable and proper, having regard to the traffic and use of the highway, or so as to endanger the life or limb of any person.

Every automobile shall be provided with good and efficient brakes, and shall also be provided with a suitable bell, horn or other signal. Every automobile shall be so constructed as to exhibit during the period from one hour after sunset to one hour before sunrise two lamps showing white lights visible within a reasonable distance in the direction toward which the automobile is proceeding, and shall also exhibit a red light visible in the reverse direction. The lamps shall be so placed as to be free from obstruction to light from other parts of said automobile.

Every person driving an automobile shall at request or signal by putting up the hand from a person driving or riding a restive horse cause the automobile to immediately stop and to remain stationary, so long as may be necessary to allow said horse to pass. This provision shall apply to automobiles going either in the same or in an opposite direction.

Any person owning or operating an automobile except such as are used for public hacks, trucks or other vehicles for hire, shall not be required to obtain any license or permit pursuant to the provisions of any local or municipal resolution or ordinance, or the rules or regulations of any commissioners, or other authorities having charge of any highway, etc., or pursuant to the provision of any municipal character or any other statute, except as herein contained. Every such automobile shall have the separate initials of the owner's name placed upon the back thereof in a conspicuous place, the letters forming such initials to be at least 3 inches in height.

The penalty for violating any of the provisions of the law relating to automobiles shall be not exceeding $25.

The Cocks Law.

Sec. 666. A person driving any vehicle upon any public highway, who unjustifiably runs the horses, or who drives an automobile upon any public highway within any city or incorporated village, at a greater rate of speed than 8 miles per hour, except where a greater rate of speed is permitted by the ordinance of a city, or upon any public highway outside of any city or incorporated village at a greater rate of speed than 20 miles per hour, or upon any bridge at a greater rate of speed than 4 miles per hour, is guilty of a misdemeanor, and shall be fined for the first offense not exceeding the sum of $50, and for the second offense not exceeding $50, or by imprisonment for a term not exceeding six months, or both.

New York City Licensing Ordinance (pending)

Following are the chief provisions of ordinance 1066, introduced by Alderman Peck:

No person shall hereafter operate any automobile until he has obtained a license to operate same. The mayor shall designate three competent persons, who shall hold office for two years and shall be known as the Board of Examiners of Automobile Operators, who shall carefully examine every applicant for a license as to such person's general and special fitness to operate such vehicle and make their written report to the mayor. Said board may adopt such rules and regulations for the performance of the duties imposed upon it as it shall deem necessary, and shall hold stated meetings in one of the public buildings of said city. They shall keep an accurate record of all their proceedings, and the salaries of the members of said board shall be paid monthly, out of the moneys paid for licenses.

Persons desiring a license shall make written application to the Bureau of Licenses, in such form as said board shall specify. Such application shall be referred to the board of examiners, who shall appoint a time and place for hearing thereon, and the secretary of said board shall notify the applicant thereof; the applicant shall personally appear before the said board at the time designated and shall submit to examination. The board in its report shall state whether the application is approved or rejected, and if rejected, the reason therefor. Such report shall forthwith be forwarded to the mayor for approval or rejection. If approved, and if the report is in favor of granting the license, the Bureau of Licenses shall at once issue the license, which shall be good for one year from its date unless sooner suspended or revoked. If the report of the board be against granting the license and if such report is approved, no license shall be granted on such application; if the mayor shall disapprove such report rejecting said application the same shall go back to the board of examiners for further hearing.

All licenses shall be by authority of the mayor, and be issued by the Bureau of Licenses; they shall be good for one year from date of issue unless sooner revoked or suspended, and may be renewed from year to year, either with or without further examination, as the board of examiners may determine, on payment of one-half the sum paid the first year. The mayor shall have power, after a hearing, to revoke the license. A license is not transferable, and must be produced whenever required by an officer of the city.

Licenses shall contain the name and address of the licensee, and state the kind of vehicle to be operated, with a sufficiently definite description; and shall be numbered and registered by the Bureau of Licenses in a book provided for that purpose, open to inspection by the public. The vehicle shall be equipped with two lamps, and there shall be securely fastened across the middle of the outside of each lamp a metal band not less than 2 inches in width, out of which the official numbers of the license shall be cut; the figures shall not be less than 1½ inches high, and the lamps shall be kept burning from one-half hour after sunset.

It shall be sufficient cause for revoking the license that the holder has violated the speed regulations or willfully violated any other law relating to the use of automobiles, or has allowed his vehicle to stand unattended on any public places or refused to display his license to officers.

The fee to be paid for licenses for any public vehicle intended to carry one or two persons is $3; if intended to carry more than two persons, $5. For any vehicle operated for private use, $10. Any person operating any vehicle without first obtaining a license or violating any of the other provisions of this ordinance, shall for each offense be fined not less than $10 nor more than $50, or shall be imprisoned not less than two days nor more than ten days, or shall suffer both fine and imprisonment.

Nothing in this ordinance shall be construed as applying to motor cycles.

BUFFALO—Ordinance in force December 22, 1899, limits speed of all vehicles to 8 miles, or around corners and at intersection of streets, 5 miles; ordinance includes usual street regulations; penalty, $5, or imprisonment for five days. A special ordinance governing automobiles is before the Board of Councilmen, the upper house, having been passed by the Board of Aldermen, the lower house. It confines the 8 mile limit to the business streets, and permits 15 miles outside. Vehicles must not be left standing on Main street, between Seneca and Exchange streets, longer than fifteen minutes; must not be left on other streets longer than ten minutes. Penalty remains the same.

YONKERS—Ordinance of May 16, 1900, 8 mile limit; penalty, $5 to $25.

NIAGARA FALLS—General vehicle ordinance limiting speed to 12 miles.

GENEVA—Now contemplating special ordinance.

UTICA—No special law at present, but one in contemplation.

RIVERHEAD—The District Attorney has advertised and posted notices of reward for conviction of automobile drivers who operate beyond speed limit of the Cocks law.

ROCHESTER—Ordinance limits speed within 1 mile of intersection of State and Exchange streets with Main street to 6 miles; otherwise within city to 8 miles. Must carry two lamps and a gong or bell.

OSWEGO—Limit of speed for all vehicles on streets and across bridges, 6 miles.

BINGHAMTON—An ordinance has just been passed limiting speed in the built up portion to 8 miles an hour, in parks to 5 miles and in other parts of the city to 15 miles. It requires good brakes, a bell, whistle or other signaling device, two lamps and initial plates. Automobiles must stop upon signal from driver of restive horse and remain stationary until the latter has passed; fine, not to exceed $25.

Massachusetts (see earlier in this appendix for state law)

WALTHAM—Ordinance limits speed to 8 miles an hour "except in such places as the superintendent of streets may determine."

WARREN—Voted that the speed of automobiles be regulated by the selectmen.

WEST NEWTON—Only state law in effect.

CHICOPEE—An ordinance enacted last December [1901] limits speed to 12 miles an hour and 5 miles an hour on the bridge over the Connecticut River at Chicopee Junction and the bridge over the Chicopee River at Chicopee Centre. Ordinance requires a suitable bell and a lamp. Penalty, not to exceed $100 or ten days' imprisonment or both. The speed limit, of course, conflicts with the limit of the State law, and is therefore void.

ADAMS—Bylaws fix speed limit at 8 miles an hour.

SOMERVILLE—Ordinance speed limit is 10 miles, the same as the limit of the State law.

NORTH ADAMS—Speed limit, 8 miles an hour.

BEVERLY—Ordinance speed limit, 10 miles an hour. One conviction under this ordinance leading to fine of $25.

NEWTON—Ordinance speed limit, 10 miles an hour; fine, not to exceed $20.

CAMBRIDGE—There are several propositions before the City Council with regard to automobile speed regulations.

LENOX—Speed is limited to 8 miles an hour in town districts.

CHELSEA—Ordinance limits speed to 8 miles an hour; fine, not to exceed $20.

Connecticut

Revised Statutes, section 2,089 (condensed).

No motor vehicle shall be run on any highway outside the limits of a city at a speed to exceed 15 miles an hour, and within the limits of any city at a speed to exceed 12 miles an hour. Upon approaching a crossing of intersecting streets or roads the driver shall have such vehicle under control, and shall reduce the speed until said crossing shall have been passed. Upon meeting or passing any vehicle drawn by a horse the driver shall reduce the speed, and if the horse drawing said vehicle appears to be frightened the person in charge of said motor vehicle shall cause it to come to a stop.

No city, town or borough shall have any power to make any ordinance, bylaw, or resolution respecting the speed of motor vehicles, and no ordinance, bylaw or resolution heretofore or hereafter made by any city, town, or borough in respect to motor vehicles shall have any force or effect. The mayor of any city, the selectmen of any town, or the warden of any borough may, upon any special occasion, or whenever in their judgment it may be deemed advisable grant permits to any person or persons or to the public to run such motor vehicles during a specified time or until such permit is revoked, upon specified portions of the public ways or highways of such city, town or borough, at any rate of speed, and may annex such other reasonable conditions to such permits as they may deem proper. Any person violating any of the provisions of this section shall be fined not more than $200 for each offense.

New Jersey

ENGLEWOOD—Eight mile limit; two arrests and convictions; fine $5; maximum penalty since raised to $100.

HACKENSACK—Ordinance July 7, 1902; 8 mile limit; lamps after dark alarm signal required; must stop on request of horse driver; owner's initials on vehicle; persons under eighteen cannot operate; penalty $50 and costs, or, in default, imprisonment not exceeding twenty days; ordinary rules of the road included in the ordinance, and non-observance punished by fine of $10, or, in default, imprisonment for not exceeding ten days.

FORT LEE—Speed limit, 8 miles; penalty, $10.

Gloucester County

Ordinance August 21, 1902, limits speed to 12 miles, in villages, towns, etc., to 8 miles, and when passing teams to 5 miles; if horse shows fright, must stop; must use alarm; penalty, $50, and, on failure to pay, fifteen days in jail; no arrests up to date.

LAWRENCEVILLE—Speed limit 12 miles; penalty, $10 to $15.

Essex County

Ordinance limiting speed in cities of first and second class and in towns, to 8 miles, and in townships to 15 miles; turning corners speed not to exceed 4 miles; penalty $10 for firs offense, $25 afterward; lamps after dark, penalty $5; efficient brakes required, penalty $5; registration with country clerk required, penalty $10; infraction of ordinary rules of the road punishable with fine of $5.

NEWARK—Ordinance of August 21, 1902; limit 8 miles, turning corners 4 miles, first offense $10, subsequent offenses $25; must sound alarm when within 100 feet of pedestrian or vehicle, penalty $5; must keep to left, overtaking or passing, and take reasonable precaution to avoid danger, penalty $5; automobiles used in Newark must be registered with county clerk, penalty $10; in case of accident must stop and give name and address, penalty $10.

Camden County

Ordinance November 13, 1901, limits speed to 10 miles; must stop for frightened horse; automobiles to be registered with county clerk and display number; must carry lamp after nightfall; penalty, $20 and costs.

FREEHOLD—Ordinance, September 1, 1902, limits speed to 6 miles; must use alarm; must show light from one hour after sunset to one hour before sunrise; penalty, $10 for first offense, $20 subsequent offenses; imprisonment for thirty days on failure to pay.

SHREWSBURY TOWNSHIP—Ordinance June 24, 1902, limits speed to 12 miles; penalty, first offense, $10; subsequent offenses, $20; must stop upon request to avoid accidents; penalty for refusal, $5 first time, $10 subsequently.

RED BANK—speed limit, 6 miles; other provisions same as Shrewsbury.

KEYPORT—Speed limit, 8 miles.

MADISON—Speed limit, 8 miles; lamp between one hour after sunset and sunrise; must use alarm; penalty, $10 to $25 and costs, or, in default, imprisonment for five to thirty days.

MORRISTOWN—Ordinance of August 3, 1900, amended October 4, 1901, imposes a fine of $250 for exceeding speed limit of 8 miles, or for failure to carry bell and lamp; about a dozen arrests and convictions.

Atlantic County

Ordinance August 6, 1902, limits speed to 10 miles; lamp after dark; must stop on request for frightened horse; penalty $25.

HAMMONTON—Ordinance, December 28, 1901; speed limit, 10 miles; penalty $10 or imprisonment for ten days.

ATLANTIC CITY—Ordinance limiting speed to 10 miles on streets between the inlet and ocean on northeast extremity and Florida avenue, and 12 miles in other parts of city; alarm when approaching intersections of streets between the inlet and Florida avenue; light after dark; penalty, not exceeding $200; or, in default, imprisonment not exceeding ninety days.

PASSAIC—No ordinance in force, but one projected; general ordinance limits speed to gait no faster than a moderate trot; penalty, $5 with costs.

Pennsylvania

SOUTH BETHLEHEM—Ordinance of December 17, 1900, limits speed to 6 miles; penalty, $10.

EATON—ordinance of June 11, 1901, limits speed to 10 miles; penalty, $20.

ERIE—Ordinance of September 17, 1901, limits speed to 10 miles, and at street intersections, 5 miles; must carry bell or gong; penalty, $10 to $50; or, in default, imprisonment from ten to thirty days.

PITTSBURGH—Ordinance introduced in council limits speed to 6 miles in busy portion, and 10 miles outside; penalty, fine of $25 to $100.

Automobiles are taxed under vehicle ordinance, a single seated vehicle $6 per annum, and vehicles with more than one seat $10 per annum.

PHILADELPHIA—bill now pending in city council provides for inspection of machines and issue of licenses; limits speed to 7 miles in portion bounded by Vine street, South street, Sixteenth street and the Delaware River, and within the buildup portion of suburban wards; 10 miles within all other parts of the city, excepting north of Erie avenue, south of Porter street, west of Fifty-second street, where 15 miles is permitted.

Speed must be reduced to 5 miles, 8 miles, 10 miles respectively, when passing horse vehicles.

Must light lamps one hour after sunset.

Drivers must not leave vehicle before subduing noise of motor.

Motor vehicles must have solidly constructed steering gear. If the weight is above 500 pounds, must have reversing mechanism; must have good and sufficient brake, a suitable bell, horn or other signal; must have means to condense or prevent unnecessary escape of steam or vapor, also improved mufflers to prevent unnecessary noise.

Machines will be examined and license granted for fee of $2, including cost of sign bearing number.

The manufacturer or owner of machine will be fined $50 if all requirements are not fulfilled, and $75 for subsequent offenses.

Penalty for violation of any provision of this ordinance by person operating the vehicle is $10; in case of second violation, license to be suspended, in addition to fine, for not more than thirty days; for third offense, in addition to fine, license suspended for three months; thereafter, license may be suspended indefinitely.

License is only required when driver remains within city limits longer than forty-eight hours.

HARRISBURG—Ordinance now pending limiting speed to 7 miles, also requiring gong and lights; penalty, $25 or imprisonment for thirty days in default.

DARBY—An ordinance has been introduced limiting speed of automobiles to 7 miles an hour; fines, $25, $50 and $100 for first, second and third offense respectively.

Ohio

COLUMBUS—Ordinance of June 16, 1902, limits speed in business streets to 7 miles; elsewhere 12 miles; penalty, $5 to $50, or imprisonment for not more than thirty days.

Penalty for not having lamp and signal, not exceeding $50.

NORWALK—Ordinance limiting speed to 10 miles.

Must carry bell or whistle and lamp; maximum fine, $25 and costs.

TOLEDO—ordinance of July 7, 1902, limits speed to 10 miles.

Penalty, fine of not more than $50, or imprisonment for not more than thirty days.

RAVENNA—Ordinance limiting speed to 5 miles, and requiring light after dark.

MADISONVILLE—Ordinance limiting speed to 5 miles.

GREENVILLE—Speed ordinance, also regulating equipments, passed; no particulars.

ELYRIA—Relies on State law, which requires automobiles to give two-thirds of road to teams.

DAYTON—Ordinance limits speed to 8 miles.

Must have gong or bell, and at night two lighted lamps.

Must stop for frightened horse.

Penalty, $25 and costs.

CLEVELAND—Must register with city clerk, fee $1, and carry numbers.

Does not apply to first visit of one day.

Speed limit, 7 miles inside business radius of ¾ mile; outside, speed limit, 15 miles; must stop on signal of horse driver.

Must carry bell or horn and lamp.

Penalty, not exceeding $100.

ALLIANCE—General ordinance limits to 9 miles.

WARREN—Ordinance limiting speed in business section to 7 miles; outside, 10 miles; at street intersections, 6 miles; must carry lamp and bell or horn; may not drive abreast.

Penalty, not exceeding $50.

MARTIN'S FERRY—Ordinance limiting speed to 10 miles.

Must show lighted lamp after dark. Penalty, not exceeding $20 and costs.

GALLIPOLIS—Ordinance of August 15, 1902, limits speed to 15 miles, and, at street corners, to 8 miles; must light lamps after dark, and ring gong at street crossings. Penalty, $1 to $10.

CINCINNATI—Speed is limited to 8 miles an hour. Horns or gongs must be sounded 100 feet ahead of street intersections. Lamps lighted from sunset to sunrise. Brakes must be efficient. Two automobiles are not allowed to travel abreast.

NEWARK—General ordinance prohibits speed of vehicles or animals of over 8 miles an hour. No arrests have ever been made. About twenty automobiles in use.

Illinois

CHICAGO—An ordinance provides that drivers must be examined and licensed by a board of examiners of operators of automobiles. License expires one year from date of issue. License fee, $3; renewal fee, $1. License may be revoked, after a hearing, if holder violates the regulations or is proved unfit. Speed is limited to 8 miles an hour. A bell or gong not less than 4 inches in diameter must be carried. One or more brakes must be provided sufficiently powerful to bring the vehicle to a stop within 10 feet when traveling at 8 miles an hour. Fine for driving without license, $5 to $25.

SPRINGFIELD—Ordinance limits speed to 12 miles per hour in the city.

PEORIA—A resolution was passed requiring the police to stop fast driving; the Park Board has prohibited the use of automobiles in the respective parks.

CHAMPAIGN—Ordinance requires a 4 inch signal bell, brake strong enough to stop vehicle in 20 feet when going 10 miles an hour, and a lighted lamp at night. Speed is limited to 10 miles per hour and to 6 miles at street intersections. Penalties, $5 to $25 fine.

BELLEVILLE—Ordinance requires a bell and the ringing of same 15 feet ahead of each street intersection, and a lamp lighted at night. Speed limit, 10 miles an hour; fine, $3 to $50.

OAK PARK—An ordinance is in force similar to that of Chicago.

EVANSTON—Ordinance requires that automobiles be equipped with a 4 inch bell and that same be sounded at street crossings, with a brake which will stop vehicle in 20 feet if running at 8 miles per hour and with a lamp or lamps. Speed limit, 8 miles per hour. Fines, $5 to $25. Very few arrests and convictions have been made under this ordinance.

WAUKEGAN—Ordinance provides that operators be licensed, the city clerk issuing licenses; license fee $2. All licenses expire on April 30 after date of issue. A numbered badge is furnished with the license and must be worn by the operator at some conspicuous place on the outside of his garment. Speed is limited to 6 miles an hour in the business district and 10 miles an hour elsewhere. When meeting any vehicle, 100 feet from said vehicle speed must be slackened to 4 miles an hour. A 4 inch alarm bell is required, a brake stopping vehicle in 15 feet at 12 miles an hour, and a lighted lamp at night. Fines, $5 to $25 for first offense and $25 to $100 for subsequent offenses.

Lake County

BELVIDERE—Ordinance limits speed to 10 miles an hour.

Rhode Island

Amendment to general laws of the State provides that any person driving faster than a common traveling pace in any of the streets of Newport or Providence or in the compact part of any town or village or in any road leading from Pawtucket to the compact part of Providence shall be fined from $5 to $20 or imprisoned for then days. For racing an automobile with a horse, vehicle, automobile or other carriage, fine of $10 or imprisonment for ten days.

NEWPORT—Ordinance limiting speed in compact part of city to 6 miles, outside 10 miles. Penalty, not exceeding $20 fine or imprisonment for ten days or both.

PROVIDENCE—Bill no pending before General Assembly to regulate use of automobiles.

WAKEFIELD—Lies between Narragansett Pier and Matunuck, and upon complaint of residents about speeding has just adopted ordinance limiting speed to 6 miles an hour in the "compact" part and to 10 miles an hour in other parts; fine, $5 to $20.

California

SAN FRANCISCO—Ordinance limits speed within the fire limits of city to 8 miles an hour, and to 12 miles an hour outside fire limits. Violations are a misdemeanor and punishable with a fine not to exceed $500 or by imprisonment not to exceed six months, or by both. Another ordinance recently passed provides that gasoline for automobiles must be stored in tanks at least 4 feet below the ground outside the walls of buildings if in excess of 5 gallons. Permits must be obtained from the fire marshal. Penalties, same as above.

An ordinance has just been introduced in the City Council to license public automobiles, the annual fee to be $10 for vehicles carrying more than four passengers, and $5 for vehicles carrying four passengers or less.

OAKLAND—Ordinance requires good and sufficient brakes, bell or horn and a lamp at each side of vehicle. The speed limit is 8 miles an hour and the fine not exceeding $50.

PASADENA—Speed limits of ordinance, 8 miles; 6 miles in certain parts of city and 4 miles at intersections of streets. Bells are required. Fine, not exceeding $300 or three months' imprisonment.

LOS ANGELES—Chamber of Commerce has petitioned City Council to limit the speed of automobiles to 4 miles an hour at certain street crossings.

NAPA—Public automobiles are licensed at $10 a year.

SAN RAFAEL—Speed is limited to 10 miles per hour; must stop when withing 300 feet of a team; a license clause of the ordinance is void.

Michigan

JACKSON—General vehicle ordinance limits speed on business streets to 6 miles.

DETROIT—Ordinance in force regulating speed only—6 to 12 miles; legislation covering whole matter now before council committee; there have been many arrests.

BAY CITY—Pending ordinance limits speed to 8 miles in business portion; 10 miles in other portions; must carry and use alarm device and lamp; penalty, $5 to $100, or imprisonment from five to ninety days, or both.

ADRIAN—Ordinance limits speed to 6 miles in business district; 10 miles outside; penalty, $1 to $10, or imprisonment not exceeding ten days.

GRAND RAPIDS—Automobile operators must procure license, fee $1, which may be revoked by the mayor; limit in business section, 7 miles; other portions, 15 miles; must use alarm bell not less than 4 inches or more than 6 inches diameter, or similar alarm device; must provide brakes and lamps; penalty, fine not exceeding $25; or, in default, jail not exceeding thirty days; one arrest has so far been made.

LANSING—Ordinance has just been passed limiting speed to 10 miles on paved and 12 miles on unpaved streets; license is required.

Wisconsin

JANESVILLE—Ordinance limiting speed to 10 miles. Bell and lamp required; penalty, $1 to $10.

MILWAUKEE—Pending ordinance limiting speed to 8 miles, and at street corners and intersections, 4 miles. Brakes must stop vehicle within 10 feet at 8 mile speed. Must carry alarm bell or gong, and lamps. Penalty, $1 to $50, or jail for not more than ninety days, or both. Ordinance limits speed to 6 miles.

Missouri

ST. LOUIS—Ordinance limits speed to 8 miles an hour in streets and 6 miles an hour in parks. Fine, $5 to $500. There has been some reckless driving recently and consequent accidents and arrests, and the press has assumed a hostile position toward high speed.

KANSAS CITY—An ordinance is now before the Common Council ordaining that the speed must not exceed 10 miles an hour in the business district and 12 miles an hour in other parts of the city. A lamp must be carried on each; vehicles must be registered and be provided with a plate bearing the registration number in figures 4 inches high. Drivers must procure a license: license fee, $3; renewal fee, $1. Licenses are issued by the board of engineers. Penalties, $1 to $500 fine.

JOPLIN—Speed is limited to 6 miles an hour; vehicles must carry a gong and lighted lamps at night.

SEDALIA—Speed limit, 6 miles an hour; two lamps are required.

Indiana

No state law and very few ordinances.

LAFAYETTE—Ordinance limits speed to 10 miles an hour and requires gong and lamp. Fine, $5 to $25 and costs.

KOKOMO—An ordinance limits speed to 10 miles an hour within a certain portion of the city; it is, however, neither observed nor enforced.

EVANSVILLE—Speed is limited to 10 miles an hour; fine $1 to $50.

CONNERSVILLE—Ordinance limits speed to 8 miles an hour.

SOUTH BEND—ordinance pending requiring license; license fee, $4.

Maryland

BALTIMORE—The regular traffic law, which limits speed to 6 miles an hour and imposes a fine of $5 on violations, is applied to automobiles. The latter are few and there have been no arrests so far. There are no special laws in force in any part of the State.

Florida

There are no special automobile regulations in any part of the State.

Georgia

SAVANNAH—City ordinance limits speed to 8 miles an hour; fine, not to exceed $100 and imprisonment not to exceed thirty days.

OAKLAND CITY—Speed limit, 8 miles; fine, not to exceed $100 and costs.

No regulations in Atlanta, Thomasville, Augusta, Rome, Brunswick or Columbus. In Macon the speed is limited to 8 miles an hour.

Maine

PORTLAND—General law limits speed to 8 miles.

BAR HARBOR—Ordinance limits speed to 7 miles, and prohibits use of two principal drives; law not tested.

New Hampshire

FRANKLIN—Automobile drivers must slow up or stop for frightened horses, as necessary; penalty, $10.

Vermont

In all this state, only the town of Manchester, Bennington County, which limits speed to 8 miles, ppears to have any law on the subject.

Virginia

No special legislation reported in any part of this state.

West Virginia

PARKERSBURG—Ordinance limits speed to 8 miles.

WHEELING—Ordinance limits speed to 5 miles; penalty, $5 and costs.

Tennessee

No special legislation reported in any part of this state.

Minnesota

MINNEAPOLIS—No special ordinance at present, but one contemplated; several arrests and fines under general vehicle law limiting speed to 7 miles.

ST. PAUL—Ordinance of August 22, 1902, limits speed to 10 miles. Lamps required; penalty, $10 to $100; or imprisonment for ten to eighty days.

WINONA—Ordinance of July 11, 1902, limits speed to 8 miles—6 miles over bridges.

Iowa

DAVENPORT—An ordinance has been introduced in the City Council limiting speed to 8 miles an hour and requiring vehicle to be stopped at once whenever a horse shies. A bell and a lamp are required. No other regulations are reported from this state.

South Carolina

No regulation of automobiles are in effect in any part of this State as far as our reports go.

North Carolina

NEWBERN—City license required; annual license fee, $50.

No other legislation reported from this State.

North Dakota

No automobile legislation in any part of the State reported.

Kansas

WICHITA—An ordinance has been drawn up limiting speed to 8 miles an hour in the business district, 6 miles in the parks and 12 miles in other parts of the city. The vehicles must have a bell or horn and a muffler to deaden the noise of exhaust. Fine, $10 for first and $20 for succeeding offenses.

Nebraska

OMAHA—No automobile ordinance; automobiles are given the same privileges as horse vehicles, and are limited to 10 miles an hour.

LINCOLN—Ordinance limits speed to 8 miles an hour; another ordinance imposes a license duty of $25 per year on automobiles for public passenger service.

Louisiana

NEW ORLEANS—Ordinance regulating speed was introduced but never passed.

BATON ROUGE—Ordinance limits speed to 8 miles per hour in the towns and 5 miles at corners.

SHREVEPORT—Must carry two lights and speed limited to 8 miles an hour.

Colorado

DENVER—Colorado Automobile Club's ordinance proposed limiting speed to 15 miles and to 8 miles within congested district. Failed to pass.

The present city vehicle ordinance limits speed to 8 miles and at street crossings to 4 miles.

Idaho

No State, county or city laws on the subject.

Kentucky

No special legislation in any part of the State.

New Mexico

No special legislation reported. "The fad has not traveled this far yet."

Oregon

PORTLAND—A speed and licensing ordinance is now pending. No other automobile legislation is reported from this State.

Washington

SPOKANE—Speed limit 8 miles within fire limits and 12 miles outside in city confines.

Utah

No special legislation reported in any part of this State.

Wyoming

No special legislation reported in any part of this State.

Montana

This State reports no special legislation.

[SOURCE: *Horseless Age*, November 5, 1902, pp. 505–511, verbatim.]

Appendix B: Some Leading Automobile Suits

November 1899–October 31, 1900. Damage suits for $3,000 and $5,000 were brought against Alonzo T. Cross, of Providence, Rhode Island, by Walter S. and Ella A. Williams, for frightening horse with automobile, overturning carriage and injuring plaintiffs. The Common Pleas Division of the Supreme Court of Rhode Island gave a verdict of $1,400 for Mr. Williams and $200 for his wife.

December 1899. Three damage suits were brought against John C. Higdon in the Circuit Court at Clayton, Missouri, by Mrs. Katharine Onslen and daughter; alleged that defendant's automobile was beyond control, frightened horse and overturned buggy, throwing out plaintiffs, one of whom died. Dismissed, defendant paying costs.

April 1900. Jonathan West, of Rochester, N. Y., sued for frightening a horse owned by Mason Brothers with his steam carriage, and judgment being secured against him, appealed before County Judge Sutherland, who reversed the judgment on the ground that the temporary inconvenience incident to these modern and practical modes of travel must be subordinate to the larger and permanent benefits resulting from the adopting of such improvements. On May 8, 1901, an appeal was taken to the Appellate Division, and Judge Sutherland's decision reversed, the court holding defendant negligent in having operated a machine that emitted so much steam. On June 19, 1901, Mr. West having died, the Automobile Club of America appealed the case for his widow but the Appellate Division refused the appeal and the verdict stands.

Dr. William L. Vroom, of Ridgewood, N. J., was sued by John L. Guyre, of Woolwick. Alleged that Vroom's automobile frightened Guyre's horse, causing it to run away, throwing out Guyre's wife, who was killed. Vroom testified that horse was frightened when 275 feet distant, and that he stopped his automobile. Judge charged finding whether automobile was a nuisance. Jury agreed it was not a nuisance.

September 1900. Wilson R. Smith, of New York, was sued by Daniel Platt, of Patchogue L. I., because Platt's horse became unmanageable at sight of Smith's automobile, throwing out Platt and wife, the latter being hurt severely; $170 damages were claimed. The court awarded $120.

January 1901. L.C. Havener and Mr. Lewis, of Worcester, Massachusetts, were sued for $2,000 damages on allegation that their motor cycle had caused runaway. Henry A. Corey, of Shrewsbury, Massachusetts, the plaintiff, was awarded a verdict of $1,400.

April 1901. Charles W. Knight vs. James F.D. Lanier. A suit for damages caused by defendant's automobile frightening plaintiff's horse. Judge William J. Gaynor, of the Supreme

Court of Nassau County (Brooklyn), N. Y., instructed the jury that the automobile has as much right to the street as the horse but that if the defendant started up his automobile, the horse, being evidently in distress, without being beckoned by the plaintiff to go on, that was negligence, for which he was responsible. The jury awarded nominal damages. The case was appealed on May 28, 1902, and judgment reaffirmed.

May 1901. Dr. T. Cook Royal, of Ballston Spa, N. Y., obtained judgment of $308.25 from Louis W. Moore for damage caused by Moore's automobile frightening Royal's horse. Defendant disputed legality of decision and entered appeal on the ground that: (1) no negligence was shown on his part; (2) the plaintiff was not free from negligence; (3) the statute (highway law of 1890, Section 155) does not apply to automobiles. The appeal was denied, the Appellate Division confirming decision of Judge Russell that a steam automobile must be preceded one-eighth of a mile by a man warning of its approach.

August 1901. A test case brought by Southampton (L. I.) village authorities to fine Sidney Allen for "running his automobile on the public highways at an unreasonable and unsafe speed" was dismissed by Justice Edward H. Foster on the ground of a defect in the papers.

September 1902. Blum Brothers, found guilty of negligence in operating automobile resulting fatally to Richard Henches and injuring John Krieger, settled by paying $2,000 to the heirs of Henches and $2,000 to Krieger. October 8 Henry L. Blum and his chauffeur were indicted for maintaining a nuisance by Bergen County (N. J.) jury and fined $500 each.

September 1902. August Dietz, chauffeur of W.D. Guthrie, of Lattingtown, Long Island, was fined $20 for violating Cocks law. Guthrie gave notice of appeal. Dietz was discharged by Justice Wallace because timing device which led to arrest was inaccurate.

August 1902. F.D. Shellbarger, of Saline, Kansas, sued in the District Court there by Jacob Gottschall and wife for "48.136.50 damages for injuries received in a runaway caused by Shellbarger's automobile."

July 1902. Edward A. Mulliken, of Quincy, Massachusetts, charged with manslaughter and violation of automobile law by State Officer Thomas A. Dexter, claimed that Ariel B. Scott's horse became frightened, throwing Mr. Scott, who received fatal injuries. August 1902. Scott's widow brought suit for $10,000. The finding of Judge Eldridge, of Duke County, was that Mulliken did not exercise reasonable care in operating his automobile.

July 1902. E.C. Wallace of New York, was fined $25 by Justice Fisher at Nyack, N. Y., for running at illegal speed. Suit for $25,000 damages was also brought by E.T. Lovatt, who, with his wife, was thrown from horse vehicle. July 1902. Supreme Court Justice Cochrane, of Brooklyn, granted order carrying Justice Fisher's judgment to the County Court of Rockland County.

May 1902. The case of Harlan W. Whipple, charged with causing a runaway near Herkimer, N. Y., by excessive speeding of his automobile, was dismissed.

May 1902. First test case under Cocks anti-speed law. Harry S. Woodworth, of Rochester, N. Y., charged by C.B. Parsons, a Brighton mail carrier, with driving his Panhard at greater speed than 20 miles an hour, frightening Parsons' horse, causing it to run away and scatter the mail. Fined $50. Appealed. Judgment sustained. Case now carried to higher court.

March 1902. Charles W. Hall, of 140 Nassau street, N. Y., arraigned for failing to carry number or initials on his automobile, under Section 531 of 1901 law. The magistrate was not conversant with the law and paroled Mr. Hall pending inquiry, which never took place.

February 1902. Thomas Wittmer, of Pittsburgh, Pennsylvania, was sued by C.C. Smith for $5,000 damages sustained by negligence on Wittmer's part in driving his automobile, causing Smith's horse to run away, and throwing Smith and a companion into a creek 30 feet below.

May 1902. In the Court of General Sessions, New York, city, Recorder Goff decided that city magistrates had no power to fine speed offenders, the offense coming under the jurisdiction of the Court of Special Sessions. This was in the case of August Paterson, charged with running his vehicle at 12 miles an hour. He was fined $50 in the Harlem Police Court, but Recorder Goff decided as above on appeal.

February 1902. C.H. Mackay, of Mineola, Long Island, whose automobile had scared a team of horses belonging to Samuel Goldberg, causing them to run away, was sued for $368. The Mineola jury awarded the plaintiff $280.

October. Judge Kellogg, at Yonkers, sentenced to six months' imprisonment W.B. Raymond, an automobile driver, whom he found guilty of negligent driving, resulting in a collision with a street car, the car upsetting and injuring twenty-two passengers. The automobile ran ahead of the car on the track and the car collided with it and was thrown from the track. The case attracted wide attention in automobile circles. The testimony, it is claimed, failed to show any greater negligence on the part of Raymond than on the part of the motorman, who, it is alleged, was racing his car at the time as is customary in this section of Yonkers. Damage suits aggregating a large amount have been brought by persons injured against the railroad company, and the automobile associations are investigating with the object of having the sentence revoked if the circumstances justify it.

October 1902. F.A. Warburg, of New York, was sued at Trenton, N. J., for $50,000 by J.B. Hughes, of New York, for having caused a team of horses driven by the latter to run away, resulting in the loss of one horse and personal injury to the complainant. Damages were awarded plaintiff to the amount of $12,070. The case established a precedent for damages done in horse runaways caused by shying at automobiles, and the case is being appealed. If necessary the American Automobile Association will fight the case for Mr. Warburg.

Judge Kirkpatrick in the suit held that: "It is not negligence per se to operate an automobile on the public highway. By that I mean that the mere operation of an automobile upon the highways does not itself constitute negligence, such negligence as the owner of the automobile would be answerable for in law for damages sustained by reason of its being on the highway. ... The highway is for the common use of everyone who has occasion to travel over it, whether it be in a carriage drawn by horses or in an automobile propelled by electricity, so to speak. But each one must use this common right with due regard to the rights of others. The use of the streets and of the highways is subordinated to a duty to exercise care that others who have equal rights may not receive an injury. One may not wantonly commit any act upon the highway which is likely to result in injury to others." The severity of the sentence has attracted the attention of the Automobile Club of America and the American Automobile Association, and an investigation is being made. The damage suit came to naught when Marble took the poor debtor's oath.

October 1898. An accident was caused in a suburb of Bridgeport, Connecticut, by a horse driven by Dr. Collard taking fright at an automobile driven by F.C. Beach of New York. The automobile (an electric carriage) was behind and to one side of the carriage. The doctor had just stepped out of the carriage and had the reins wrapped around one hand. The horse took fright, ran and pulled him over and he was dragged 50 feet. It was alleged that the peculiar appearance of the machine was calculated to frighten horses of ordinary gentleness. Plaintiff served papers on Mr. Beach in New York, and the case came to trial in October 1901, before Judge McLean. The verdict was unanimous in favor of defendant. The judge reopened the case on the ground that he had omitted in his charge to the jury a citation which might have influenced the verdict. The case was again argued by counsel before the judge, and the latter decided on a new trial. Defendant took an appeal from the judge's decision to the Appellate Division, which will be argued the present fall.

Herbert A. Marble, driver for a New York automobile storage company, who, while in New Haven for the purpose of bringing an automobile to New York, took a spin out North Haven way, collided with a horse and buggy and killed Christian Molz and injured his son, was convicted of manslaughter at Wallingford and sentenced to six months in the penitentiary.

December 1901. The Supreme Court of Indiana held that automobiles have equal rights on the road, and the mere face of a horse taking fright is not sufficient ground for suit.

January 1902. Max Altman, of Tonawanda, N. Y., brought suit against the Mobile Company of America because his horse was frightened by a mobile and ran away, wrecking the carriage and injuring itself. Altman claimed $200 and was awarded $170 and costs, $11.95. The Mobile Company filed notice of appeal.

June 1902. The grand jury of Richmond decided not to indict W.C. Baker and O.E. Denzer, the operators of the electric car that ran amuck at the Staten Island races, killing three persons.

July 1902. First automobile damage suit in San Francisco. E. Courtney Ford sued for $5,000 damages by a salesman for a tailoring firm, who was run over and sustained injuries by Ford's automobile.

September 1902. At Southampton, N. Y., the case against Gerald May for alleged violation of Cocks law was dismissed, because the State failed to show the village was incorporated.

[Source: *Horseless Age*, November 5, 1902, pp. 512–513, verbatim.]

Appendix C: Motor Vehicle Deaths in U.S. by Year

Year	Deaths	VMT—Vehicle miles traveled (billions)	Fatalities per 100 million VMT	Population	Fatalities per 100,000 population
1899	26				
1900	36			76,094,000	0.05
1901	54			77,584,000	0.07
1902	79			79,163,000	0.10
1903	117			80,632,000	0.15
1904	172			82,166,000	0.21
1905	252			83,822,000	0.30
1906	338			85,450,000	0.40
1907	581			87,008,000	0.67
1908	751			88,710,000	0.85
1909	1,174			90,490,000	1.30
1910	1,599			92,407,000	1.73
1911	2,043			93,863,000	2.18
1912	2,968			95,335,000	3.11
1913	4,079			97,225,000	4.20
1914	4,468			99,111,000	4.51
1915	6,779			100,546,000	6.74
1916	7,766			101,961,000	7.62
1917	9,630			103,268,000	9.33
1918	10,390			103,208,000	10.07
1919	10,896			104,514,000	10.42
1920	12,155			106,461,000	11.42
1921	13,253	55	24.09	108,538,000	12.21
1922	14,859	67	21.95	110,049,000	13.50
1923	17,870	85	21.03	111,947,000	15.96

Year	Deaths	VMT—Vehicle miles traveled (billions)	Fatalities per 100 million VMT	Population	Fatalities per 100,000 population
1924	18,400	104	17.55	114,109,000	16.13
1925	20,771	122	16.98	115,829,000	17.93
1926	22,194	140	15.77	117,397,000	18.91
1927	24,470	158	15.44	119,035,000	20.56
1928	26,557	172	15.36	120,509,000	22.04
1929	29,592	197	14.97	121,767,000	24.30
1930	31,204	206	15.12	123,076,741	25.35
1931	31,963	216	14.79	124,039,648	25.77
1932	27,979	200	13.95	124,840,471	22.41
1933	29,746	200	14.83	125,578,763	23.69
1934	34,240	215	15.88	126,373,773	27.09
1935	34,494	228	15.09	127,250,232	27.11
1936	36,126	252	14.33	128,053,180	28.21
1937	37,819	270	14.00	128,824,829	29.36
1938	31,083	271	11.46	129,824,939	23.94
1939	30,895	285	10.83	130,879,718	23.61
1940	32,914	302	10.89	132,122,446	24.91
1941	38,142	333	11.43	133,402,471	28.59
1942	27,007	268	10.07	134,859,553	20.03
1943	22,727	208	10.92	136,739,353	16.62
1944	23,165	212	10.89	138,397,345	16.74
1945	26,785	250	10.71	139,928,165	19.14
1946	31,874	340	9.35	141,388,566	22.54
1947	31,193	370	8.41	144,126,071	21.64
1948	30,775	397	7.73	146,631,302	21.00
1949	30,246	424	7.13	149,188,130	20.27
1950	33,186	458	7.24	152,271,417	21.79
1951	35,309	491	7.19	154,877,889	22.80
1952	36,088	513	7.03	157,552,740	22.91
1953	36,190	544	6.65	160,184,192	22.59
1954	33,890	561	6.03	163,025,854	20.79
1955	36,688	605	6.06	165,931,202	22.11
1956	37,965	627	6.05	168,903,031	22.48
1957	36,932	647	5.71	171,984,130	21.47
1958	35,331	664	5.32	174,881,904	20.20
1959	36,223	700	5.17	177,829,628	20.37

Year	Deaths	VMT—Vehicle miles traveled (billions)	Fatalities per 100 million VMT	Population	Fatalities per 100,000 population
1960	36,399	718	5.06	180,671,158	20.15
1961	36,285	737	4.92	183,691,481	19.75
1962	38,980	766	5.08	186,537,737	20.90
1963	41,723	805	5.18	189,241,798	22.05
1964	45,645	846	5.39	191,888,791	23.79
1965	47,089	887	5.30	194,302,963	24.24
1966	50,894	925	5.50	196,560,338	25.89
1967	50,724	964	5.26	198,712,056	25.53
1968	52,725	1,015	5.19	200,706,052	26.27
1969	53,543	1,061	5.04	202,676,946	26.42
1970	52,627	1,109	4.74	205,052,174	25.67
1971	52,542	1,178	4.46	207,660,677	25.30
1972	54,589	1,259	4.33	209,896,021	26.01
1973	54,052	1,313	4.12	211,908,788	25.51
1974	45,196	1,280	3.53	213,853,928	21.13
1975	44,525	1,327	3.35	215,973,199	20.62
1976	45,523	1,402	3.25	218,035,164	20.88
1977	47,878	1,467	3.26	220,239,425	21.74
1978	50,331	1,544	3.26	222,584,545	22.61
1979	51,093	1,529	3.34	225,055,487	22.70
1980	51,091	1,527	3.35	227,224,681	22.48
1981	49,301	1,552	3.18	229,465,714	21.49
1982	43,945	1,595	2.76	231,664,458	18.97
1983	42,589	1,652	2.58	233,791,994	18.22
1984	44,257	1,720	2.57	235,824,902	18.77
1985	43,825	1,774	2.47	237,923,795	18.42
1986	46,087	1,834	2.51	240,132,887	19.19
1987	46,390	1,921	2.42	242,288,918	19.15
1988	47,087	2,025	2.32	244,498,982	19.26
1989	45,582	2,096	2.17	246,819,230	18.47
1990	44,599	2,144	2.08	249,464,396	17.88
1991	41,508	2,172	1.91	252,153,092	16.46
1992	39,250	2,247	1.75	255,029,699	15.39
1993	40,150	2,296	1.75	257,782,608	15.58
1994	40,716	2,358	1.73	260,327,021	15.64
1995	41,817	2,423	1.73	262,803,276	15.91

Year	Deaths	VMT—Vehicle miles traveled (billions)	Fatalities per 100 million VMT	Population	Fatalities per 100,000 population
1996	42,065	2,486	1.69	265,228,572	15.86
1997	42,013	2,562	1.64	267,783,607	15.69
1998	41,501	2,632	1.58	270,248,003	15.36
1999	41,717	2,691	1.55	272,690,813	15.30
2000	41,945	2,747	1.53	282,216,952	14.86
2001	42,196	2,797	1.51	285,226,284	14.79
2002	43,005	2,856	1.51	288,125,973	14.93
2003	42,884	2,890	1.48	290,796,023	14.75
2004	42,836	2,965	1.44	293,638,158	14.59
2005	43,510	2,989	1.46	296,507,061	14.67
2006	42,708	3,014	1.42	299,398,484	14.27
2007	41,259	3,031	1.36	301,139,947	13.70
2008	37,423	2,977	1.26	303,824,640	12.32
2009	33,883	2,957	1.15	306,700,000	11.05
2010	32,999	2,967	1.11	309,326,000	10.67
2011	32,479	2,950	1.10	311,588,000	10.42
2012	33,782	2,969	1.14	313,914,000	10.75
2013	32,893	2,988	1.10	316,129,000	10.40
2014	32,744	3,026	1.08	318,860,000	10.28
2015	35,485	3,095	1.15	321,370,000	11.06
2016	37,806	3,174	1.19	323,121,000	11.59
2017	37,473	3,213	1.16	326,213,213	11.40
2018	36,835	3,223	1.13	327,096,265	11.18
2019	36,355	3,248	1.10	328,231,337	10.99
2020	38,824	2,904	1.34	331,449,281	11.67
2021	42,939	3,230	1.37	332,915,073	12.89
2022	42,795		1.35	338,289,857	

SOURCE: https://en.wikipedia.org/wiki/Motor_vehicle_fatality_rate_in_U.S._by_year

Chapter Notes

Chapter 1

1. "The horseless age." *Horseless Age*, Nov. 1895, pp. 7–8.
2. "Adieu to the bicycle." *Kansas City Journal* (MO), Nov. 30, 1896.
3. No title. *Daily Ardmoreite* (Ardmore, OK), July 24, 1899; No title. *Rock Island Argus* (IL), Sept. 21, 1901.
4. "Racing in automobiles." *New York Tribune*, Oct. 14, 1900.
5. "No discrimination." *Evening Star* (Washington, D.C.), Mar. 26, 1902.
6. "Death for automobilists." *Wood County Reporter* (Grand Rapids, WI), May 29, 1902.
7. No title. *Atlanta Journal* (GA), Aug. 25, 1902.
8. "Millionaires in craze for speed." *Evening World* (NY), Aug. 29, 1902.
9. No title. *The Watchman and Southron* (Sumter, SC), Oct. 22, 1902.
10. "To conciliate the masses." *Horseless Age*, Sept. 10, 1902, p. 266.
11. "Abuses of chauffeurs to be checked." *Horseless Age*, Mar. 18, 1903, p. 364.
12. "A Rothschild in jail." *Spokane Press* (WA), Sept. 24, 1903.
13. "New auto road." *Jersey City News* (NJ), Feb. 11, 1903.
14. "Automobilism in New York." *Evening Star* (Washington, D.C.), Apr. 23, 1903.
15. "Aphorisms of an artless actor." *Evening World* (NY), May 20, 1903; "More trouble for the poor." *Omaha Bee* (NE), Oct. 21, 1903.
16. "Evils of the power of wealth." *Red Cloud Chief* (NE), Nov. 17, 1903.
17. "An open challenge." *Times Dispatch* (Richmond, VA), June 14, 1904.
18. "Automobiles and class hatred." *Evening Star* (Washington, D.C.), June 4, 1904.
19. No title. *Seattle Republican* (WA), Sept. 30, 1904.
20. Julius W. Muller. "On the edge of the future." *Evening Star* (Washington, D.C.), Dec. 24, 1904.

Chapter 2

1. "The horseless carriage." *Scranton Tribune* (PA), Aug. 10, 1895.
2. "Horseless carriages in Paris." *Edgefield Advertiser* (SC), Dec. 2, 1896.
3. "The prevention of noise." *Horseless Age*, May 1897, p. 1.
4. "The horse and the dynamo." *Wichita Eagle* (KS), June 4, 1897.
5. "Prejudice at Washington." *Horseless Age*, July 1897, p. 1.
6. "The horse an unruly brute." *Horseless Age*, July 1897, p. 2.
7. "The tortured horse." *Orleans County Monitor* (Barton, VT), Oct. 25, 1897.
8. "Terminal transfer." *Horseless Age*, Apr. 1898, p. 1.
9. "Liability of motor vehicle owners." *Horseless Age*, July 1898, p. 4.
10. "Driving out the horse." *Anderson Intelligencer* (SC), Oct. 19, 1898.
11. "Cold comfort for carriage builders." *Horseless Age*, Dec. 1898, pp. 5–6.
12. "Horses and automobiles." *Wichita Eagle* (KS), Jan. 26, 1899.
13. Charles E. Duryea. "Comicalities of the horse." *Horseless Age*, May 10, 1899, p. 14.
14. "Appeal in the West case." *Horseless Age*, June 28, 1899, p. 15.
15. "A judgment reversed." *Horseless Age*, Apr. 25, 1900, p. 11.
16. "The advent of the automobile." *Virginian-Pilot* (Norfolk, VA), July 23, 1899.
17. "Careless drivers of horses." *Horseless Age*, Aug. 9, 1899, p. 6.
18. "Damage suit in Rhode Island." *Horseless Age*, Nov. 15, 1899, p. 6.
19. "A chance for the automobile." *Horseless Age*, Dec. 27, 1899, p. 14.
20. "Equal rights upon the road." *Horseless Age*, Jan. 10, 1900, p. 7.
21. "Responsibility of the horse owner." *Horseless Age*, Mar. 14, 1900, p. 10; "Educates his neighbors' horses to the automobile." *Horseless Age*, Mar. 7, 1900, p. 11.
22. "To guard Queen Victoria." *County Record* (Kingstree, SC), Mar. 1, 1900.
23. "To drive out fear." *Telegraph-Courier* (Kenosha, WI), June 12, 1902.
24. "Automobile lady horse trainer." *St. Paul Globe* (MN), Sept. 12, 1902.

25. "Cost of horse and auto." *New York Tribune*, Aug. 6, 1900.
26. No title. *Omaha Bee* (NE), June 21, 1901.
27. "The automobile not a nuisance." *Horseless Age*, Sept 26, 1900, p. 10.
28. "Damages awarded against the automobile." *Horseless Age*, Oct. 31, 1900, p. 12.
29. "The noise question." *Horseless Age*, Dec. 19, 1900, pp. 11–12.
30. "The law of the road for automobiles." *Horseless Age*, Apr. 24, 1901, pp. 73–74.
31. "Adverse decision at Rochester." *Horseless Age*, May 8, 1901, p. 121.
32. "Automobile club appeals West case." *Horseless Age*, May 8, 1901, p. 138.
33. "$50,000 automobile damage suit." *Horseless Age*, Oct. 30, 1901, p. 641.
34. "An interesting automotive damage case." *Horseless Age*, Dec. 25, 1901, pp. 837–38.
35. "Runaway in Fifth Ave." *New York Tribune*, Apr. 7, 1902.
36. "Horses and automobiles." *Evening World* (NY), May 23, 1902.
37. "Jury wants auto speed cut down." *Evening World* (NY), June 3, 1902.
38. "Legislative and legal." *Horseless Age*, Oct. 15, 1902, p. 403; "$500 fine for man's death." *Evening World* (NY), Oct. 27, 1902.
39. "The dangers of horse traffic." *Horseless Age*, July 16, 1902, p. 66.
40. "Automobile and horse regulations." *Horseless Age*, Nov. 12, 1902, p. 524.
41. Public road question." *Middlebury Register* (VT), Nov. 14, 1902.
42. "Legislative and legal." *Horseless Age*, Nov. 19, 1902, pp. 568–69.
43. *Ibid.*
44. "Stop that cough." *Minneapolis Journal* (MN), Nov. 22, 1902.
45. "Suffolk wants no automobiles." *Times Dispatch* (Richmond, VA), May 3, 1903.
46. "Horses and automobiles." *Evening World* (NY), May 23, 1902.
47. William A. Clarke. "Automobile versus horse." *Bridgeton Pioneer* (NJ), July 17, 1902.
48. "Unmanageable automobiles." *New York Tribune*, May 12, 1903.
49. "Automobiles and horses." *Evening Star* (Washington, D.C.), Dec. 12, 1903.

Chapter 3

1. "Motor carriages excluded from Boston parks." *Horseless Age*, Mar. 1899, p. 7.
2. *Ibid.*
3. *Ibid.*
4. *Ibid.*
5. "Barred out of Boston's sacred parks." *Horseless Age*, Mar. 1899, p. 6.
6. *Ibid.*
7. *Ibid.*
8. "License numbers required in Boston parks, too." *Horseless Age*, Nov. 14, 1900, p. 38.
9. "Automobiles for park police." *New York Tribune*, July 17, 1903.
10. "Excluded from Chicago parks." *Horseless Age*, June 21, 1899, p. 6.
11. *Ibid.*
12. "To test the law." *Horseless Age*, June 21, 1899, p. 11.
13. "The automobile wins." *Evening World* (Shenandoah, PA), June 22, 1899.
14. "Chicago judge does not support park commissioners." *Horseless Age*, June 28, 1899, p. 14.
15. *Ibid.*
16. "Harmless horseless carriages." *Albuquerque Citizen* (NM), July 5, 1899.
17. "Win the right to the road." *San Francisco Call*, July 6, 1899.
18. "In favor of automobiles." *Evening Times* (Washington, D.C.), July 6, 1899.
19. "The motor vehicle wins in Chicago." *Horseless Age*, July 12, 1899, p. 17.
20. "Make way for the automobile." *San Francisco Call*, July 14, 1899.
21. "The coming vehicles." *Record-Union* (Sacramento, CA), July 16, 1899.
22. "Authorities relenting." *Horseless Age*, June 28, 1899, pp. 5–6.
23. "Automobiles in parks." *San Antonio Light* (TX), July 5, 1899.
24. "The automobile age." *Kansas City Journal* (MO), Nov. 15, 1899.
25. "To test the law." *Horseless Age*, June 21, 1899, p. 11.
26. "Willing to be convinced." *Horseless Age*, July 5, 1899, p. 6.
27. "No permit for motor carriages in Central Park." *Horseless Age*, July 5, 1899, p. 10.
28. "Short stories of the day." *Omaha Bee* (NE), Aug. 13, 1899.
29. "Central Park recalcitrance." *Horseless Age*, Nov. 8, 1899, pp. 5–6.
30. "Automobile a pleasure carriage?" *Sun* (NY), Oct. 29, 1899.
31. "Victory for the automobile." *Horseless Age*, Nov. 8, 1899, p. 8.
32. "Park board acts on automobiles." *New York Tribune*, Nov. 3, 1899.
33. "Automobiles in the park." *New York Tribune*, Nov. 10, 1899.
34. "Hearing before the park board." *Horseless Age*, Nov. 15, 1899, p. 10; "Park authorities wavering." *Horseless Age*, Nov. 15, 1899, p. 7.
35. "Park rules relaxed." *Horseless Age*, Nov. 22, 1899, p. 5.
36. "Automobile wins the day." *New York Tribune*, Nov. 21, 1899.
37. "More park permits." *Horseless Age*, Dec. 13, 1899, p. 8.
38. "Automobiles in parks." *New York Tribune*, May 20, 1899.
39. "Police block test case." *New York Tribune*, May 5, 1901.

40. "Fairmont park opens." *Horseless Age*, Oct. 11, 1899, p. 5.
41. "Philadelphia parks open." *Horseless Age*, Oct. 3, 1900, p. 16.
42. "Automobiles in the park." *San Francisco Call*, Feb. 23, 1900.
43. "Barred from Golden Gate Park." *Horseless Age*, Mar. 7, 1900, p. 19.
44. "Golden Gate Park open on permit." *Horseless Age*, Oct. 24, 1900, p. 13.
45. "Object to Automobiles in park." *San Francisco Call*, Dec. 10, 1901.
46. "Police watch chauffeurs." *San Francisco Call*, Mar. 16, 1903.
47. "Baltimore parks barred." *Horseless Age*, Mar. 23, 1900, p. 11.
48. "Park exclusion case to be tested at Baltimore." *Horseless Age*, Jan. 9, 1901, p. 13.
49. "Puts ban on devil wagons." *Omaha Bee* (NE), Aug. 1, 1902.
50. "Memphis park board passes offensive measure." *Horseless Age*, June 24, 1903, p. 743.

Chapter 4

1. "The policy of the Motor League." *Horseless Age*, Dec. 1895, p. 8.
2. *Ibid.*
3. "S. W. Elston appointed." *Indianapolis Journal*, Apr. 3, 1902.
4. "American Motor League." *Norfolk News-Journal* (NE), May 7, 1902.
5. "Elects I.B. Potter president." *New York Tribune*, Jan. 23, 1903.
6. "Automobiling." *New York Tribune*, June 24, 1903.
7. "Opposed to auto races." *Sun* (NY), June 25, 1903.
8. "League being organized for protecting motorists." *Savannah Morning News* (GA), July 6, 1903.
9. "Auto notes." *Providence News* (RI), July 20, 1903.
10. No title. *Minneapolis Journal* (MN), July 22, 1903.
11. "Guides for autoists." *Morris Tribune* (MN), Sept. 26, 1903.
12. "Auto makers organize." *New York Tribune*, Dec. 4, 1900.
13. "Good roads movement." *Jersey City News* (NJ), Nov. 15, 1900.
14. "Movement for a joint show." *New York Tribune*, Nov. 22, 1901.
15. "Of interest to automobilists." *New York Tribune*, Dec. 5, 1902.
16. "Chicago's auto show." *Free Press* (Poplarville, MS), Mar. 6, 1902.
17. "New York automobile show opens Saturday." *Rock Island Argus* (IL), Jan. 15, 1903.
18. "Automobiling." *New York Tribune*, Jan. 17, 1903.
19. "To fight Bedell bill to-day." *New York Tribune*, May 6, 1903.
20. "A progressive governor." *Horseless Age*, Apr. 1897, p. 17.
21. "Automobile club organized." *Horseless Age*, June 14, 1899, p. 6.
22. "Automobile riders confer." *Evening Times* (Washington, D.C.), June 8, 1899.
23. "Automobile club." *Topeka State Journal* (KS), June 8, 1899.
24. "Automobile club dines." *New York Tribune*, Apr. 3, 1900.
25. "The automobile club." *New York Tribune*, Apr. 8, 1900.
26. "The automobile test." *New York Tribune*, Oct. 10, 1902.
27. "Automobile war is growing." *New York Tribune*, June 5, 1900.
28. "A national automobile association." *Indianapolis Journal*, Mar. 5, 1902.
29. "Automobile topics." *New York Tribune*, Mar. 7, 1902.
30. "Official blacklist for speedy chauffeurs." *Washington Evening Times* (Washington, D.C.), May 7, 1902.
31. "Fight for control of automobile racing." *Evening World* (NY), Dec. 24, 1903.
32. "Investigating before legislating." *Horseless Age*, June 28, 1899, p. 14.
33. "The automobile club." *Horseless Age*, July 5, 1899, pp. 5–6; C.E. Corrigan. "Favors a national protective association." *Horseless Age*, July 12, 1899, p. 19.
34. "A national protective association." *Horseless Age*, July 19, 1899, p. 6.
35. "Work for the automobile club." *Horseless Age*, Oct. 11, 1899, p. 5.
36. "Constitution and by-laws of the Automobile Club of America." *Horseless Age*, Oct. 11, 1899, p. 6.
37. "Resume." *Horseless Age*, Jan. 24, 1900, pp. 9–10.
38. "A simon pure automobile exhibition needed." *Horseless Age*, Jan. 24, 1900, p. 10; "The automobile club's exhibition." *Horseless Age*, Mar. 7, 1900, p. 11.
39. "Advocating good roads." *Horseless Age*, Mar. 7 ,1900, p. 11.
40. "Good roads." *Horseless Age*, Mar. 14, 1900, pp. 9–10.
41. "Bicyclists and motorists part company." *Horseless Age*, Mar. 21, 1900, p. 10.
42. "A plea for good roads." *Horseless Age*, Mar. 14, 1900, pp. 26–28.
43. "Good roads indorsed." *Horseless Age*, July 4, 1900, p. 9.
44. "Automobile clubs." *Horseless Age*, Jan. 9, 1901, p. 11.
45. "American automobile clubs." *Horseless Age*, Jan. 9, 1901, pp. 16–18.
46. "Membership and constitution of the national association." *Horseless Age*, Jan. 16, 1901, p. 17.

47. "Manufacturer's Association endorses Boston show." *Horseless Age,* Feb. 13, 1901, p. 13.
48. "Chauffeurs to run to crystal Springs dam." *San Francisco Call,* Sept. 28, 1901.
49. "Doings of the A.C.A." *Horseless Age,* Dec. 25, 1901, p. 838.
50. "Review of the year." *Horseless Age,* Jan. 1, 1902, p. 1.
51. "Who are the enemies of the automobile industry?" *Horseless Age,* Jan. 1, 1902, pp. 4–5.
52. "Club affiliation in Indiana." *Horseless Age,* Jan. 15, 1902, p. 67.
53. Charles E. Duryea. "Proposal to revive." *Horseless Age,* Jan. 22, 1902, p. 120.
54. Charles E. Duryea. "The question of automobile organization." *Horseless Age,* Jan. 29, 1902, p. 147.
55. "The question of automobile organization." *Horseless Age,* Jan. 22, 1902, p. 98.
56. "Club affiliation abandoned." *Horseless Age,* Feb. 19, 1902, p. 244.
57. "Automobilists in convention at Chicago." *Times* (Washington, D.C.), Mar. 2, 1902.
58. "The American Automobile Association." *Horseless Age,* Mar. 12, 1902, p. 317.
59. "Third annual banquet." *Horseless Age,* Mar. 12, 1902, pp. 334–36.
60. "Meeting of the American Motor League." *Horseless Age,* Mar. 12, 1902, p. 341.
61. "American Automobile Association meeting." *Horseless Age,* Apr. 2, 1902, p. 430.
62. Winthrop E. Scarritt. "Invitation extended." *Horseless Age,* Apr. 23, 1902, p. 511.
63. "The good roads movement." *Horseless Age,* Mar. 12, 1902, pp. 318–19.
64. "Speed excesses punished." *Horseless Age,* May 28, 1902, p. 626.
65. "Automobile war is growing." *New York Tribune,* June 5, 1902.
66. "List of automobile clubs and organizations." *Horseless Age,* Oct. 1, 1902, p. 370.
67. "The old year and the new." *Horseless Age,* Jan. 7, 1903, p. 1.
68. "A.A.A. annual meeting." *Horseless Age,* Jan. 14, 1903, p. 114.
69. "Automobile legislation in Cincinnati." *Horseless Age,* Feb. 25, 1903, p. 309.
70. "Legislative and legal." *Horseless Age,* Mar. 11, 1903, p. 359.
71. "New Jersey automobile law comprised." *Horseless Age,* Feb. 25, 1903, p. 309.
72. *Ibid.*
73. "A.C.A. affairs." *Horseless Age,* Apr. 8, 1903, p. 464.
74. "Club notes." *Horseless Age,* May 13, 1903, p. 587.
75. "Probable expansion of the A.A.A." *Horseless Age,* Sept. 23, 1903, p. 322.

Chapter 5

1. "The status of the race." *Horseless Age,* Dec. 1895, pp. 5–6; "Paid his fine." *Evening Star* (Washington, D.C.), Apr. 4, 1902.
2. Charles Duryea. "Charles Duryea on the speed craze." *Horseless Age,* Feb. 1896, p. 19.
3. "The road vehicle and the track vehicle." *Horseless Age,* Apr. 1896, pp. 3–4.
4. "Hasten slowly." *Horseless Age,* July 1898, p. 4.
5. "The speed limit in France." *Horseless Age,* Aug. 1898, p. 4.
6. "The law puts on the brake in France." *Horseless Age,* Feb. 1899, p. 6.
7. "Crusade against reckless motoring in France." *Horseless Age,* Sept. 6, 1899, p. 6.
8. "Speed of automobiles." *Sun* (NY), May 6, 1900.
9. "Automobiles must not run too fast," *New York Tribune,* May 23, 1900.
10. "Mr. Vanderbilt's fast auto." *New York Tribune,* June 12, 1900.
11. "Automobiles in Newport." *Sun* (NY), June 13, 1900.
12. "Laws and automobiles." *New York Tribune,* July 22, 1900.
13. "Make the punishment fit the crime." *Horseless Age,* Sept. 19, 1900, p. 10.
14. "Horses willingly sacrificed to the Vanderbilt automobile." *Horseless Age,* Jan. 2, 1901, p. 13.
15. "Orders speedy automobile." *St. Louis Republic,* Feb. 1, 1901.
16. "Racing in automobiles." *New York Tribune,* Oct. 14, 1900.
17. "Attacks Vanderbilt's White Ghost." *New York Tribune,* May 18, 1901; "How fast autos should go." *Sun* (NY), May 18, 1901.
18. "W.K. Vanderbilt is fined." *Omaha Bee* (NE), Aug. 31, 1901.
19. "Vanderbilt is disgusted." *Wichita Eagle* (KS), Nov. 30, 1910.
20. "To restrict speed in Tarrytown." *New York Tribune,* June 19, 1900.
21. "The legal idea of speed." *Horseless Age,* Sept. 5, 1900, p. 23.
22. "Fined for fast driving." *Horseless Age,* Jan. 16, 1901, pp. 16–17.
23. "Automobile speed laws in Connecticut." *Horseless Age,* Feb. 13, 1901, pp. 13–14.
24. "Automobile club frowns down unlawful speed." *Horseless Age,* Feb. 13, 1901, p. 12.
25. "Road racing forces attention at last." *Horseless Age,* Feb. 13, 1901, p. 30.
26. "Stand fast on the speed question." *Horseless Age,* Feb. 20, 1901, p. 13.
27. "To check speed in Chicago." *Horseless Age,* Feb. 20, 1901, p. 27.
28. "Manufacturers' Association to be heard on the speed question." *Horseless Age,* Feb. 27, 1901, p. 15.
29. "Clubs advocate a uniform speed law." *Horseless Age,* Feb. 27, 1901, p. 15.
30. "The automobile club's substitute speed bill." *Horseless Age,* Mar. 6, 1901, pp. 14–15.
31. "Look for it here." *Public Ledger* (Maysville, KY), Feb. 28, 1901.

32. "Speed on the streets." *New York Tribune*, Mar. 25, 1901.
33. "The new glory of automobilism." *Horseless Age*, May 15, 1901, p. 141.
34. "To regulate speed of automobiles." *St. Louis Republic*, Aug. 2, 1901.
35. "Mobiles must travel slowly." *San Francisco Call*, Aug. 21, 1901.
36. "Police issue waring to racing association." *Horseless Age*, Aug. 28, 1901, p. 464.
37. "Observations." *Courier* (Lincoln, NE), Sept. 14, 1901.
38. "Heroic measures to stop speeding of automobiles." *Horseless Age*, Oct. 16, 1901, p. 500.
39. "To curb speed of automobiles." *Evening World* (NY), Oct. 8, 1901.
40. "After the Long Island scorcher." *Horseless Age*, Oct. 23, 1901, p. 628.
41. "No municipal paternalism needed." *Horseless Age*, Oct. 30, 1901, pp. 631–632.

Chapter 6

1. "The flurry of anti-speed legislation." *Horseless Age*, Jan. 15, 1902, p. 65.
2. *Ibid.*
3. *Ibid.*
4. "Anti-speed legislation—an interview with Mr. Chamberlin." *Horseless Age*, Jan. 15, 1902, p. 67.
5. "Westchester County anti-speed." *Horseless Age*, Jan. 15, 1902, p. 67.
6. "Automobile laws." *Sun* (NY), Jan. 16, 1902.
7. "Speed limit for autos." *Columbus Journal* (NC), Jan. 22, 1902.
8. "Speed of motor vehicles." *Horseless Age*, Jan. 22, 1902, p. 127.
9. "Fined for fast driving." *Horseless Age*, Jan. 22, 1902, p. 127.
10. "Protest against the automobile." *Horseless Age*, Feb. 19, 1902, p. 244.
11. "Automobiling." *Evening Star* (Washington, D.C.), Mar. 27, 1902.
12. "Massachusetts speed legislation." *Horseless Age*, Apr. 2, 1902, p. 429; "Minor mention." *Horseless Age*, Apr. 9, 1902, p. 460.
13. "Speed madness." *New York Tribune*, Apr. 3, 1902.
14. "The question of speed under the new law." *Horseless Age*, Apr. 9, 1902, p. 454.
15. "To begin auto speed crusade." *New York Tribune*, Apr. 13, 1902.
16. "Speed of automobiles." *Evening Star* (Washington, D.C.), Apr. 25, 1902.
17. "Sowing the wind, reaping the whirlwind." *Horseless Age*, May 14, 1902, p. 572.
18. "To test the New York State law." *Horseless Age*, May 14, 1902, p. 572; "New York speed violation cases." *Horseless Age*, May 21, 1902, p. 620.
19. "Mounted policemen." *Minneapolis Journal* (MN), May 21, 1902.
20. "Chauffeurs not allowed to scorch." *St. Louis Republic*, June 17, 1902.
21. "Police traps on the Merrick Road, L.I." *Horseless Age*, July 9, 1902, p. 47.
22. "Legislative and legal." *Horseless Age*, July 16, 1902, p. 76.
23. "The automobile war on the north shore, Chicago." *Horseless Age*, July 30, 1902, p. 123.
24. "Police traps in Evanston, Ill." *Horseless Age*, Aug. 27, 1902, p. 215.
25. "Legislative and legal." *Horseless Age*, Oct. 1, 1902, pp. 364–65.
26. "Speed restrictions and police traps in Massachusetts." *Horseless Age*, Dec. 10, 1902, p. 627.
27. "A. H. Marks." *Akron Democrat* (OH), July 11, 1902; "Made no case." *Akron Democrat* (OH), July 14, 1902.
28. "Doctors and the speed laws." *Horseless Age*, July 23, 1902, p. 83.
29. "New York courts to deal with speed offenders." *Horseless Age*, July 30, 1902, p. 110.
30. "New York court will not spare reckless automobilists." *Horseless Age*, July 30, 1902, p. 113.
31. "Speedometers required by law." *Horseless Age*, July 30, 1902, p. 111.
32. "Oppressive speed ordinances." *Horseless Age*, Aug. 27, 1902, p. 210.
33. "An example of liberal speed legislation." *Horseless Age*, Sept. 3, 1902, pp. 237–38.
34. "Violates law relating to speed." *Evening Star* (Washington, D.C.), Sept. 6, 1902.
35. No title. *Stark County Democrat* (Canton, OH), Sept. 23, 1902.
36. "Automaniacs, beware!" *Horseless Age*, Oct. 1, 1902, pp. 349–50.
37. "Legislative and legal." *Horseless Age*, Oct. 22, 1902, p. 462.
38. "Automania in a new light." *Horseless Age*, Apr. 29, 1903, pp. 519–20.
39. "Speed of automobiles." *Indianapolis Journal* (IN), Apr. 30, 1903; "Braking/stopping distances." nacto.org, downloaded Nov. 28, 2018.
40. "Legislation and legal," *Horseless Age*, May 6, 1903, p. 564.
41. "Legislative and legal." *Horseless Age*, May 20, 1903, p. 613.
42. "Races and furious driving on the highways." *Horseless Age*, June 3, 1903, p. 643.
43. "Police are instructed to enforce ordinance." *Stark County Democrat* (Canton, OH), Aug. 14, 1903.
44. "Enforce speed law." *Indianapolis Journal*, Dec. 10, 1903.
45. "Death blow to street races." *New York Tribune*, June 4, 1902.
46. "Automobile war is growing." *New York Tribune*, June 5, 1902.
47. "Auto club of America behind the movement." *Topeka State Journal* (KS), June 18, 1902.
48. "To stop dangerous auto-speeding." *Wauwatosa News* (WI), June 27, 1903.

49. "Millionaires in craze for speed." *Evening World* (NY), Aug. 29, 1902.

Chapter 7

1. "Reckless driving in France." *Horseless Age*, June 1898, p. 1.
2. "Motor vehicle accident insurance." *Horseless Age*, Jan. 10, 1900, p. 13.
3. "Apportioning the blame." *Horseless Age*, July 25, 1900, p. 10.
4. "Reckless automobiling." *Evening Star* (Washington, D.C.), Dec. 20, 1900.
5. "Careless operations in cities—insurance." *Horseless Age*, May 15, 1901, p. 142.
6. "Automobile insurance." *Horseless Age*, Sept. 4, 1901, p. 469.
7. "Automobiles and fire insurance rates." *Horseless Age*, Sept. 18, 1901, p. 511.
8. "Freak racer a juggernaut." *New York Tribune*, June 1, 1902.
9. "Automobilists held to answer for murder." *St. Paul Globe*, June 16, 1902.
10. "Automobile war is growing." *New York Tribune*, June 5, 1902.
11. "Death due to automobile." *New York Tribune*, June 8, 1902.
12. Mr. And Mrs. Charles Fair instantly killed." *Evening Bulletin* (Honolulu, HI), Aug. 23, 1902.
13. "Mr. And Mrs. Charles Fair killed by automobile." *St. Louis Republic*, Aug. 15, 1902.
14. "Wife of United States senator." *San Francisco Call*, Sept. 13, 1902.
15. "Killed by racing auto." *New York Tribune*, June 6, 1902.
16. "Insurance against damage suits." *Horseless Age*, July 9, 1902, pp. 27–28.
17. "Automobile accident insurance." *Horseless Age*, July 30, 1902, p. 123.
18. Edward Sephton. "Why there are so many auto accidents." *Deseret News* (Salt Lake City, UT), Sept. 20, 1902.
19. "Prison shave for Raymond." *Evening World* (NY), Oct. 31, 1902.
20. "Woman barely escapes death." *San Francisco Call*, Mar. 16, 1903.
21. "Legislative and legal." *Horseless Age*, Nov. 12, 1902, p. 541.
22. "Legislative and legal." *Horseless Age*, Nov. 26, 1902, p. 596.
23. "Big auto fells horse." *New York Tribune*, Apr. 8, 1903.
24. "Serious charge against automobile driver." *Horseless Age*, June 24, 1903, p. 744.
25. "Legislative and legal." *Horseless Age*, July 15, 1903, pp. 79–80.
26. "Fatal accidents—warning." *Horseless Age*, July 29, 1903, pp. 112–13.
27. Charles E. Duryea. "Accidents and their remedy." *Horseless Age*, Aug. 5, 1903, p. 151.
28. "Automobile insurance." *New Haven Morning Journal* (CT), Nov. 2, 1902.

Chapter 8

1. "Taxes and licenses." *Horseless Age*, May 17, 1899, p. 3.
2. *Ibid.*
3. *Ibid.*
4. "Want all motor vehicles licensed." *Horseless Age*, June 21,1899, p. 6.
5. "Anti-motor legislation in Chicago." *Horseless Age*, July 5, 1899, p. 5.
6. *Ibid.*
7. "Chicago wants motor drivers licensed." *Horseless Age*, July 12, 1899, pp. 5–6.
8. *Ibid.*
9. *Ibid.*
10. "Topics of the times." *Evening Times-Republican* (Marshalltown, IA), Mar. 19, 1900; "Gathered here and there." *New York Tribune*, Mar. 27, 1900.
11. "Automobiles not dangerous." *Horseless Age*, Feb. 13, 1901, p. 30.
12. "Legislative and legal." *Horseless Age*, Jan. 28, 1903, p. 189; "Identification numbers in Chicago." *Horseless Age*, Feb. 4, 1903, p. 191.
13. "Identification numbers in Chicago." *Horseless Age*, Feb. 4, 1903, p. 191.
14. "Steam vehicle licenses." *Horseless Age*, Nov. 8, 1899, p. 5.
15. "Graded license meets with approval." *Horseless Age*, Nov. 8, 1899, p. 8.
16. "Steam vehicle licenses." *Horseless Age*, Dec. 6, 1899, pp. 11–12.
17. "Steam vehicle licenses." *Horseless Age*, Dec. 13, 1899, pp. 7–8.
18. "To arrest steam drivers." *New York Tribune*, June 17, 1900.
19. "Call a meeting." *Horseless Age*, July 4, 1900, pp. 9–10.
20. "The New York license." *Horseless Age*, Mar. 14, 1900, pp. 10–11.
21. "Manchester denied automobile license." *St. Louis Republic*, Dec. 20, 1900.
22. "Whalen on automobile licenses." *New York Tribune*, May 21, 1901.
23. "The proposed New York licensing ordinance." *Horseless Age*, Oct. 8, 1902, pp. 395–96.
24. *Ibid.*
25. "Automobile drivers." *Indianapolis Journal*, Nov. 17, 1901.
26. "License on automobile operators." *San Francisco Call*, Nov. 28, 1901.
27. "Mayor gets first licenses." *St. Louis Republic*, Dec. 25, 1901.
28. "Notice too owners of vehicles and automobiles." *St. Louis Republic*, Feb. 4, 1902.
29. "Anti-speed legislation in Massachusetts." *Horseless Age*, Feb. 26, 1902, p. 278.
30. "The automobile." *Minneapolis Journal* (MN), June 24, 1902.
31. "The proposed licensing of automobile drivers." *Horseless Age*, June 25, 1902, p. 747.
32. "Uniform federal license law." *Horseless Age*, July 2, 1901, p. 3.

33. "National drivers' license again." *Horseless Age*, Dec. 10, 1902, p. 629.
34. "Automobile licenses." *Sun* (NY), Sept. 24, 1902.
35. "Legislative and legal." *Horseless Age*, Oct. 1, 1902, pp. 364–65.
36. "Numbering autos." *St. Louis Republic*, Dec. 11, 1902; "Auto ordinance vetoes in Chicago." *Sun* (NY), Dec. 17, 1902.
37. "Legislative and legal." *Horseless Age*, Feb. 11, 1903, p. 248.
38. "Board to control automobile permits." *Evening Times* (Washington, D.C.), May 19, 1903.
39. "Constitutionality of license suspension to be tested." *Horseless Age*, July 1, 1903, p. 2.
40. "Against age limit for auto operators." *Evening Times* (Washington, D.C.), Sept. 6, 1903.
41. "Restricted license in Massachusetts." *Horseless Age*, Oct. 28, 1903, p. 467.

Chapter 9

1. "Legislation against petroleum boats." *Horseless Age*, Feb. 1896, p. 4.
2. "American motor league." *Horseless Age*, Feb. 1896, p. 34.
3. Charles E. Duryea, "Charles Duryea on the speed craze." *Horseless Age*, Feb. 1896, p. 19.
4. "Regulations regarding the use of vehicles in New York City." *Horseless Age*, Mar. 1896, p. 22.
5. "Ran foul of the police board." *Horseless Age*, Apr. 1896, p. 24.
6. "Can't go through this town." *Horseless Age*, July 1896, p. 42.
7. Charles De. Duryea. "Bogies." *Horseless Age*, Aug. 1896, pp. 3–4.
8. "Massachusetts motor vehicle bill." *Horseless Age*, Mar. 1897, pp. 1–2.
9. *Ibid.*
10. "Bill to license motor vehicles on the highways of Massachusetts." *Horseless Age*, Mar. 1897, p. 7.
11. *Ibid.*
12. "Committee on ordinances." *Morning Journal and Courier* (New Haven, CT), Nov. 5, 1897.
13. "New ordinances presented." *Record-Union* (Sacramento, CA), Feb. 15, 1898.
14. "Cannot prohibit them." *Horseless Age*, May 10, 1899, p. 9.
15. "No law to cover motor vehicles." *Horseless Age*, June 28, 1899, p. 14.
16. "Chicago to license all automobiles." *San Francisco Call*, June 29, 1899.
17. John McNaught. "Editorial variations." *San Francisco Call*, July 2, 1899.
18. "Barred from Bar Harbor." *Horseless Age*, July 5, 1899, p. 6.
19. "Proposed motor vehicle regulations at Chicago." *Horseless Age*, July 12, 1899, p. 18.
20. "Automobiles in Boston." *Times* (Washington, D.C.), July 17, 1899.
21. "Regulations for automobiles." *San Francisco Call*, July 21, 1899.
22. "Regulations for automobiles." *San Francisco Call*, July 24, 1899.
23. "A sound legal opinion." *Horseless Age*, Sept. 6, 1899, p. 6.
24. "Liability of fire." *Horseless Age*, Oct. 11, 1899, p. 5.
25. "Storage of gasoline." *Horseless Age*, Dec. 27, 1899, pp. 7–8.
26. "Storage of gasoline in New York." *Horseless Age*, Dec. 27, 1899, p. 10.

Chapter 10

1. "The explosive motor." *Horseless Age*, Jan. 17, 1900, p. 11.
2. "Storage of gasoline." *Horseless Age*, Jan. 24, 1900, p. 14.
3. "Gasoline on ferry boats." *Horseless Age*, Dec. 5, 1900, p. 15.
4. "Automobiles on ferryboats." *New York Tribune*, Jan. 10, 1901.
5. "Gasoline on ferries' bill." *Horseless Age*, Feb. 20, 1901, p. 19; "Gasoline on ferries bill becomes law." *Horseless Age*, Feb. 29, 1901, p. 15.
6. "Further ferry accommodations." *Horseless Age*, June 3, 1903, p. 644.
7. A steam automobile." *Times* (Washington, D.C.), Oct. 26, 1899.
8. "Scared by Billings." *Chicago Eagle*, Oct. 28, 1899.
9. *Ibid.*
10. "Contemporary comment." *Kansas City Journal* (MO), Nov. 15, 1899.
11. "Fenders for automobiles." *New York Tribune*, Jan. 21, 1900.
12. "No motor vehicles in this cemetery." *Horseless Age*, Feb. 14, 1900, p. 12.
13. "Automobile regulations of Brookline, Mass." *Horseless Age*, Feb. 14, 1900, p. 12.
14. "Provision for automobiles." *New York Tribune*, Mar. 3, 1900.
15. "Red Flag law in Vermont." *Horseless Age*, Sept. 5, 1900, p. 21.
16. "Decision adverse to the steam carriage." *Horseless Age*, Feb. 20, 1901, p. 14.
17. "Runners for automobiles." *Evening Star* (Washington, D.C.), Feb. 9, 1901.
18. "Present automobile laws in New York State." *Horseless Age*, Feb. 27, 1901, pp. 19–20.
19. "Automobile club's bill becomes law." *Horseless Age*, May 1, 1901, pp. 98–99.
20. "Automobile regulations of Grand Rapids, Mich." *Horseless Age*, Nov. 21, 1900, p. 22.
21. "Automobile regulations." *Horseless Age*, Jan. 9, 1901, p. 14.
22. "Automobile regulations in Madison, N.J." *Horseless Age*, Jan. 23, 1901, p. 19.
23. "Cincinnati automobile ordinance." *Horseless Age*, Feb. 13, 1901, p. 30.

24. "The fender question." *Horseless Age*, May 22, 1901, p. 166.
25. "Bicycles and automobiles." *Scranton Tribune* (PA), June 26, 1901.
26. "To increase the city's revenue." *St. Louis Republic*, June 26, 1901.
27. "Would keep out the automobile." *San Francisco Call*, July 7, 1901.
28. "Affairs of the district." *Evening Times* (Washington, D.C.), Feb. 23, 1901.
29. "The legislative era." *Horseless Age*, Feb. 27, 1901, p. 11.
30. "Automobile law for South Carolina." *Horseless Age*, Mar. 6, 1901, p. 15.
31. "Automobile men pleased." *New York Tribune*, Mar. 27, 1901.
32. "Automobile club's bill becomes laws." *Horseless Age*, May 1, 1901, pp. 98–99.
33. "The crisis in Massachusetts." *Horseless Age*, Apr. 3, 1901, pp. 1–2.
34. "To minimize the dangers." *Evening Times* (Washington, D.C.), Apr. 24, 1901.
35. "Indiana Supreme Court on the rights of the automobile." *Horseless Age*, Apr. 24, 1902, pp. 76–77.
36. "Automobile owners registering." *New York Tribune*, Sept. 4, 1901.
37. "Automobile regulation." *New York Tribune*, Nov. 17, 1901.
38. "Automobile safeguards." *New York Tribune*, Dec. 29, 1901.

Chapter 11

1. "The New York automobile bills." *Horseless Age*, Feb. 5, 1902, p. 162.
2. "New York State speed bills." *Horseless Age*, Feb. 5, 1902, pp. 186–87.
3. "Sharp debate on auto bill." *New York Tribune*, Feb. 21, 1902.
4. "Cocks bill becomes law." *Horseless Age*, Apr. 2, 1902, p. 430.
5. "Gov Odell's plans." *Sun* (NY), Mar. 27, 1902.
6. "To control automobiles." *Omaha Bee*, Feb. 14, 1902.
7. "Anti-speed legislation in Massachusetts." *Horseless Age*, Feb. 26, 1902, p. 278.
8. "New Jersey automobile legislation." *Horseless Age*, Mar. 12, 1902, p. 341.
9. "Motor vehicle laws endorsed." *Evening Times* (Washington, D.C.), Mar. 25, 1902.
10. "National legislation." *Horseless Age*, Apr. 23, 1902, p. 493.
11. "Rhode Island automobile law." *Horseless Age*, Apr. 23, 1902, p. 511.
12. "Mayor vetoes automobile law." *New York Tribune*, Sept. 4, 1902.
13. "Legislative and legal." *Horseless Age*, Oct. 1, 1902, pp. 364–65.
14. *Ibid.*
15. *Ibid.*
16. "Some advantages of the automobile." *Horseless Age*, Oct. 8, 1902, p. 377.
17. "Legislative and legal." *Horseless Age*, Oct. 15, 1902, p. 403.
18. "Kansas City vehicle ordinance." *Horseless Age*, Oct. 22, 1902, p. 462.
19. "Automobile legislation." *Horseless Age*, Nov. 5, 1902, pp. 491–98.
20. *Ibid.*
21. *Ibid.*
22. *Ibid.*
23. *Ibid.*
24. *Ibid.*
25. *Ibid.*
26. *Ibid.*
27. *Ibid.*
28. *Ibid.*
29. "Automobiles and road laws." *New York Tribune*, Nov. 15, 1902.
30. "Automobiles abroad." *Evening Star* (Washington, D.C.), Nov. 20, 1902.
31. "Automobile ordinance." *Topeka State Journal* (KS), Nov. 22, 1902.
32. "Legislative and legal." *Horseless Age*, Nov. 26, 1902, p. 596.
33. "Numbering autos." *St. Louis Republic*, Dec. 11, 1902.
34. "Legislative and legal." *Horseless Age*, Jan. 21, 1903, p.150.
35. "Oppressive regulations proposed in New Jersey." *Horseless Age*, Jan. 28, 1903, p. 154.
36. "The Scovel automobile law." *Horseless Age*, Mar. 25, 1903, pp. 409–411.
37. "An outrageous automobile bill in Pennsylvania legislature." *Horseless Age*, Mar. 18, 1903, p. 365.
38. "The automobile law of Indiana." *Horseless Age*, Mar. 25, 1903, pp. 390–91.
39. "Automobile regulation." *Evening Star* (Washington, D.C.), Apr. 7, 1903.
40. "Public to be heard." *Evening Star* (Washington, D.C.), Apr. 8, 1903.
41. "Automobile regulation." *Evening Times* (Washington, D.C.), Apr. 8, 1903.
42. "Regulation of autos." *Evening Star* (Washington, D.C.), Apr. 14, 1903.
43. "Automobile regulation." *Evening Times* (Washington, D.C.), Apr. 18, 1903.
44. "Must be registered." *Evening Star* (Washington, D.C.), Apr. 21, 1903; "New regulations for automobilists." *Evening Times* (Washington, D.C.), Apr. 21, 1903.
45. "Automobilists to fight regulations." *Evening Times* (Washington, D.C.), May 20, 1903; "Not worried by views of owners." *Evening Times* (Washington, D.C.), May 22, 1903.
46. "C.J. Lockwood is the autoists' champion." *Evening Times* (Washington, D.C.), June 2, 1903.
47. "Presents the case of automobilists." *Evening Times* (Washington, D.C.), June 5, 1903.
48. "The auto regulations." *Evening Star* (Washington, D.C.), June 8, 1903; "Surprise sprung on

District by autoists." *Evening Times* (Washington, D.C.), June 9, 1903.
49. "Auto injunction case." *Evening Star* (Washington, D.C.), July 3, 1903; "Commissioners gratified." *Evening Star* (Washington, D.C.), July 16, 1903.
50. "Major Sylvester's school for police to open this week." *Times* (Washington, D.C.), Aug. 22, 1903.
51. "Auto regulations." *Evening Star* (Washington, D.C.), Dec. 5, 1903.
52. "The automobile regulations." *Evening Star* (Washington, D.C.), Dec. 11, 1903.
53. "Regulating the automobile." *Minneapolis Journal*, Apr. 9, 1903.
54. "Race up the hill." *Minneapolis Journal*, Apr. 28, 1903.
55. "Automobile legislation this year." *Sun* (NY), Apr. 13, 1903.
56. "Legislative and legal." *Horseless Age*, Apr. 29, 1903, pp. 540–41.
57. "New automobile bill." *Sun* (NY), Mar. 12, 1903.
58. "Club won't fight bill." *New York Tribune*, May 3, 1903.
59. "No disruption in the A.C.A." *Horseless Age*, May 6, 1903, pp. 545–46.
60. *Ibid.*
61. "The public hearing on the Doughty-Bailey bill." *Horseless Age*, May 13, 1903, pp. 585–87.
62. "The Bailey bill now a law." *Horseless Age*, May 20, 1903, pp. 593–94.
63. "New York State register." *Horseless Age*, June 17, 1903, p. 713.
64. "Automobile regulation." Evening Star (Washington, D.C.), Aug. 8, 1903.
65. "Numbering section of Bailey law declared unconstitutional" *Horseless Age*, Aug. 12, 1903, p. 161.
66. "Legislative and legal." *Horseless Age*, May 6, 1903, p. 564; "Legislative and legal." *Horseless Age*, Aug. 26, 1903, pp. 230–31.
67. "Signed by the mayor." *Indianapolis Journal*, May 10, 1903.
68. "Propose to brand the horseless." *St. Paul Globe*, May 12, 1903.
69. "Auto drivers now have hope." *San Francisco Call*, May 19, 1903.
70. "Will test automobile ordinance." *San Francisco Call*, June 25, 1903.
71. "Automobile racing by moonlight in St. Louis County." *St. Louis Republic*, June 14, 1903.
72. "Missouri's drastic law." *Horseless Age*, June 24, 1903, p. 722.
73. "The automobile ordinance." *Watchman and Southron* (Sumter, SC), July 1, 1903.
74. "Legislative and legal." *Horseless Age*, July 8, 1903, pp. 49–50.
75. "The automobile industry." *Evening World* (NY), July 30, 1903.
76. "Auto regulation." *St. Louis Republic*, July 31, 1903.
77. "Legislative and legal." *Horseless Age*, Aug. 19, 1903, p. 206.
78. "Regulate automobiles." *St. Louis Republic*, Aug. 23, 1903.
79. "The healthfulness of automobiling." *Horseless Age*, Oct. 21, 1903.
80. F.A. Hyde. "Wonderful development of automobiling." *San Francisco Call*, Nov. 1, 1903.

Bibliography

"A.A.A. annual meeting." *Horseless Age*, Jan. 14, 1903, p. 114.
"Abuses of chauffeurs to be checked." *Horseless Age*, Mar. 18, 1903, p. 364.
"A.C.A. affairs." *Horseless Age*, Apr. 8, 1903, p. 464.
"Adieu to the bicycle." *Kansas City Journal* (MO), Nov. 30, 1896.
"The advent of the automobile." *Virginian-Pilot* (Norfolk, VA), July 23, 1899.
"Adverse decision at Rochester." *Horseless Age*, May 8, 1901, p. 121.
"Advocating good roads." *Horseless Age*, Mar. 7, 1900, p. 11.
"Affairs of the district." *Evening Times* (Washington, D.C.), Feb. 23, 1901.
"After the Long Island scorcher." *Horseless Age*, Oct. 23, 1901, p. 628.
"Against age limit for auto operators." *Evening Times* (Washington, D.C.), Sept. 6, 1903.
"A.H. Marks." *Akron Democrat* (OH), July 11, 1902.
"The American Automobile Association." *Horseless Age*, Mar. 12, 1902, p. 317.
"American Automobile Association meeting." *Horseless Age*, Apr. 2, 1902, p. 430.
"American automobile clubs." *Horseless Age*, Jan. 9, 1901, pp. 16–18.
"American motor league." *Horseless Age*, Feb. 1896, p. 34.
"American Motor League." *Norfolk News-Journal* (NE), May 7, 1902.
"Anti-motor legislation in Chicago." *Horseless Age*, July 5, 1899, p. 5.
"Anti-speed legislation—an interview with Mr. Chamberlin." *Horseless Age*, Jan. 15, 1902, p. 67.
"Anti-speed legislation in Massachusetts." *Horseless Age*, Feb. 26, 1902, p. 278.
"Aphorisms of an artless actor." *Evening World* (NY), May 20, 1903.
"Appeal in the West case." *Horseless Age*, June 28, 1899, p. 15.
"Apportioning the blame." *Horseless Age*, July 25, 1900, p. 10.
"Attacks Vanderbilt's White Ghost." *New York Tribune*, May 18, 1901.
"Authorities relenting." *Horseless Age*, June 28, 1899, pp. 5–6.
"Auto club of America behind the movement." *Topeka State Journal* (KS), June 18, 1902.
"Auto drivers now have hope." *San Francisco Call*, May 19, 1903.
"Auto injunction case." *Evening Star* (Washington, D.C.), July 3, 1903.
"Auto makers organize." *New York Tribune*, Dec. 4, 1900.
"Auto notes." *Providence News* (RI), July 20, 1903.
"Auto ordinance vetoes in Chicago." *Sun* (NY), Dec. 17, 1902.
"Auto regulation." *St. Louis Republic*, July 31, 1903.
"The auto regulations." *Evening Star* (Washington, D.C.), June 8, 1903.
"Auto regulations." *Evening Star* (Washington, D.C.), Dec. 5, 1903.
"Automania in a new light." *Horseless Age*, Apr. 29, 1903, pp. 519–20.
"Automaniacs, beware!" *Horseless Age*, Oct. 1, 1902, pp. 349–50.
"The automobile." *Minneapolis Journal* (MN), June 24, 1902.
"Automobile a pleasure carriage?" *Sun* (NY), Oct. 29, 1899.
"Automobile accident insurance." *Horseless Age*, July 30, 1902, p. 123.
"The automobile age." *Kansas City Journal* (MO), Nov. 15, 1899.
"Automobile and horse regulations." *Horseless Age*, Nov. 12, 1902, p. 524.
"The automobile club." *Horseless Age*, July 5, 1899, pp. 5–6.
"The automobile club." *New York Tribune*, Apr. 8, 1900.
"Automobile club." *Topeka State Journal* (KS), June 8, 1899.
"Automobile club appeals West case." *Horseless Age*, May 8, 1901, p. 138.
"Automobile club dines." *New York Tribune*, Apr. 3, 1900.
"Automobile club frowns down unlawful speed." *Horseless Age*, Feb. 13, 1901, p. 12.
"Automobile club organized." *Horseless Age*, June 14, 1899, p. 6.
"Automobile clubs." *Horseless Age*, Jan. 9, 1901, p. 11.
"Automobile club's bill becomes law." *Horseless Age*, May 1, 1901, pp. 98–99.

"The automobile club's exhibition." *Horseless Age*, Mar. 7, 1900, p. 11.
"The automobile club's substitute speed bill." *Horseless Age*, Mar. 6, 1901, pp. 14–15.
"Automobile drivers." *Indianapolis Journal*, Nov. 17, 1901.
"The automobile industry." *Evening World* (NY), July 30, 1903.
"Automobile insurance." *Horseless Age*, Sept. 4, 1901, p. 469.
"Automobile insurance." *New Haven Morning Journal* (CT), Nov. 2, 1902.
"Automobile lady horse trainer." *St. Paul Globe* (MN), Sept. 12, 1902.
"Automobile law for South Carolina." *Horseless Age*, Mar. 6, 1901, p. 15.
"The automobile law of Indiana." *Horseless Age*, Mar. 25, 1903, pp. 390–91.
"Automobile laws." *Sun* (NY), Jan. 16, 1902.
"Automobile legislation." *Horseless Age*, Nov. 5, 1902, pp. 491–98.
"Automobile legislation in Cincinnati." *Horseless Age*, Feb. 25, 1903, p. 309.
"Automobile legislation this year." *Sun* (NY), Apr. 13, 1903.
"Automobile licenses." *Sun* (NY), Sept. 24, 1902.
"Automobile men pleased." *New York Tribune*, Mar. 27, 1901.
"The automobile not a nuisance." *Horseless Age*, Sept. 26, 1900, p. 10.
"Automobile ordinance." *Topeka State Journal* (KS), Nov. 22, 1902.
"The automobile ordinance." *Watchman and Southron* (Sumter, SC), July 1, 1903.
"Automobile owners registering." *New York Tribune*, Sept. 4, 1901.
"Automobile racing by moonlight in St. Louis County." *St. Louis Republic*, June 14, 1903.
"Automobile regulation." *Evening Times* (Washington, D.C.), Apr. 8, 1903.
"Automobile regulation." *Evening Times* (Washington, D.C.), Apr. 18, 1903.
"Automobile regulation." *Evening Star* (Washington, D.C.), Apr. 7, 1903.
"Automobile regulation." *Evening Star* (Washington, D.C.), Aug. 8, 1903.
"Automobile regulation." *New York Tribune*, Nov. 17, 1901.
"The automobile regulations." *Evening Star* (Washington, D.C.), Dec. 11, 1903.
"Automobile regulations." *Horseless Age*, Jan. 9, 1901, p. 14.
"Automobile regulations in Madison, N.J." *Horseless Age*, Jan. 23, 1901, p. 19.
"Automobile regulations of Brookline, Mass." *Horseless Age*, Feb. 14, 1900, p. 12.
"Automobile regulations of Grand Rapids, Mich." *Horseless Age*, Nov. 21, 1900, p. 22.
"Automobile riders confer." *Evening Times* (Washington, D.C.), June 8, 1899.
"Automobile safeguards." *New York Tribune*, Dec. 29, 1901.
"Automobile speed laws in Connecticut." *Horseless Age*, Feb. 13, 1901, pp. 13–14.
"The automobile test." *New York Tribune*, Oct. 10, 1902.
"Automobile topics." *New York Tribune*, Mar. 7, 1902.
"Automobile war is growing." *New York Tribune*, June 5, 1900.
"Automobile war is growing." *New York Tribune*, June 5, 1902.
"The automobile war on the north shore, Chicago." *Horseless Age*, July 30, 1902, p. 123.
"The automobile wins." *Evening World* (Shenandoah, PA), June 22, 1899.
"Automobile wins the day." *New York Tribune*, Nov. 21, 1899.
"Automobiles abroad." *Evening Star* (Washington, D.C.), Nov. 20, 1902.
"Automobiles and class hatred." *Evening Star* (Washington, D.C.), June 4, 1904.
"Automobiles and fire insurance rates." *Horseless Age*, Sept. 18, 1901, p. 511.
"Automobiles and horses." *Evening Star* (Washington, D.C.), Dec. 12, 1903.
"Automobiles and road laws." *New York Tribune*, Nov. 15, 1902.
"Automobiles for park police." *New York Tribune*, July 17, 1903.
"Automobiles in Boston." *Times* (Washington, D.C.), July 17, 1899.
"Automobiles in Newport." *Sun* (NY), June 13, 1900.
"Automobiles in parks." *New York Tribune*, May 20, 1899.
"Automobiles in parks." *San Antonio Light* (TX), July 5, 1899.
"Automobiles in the park." *New York Tribune*, Nov. 10, 1899.
"Automobiles in the park." *San Francisco Call*, Feb. 23, 1900.
"Automobiles must not run too fast." *New York Tribune*, May 23, 1900.
"Automobiles not dangerous." *Horseless Age*, Feb. 13, 1901, p. 30.
"Automobiles on ferryboats." *New York Tribune*, Jan. 10, 1901.
"Automobiling." *Evening Star* (Washington, D.C.), Mar. 27, 1902.
"Automobiling." *New York Tribune*, Jan. 17, 1903.
"Automobiling." *New York Tribune*, June 24, 1903.
"Automobilism in New York." *Evening Star* (Washington, D.C.), Apr. 23, 1903.
"Automobilists held to answer for murder." *St. Paul Globe*, June 16, 1902.
"Automobilists in convention at Chicago." *Times* (Washington, D.C.), Mar. 2, 1902.
"Automobilists to fight regulations." *Evening Times* (Washington, D.C.), May 20, 1903.
"The Bailey bill now a law." *Horseless Age*, May 20, 1903, pp. 593–94.
"Baltimore parks barred." *Horseless Age*, May 23, 1900, p. 11.

"Barred from Bar Harbor." *Horseless Age*, July 5, 1899, p. 6.
"Barred from Golden Gate Park." *Horseless Age*, Mar. 7, 1900, p. 19.
"Barred out of Boston's sacred parks." *Horseless Age*, Mar. 1899, p. 6.
"Bicycles and automobiles." *Scranton Tribune* (PA), June 26, 1901.
"Bicyclists and motorists part company." *Horseless Age*, Mar. 21, 1900, p. 10.
"Big auto fells horse." *New York Tribune*, Apr. 8, 1903.
"Bill to license motor vehicles on the highways of Massachusetts." *Horseless Age*, Mar. 1897, p. 7.
"Board to control automobile permits." *Evening Times* (Washington, D.C.), May 19, 1903.
"Braking/stopping distances." nacto.org, downloaded Nov. 28, 2018.
"Call a meeting." *Horseless Age*, July 4, 1900, pp. 9–10.
"Cannot prohibit them." *Horseless Age*, May 10, 1899, p. 9.
"Can't go through this town." *Horseless Age*, July 1896, p. 42.
"Careless drivers of horses." *Horseless Age*, Aug. 9, 1899, p. 6.
"Careless operations in cities—insurance." *Horseless Age*, May 15, 1901, p. 142.
"Central Park recalcitrance." *Horseless Age*, Nov. 8, 1899, pp. 5–6.
"A chance for the automobile." *Horseless Age*, Dec. 27, 1899, p. 14.
"Chauffeurs not allowed to scorch." *St. Louis Republic*, June 17, 1902.
"Chauffeurs to run to crystal Springs dam." *San Francisco Call*, Sept. 28, 1901.
"Chicago judge does not support park commissioners." *Horseless Age*, June 28, 1899, p. 14.
"Chicago to license all automobiles." *San Francisco Call*, June 29, 1899.
"Chicago wants motor drivers licensed." *Horseless Age*, July 12, 1899, pp. 5–6.
"Chicago's auto show." *Free Press* (Poplarville, MS), Mar. 6, 1902.
"Cincinnati automobile ordinance." *Horseless Age*, Feb. 13, 1901, p. 30.
"C.J. Lockwood is the autoists' champion." *Evening Times* (Washington, D.C.), June 2, 1903.
Clarke, William A. "Automobile versus horse." *Bridgeton Pioneer* (NJ), July 17, 1902.
"Club affiliation abandoned." *Horseless Age*, Feb. 19, 1902, p. 244.
"Club affiliation in Indiana." *Horseless Age*, Jan. 15, 1902, p. 67.
"Club notes." *Horseless Age*, May 13, 1903, p. 587.
"Club won't fight bill." *New York Tribune*, May 3, 1903.
"Clubs advocate a uniform speed law." *Horseless Age*, Feb. 27, 1901, p. 15.
"Cocks bill becomes law." *Horseless Age*, Apr. 2, 1902, p. 430.
"Cold comfort for carriage builders." *Horseless Age*, Dec. 1898, pp. 5–6.
"The coming vehicles." *Record-Union* (Sacramento, CA), July 16, 1899.
"Commissioners gratified." *Evening Star* (Washington, D.C.), July 16, 1903.
"Committee on ordinances." *Morning Journal and Courier* (New Haven, CT), Nov. 5, 1897.
"Constitution and by-laws of the Automobile Club of America." *Horseless Age*, Oct. 11, 1899, p. 6.
"Constitutionality of license suspension to be tested." *Horseless Age*, July 1, 1903, p. 2.
"Contemporary comment." *Kansas City Journal* (MO), Nov. 15, 1899.
Corrigan, C.E. "Favors a national protective association." *Horseless Age*, July 12, 1899, p. 19.
"Cost of horse and auto." *New York Tribune*, Aug. 6, 1900.
"The crisis in Massachusetts." *Horseless Age*, Apr. 3, 1901, pp. 1–2.
"Crusade against reckless motoring in France." *Horseless Age*, Sept. 6 1899, p. 6.
"Damage suit in Rhode Island." *Horseless Age*, Nov. 15, 1899, p. 6.
"Damages awarded against the automobile." *Horseless Age*, Oct. 31, 1900, p. 12.
"The dangers of horse traffic." *Horseless Age*, July 16, 1902, p. 66.
"Death blow to street races." *New York Tribune*, June 4, 1902.
"Death due to automobile." *New York Tribune*, June 8, 1902.
"Death for automobilists." *Wood County Reporter* (Grand Rapids, WI), May 29, 1902.
"Decision adverse to the steam carriage." *Horseless Age*, Feb. 20, 1901, p. 14.
"District by autoists." *Evening Times* (Washington, D.C.), June 9, 1903.
"Doctors and the speed laws." *Horseless Age*, July 23, 1902, p. 83.
"Doings of the A.C.A." *Horseless Age*, Dec. 25, 1901, p. 838.
"Driving out the horse." *Anderson Intelligencer* (SC), Oct. 19. 1898.
Duryea, Charles E. "Accidents and their remedy." *Horseless Age*, Aug. 5, 1903, p. 151.
Duryea, Charles E. "Bogies." *Horseless Age*, Aug. 1896, pp. 3–4.
Duryea, Charles E. "Charles Duryea on the speed craze." *Horseless Age*, Feb. 1896, p. 19.
Duryea, Charles E. "Comicalities of the horse." *Horseless Age*, May 10, 1899, p. 14.
Duryea, Charles E. "Proposal to revive." *Horseless Age*, Jan. 22, 1902, p. 120.
Duryea, Charles E. "The question of automobile organization." *Horseless Age*, Jan. 29, 1902, p. 147.
"Educates his neighbors' horses to the automobile." *Horseless Age*, Mar. 7, 1900, p. 11.
"Elects I.B. Potter president." *New York Tribune*, Jan. 23, 1903.
"Enforce speed law." *Indianapolis Journal*, Dec. 10, 1903.
"Equal rights upon the road." *Horseless Age*, Jan. 10, 1900, p. 7.

"Evils of the power of wealth." *Red Cloud Chief* (NE), Nov. 17, 1903.
"An example of liberal speed legislation." *Horseless Age*, Sept. 3, 1902, pp. 237–38.
"Excluded from Chicago parks." *Horseless Age*, June 21, 1899, p. 6.
"The explosive motor." *Horseless Age*, Jan. 17, 1900, p. 11.
"Fairmont park opens." *Horseless Age*, Oct. 11, 1899, p. 5.
"Fatal accidents—warning." *Horseless Age*, July 29, 1903, pp. 112–13.
"The fender question." *Horseless Age*, May 22, 1901, p. 166.
"Fenders for automobiles." *New York Tribune*, Jan. 21, 1900.
"$50,000 automobile damage suit." *Horseless Age*, Oct. 30, 1901, p. 641.
"Fight for control of automobile racing." *Evening World* (NY), Dec. 24, 1903.
"Fined for fast driving." *Horseless Age*, Jan. 16, 1901, pp. 16–17.
"Fined for fast driving." *Horseless Age*, Jan. 22, 1902, p. 127.
"$500 fine for man's death." *Evening World* (NY), Oct. 27, 1902.
"The flurry of anti-speed legislation." *Horseless Age*, Jan. 15, 1902, p. 65.
"Freak racer a juggernaut." *New York Tribune*, June 1, 1902.
"Further ferry accommodations." *Horseless Age*, June 3, 1903, p. 644.
"Gasoline on ferries' bill." *Horseless Age*, Feb. 20, 1901, p. 19.
"Gasoline on ferries bill becomes law." *Horseless Age*, Feb. 29, 1901, p. 15.
"Gasoline on ferry boats." *Horseless Age*, Dec. 5, 1900, p. 15.
"Gathered here and there." *New York Tribune*, Mar. 27, 1900.
"Golden Gate Park open on permit." *Horseless Age*, Oct. 24, 1900, p. 13.
"Good roads." *Horseless Age*, Mar. 14, 1900, pp. 9–10.
"Good roads indorsed." *Horseless Age*, July 4, 1900, p. 9.
"The good roads movement." *Horseless Age*, Mar. 12, 1902, pp. 318–19.
"Good roads movement." *Jersey City News* (NJ), Nov. 15, 1900.
"Gov Odell's plans." *Sun* (NY), Mar. 27, 1902.
"Graded license meets with approval." *Horseless Age*, Nov. 8, 1899, p. 8.
"Guides for autoists." *Morris Tribune* (MN), Sept. 26, 1903.
"Harmless horseless carriages." *Albuquerque Citizen* (NM), July 5, 1899.
"Hasten slowly." *Horseless Age*, July 1898, p. 4.
"The healthfulness of automobiling." *Horseless Age*, Oct. 21, 1903.
"Hearing before the park board." *Horseless Age*, Nov. 15, 1899, p. 10.
"Heroic measures to stop speeding of automobiles." *Horseless Age*, Oct. 16, 1901, p. 500.
"The horse an unruly brute." *Horseless Age*, July 1897, p. 2.
"The horse and the dynamo." *Wichita Eagle* (KS), June 4, 1897.
"The horseless age." *Horseless Age*, Nov. 1895, pp. 7–8.
"The horseless carriage." *Scranton Tribune* (PA), Aug. 10, 1895.
"Horseless carriages in Paris." *Edgefield Advertiser* (SC), Dec. 2, 1896.
"Horses and automobiles." *Evening World* (NY), May 23, 1902.
"Horses and automobiles." *Wichita Eagle* (KS), Jan. 26, 1899.
"Horses willingly sacrificed to the Vanderbilt automobile." *Horseless Age*, Jan. 2, 1901, p. 13.
"How fast autos should go." *Sun* (NY), May 18, 1901.
Hyde, F.A. "Wonderful development of automobiling." *San Francisco Call*, Nov. 1, 1903.
"Identification numbers in Chicago." *Horseless Age*, Feb. 4, 1903, p. 191.
"In favor of automobiles." *Evening Times* (Washington, D.C.), July 6, 1899.
"Indiana Supreme Court on the rights of the automobile." *Horseless Age*, Apr. 24, 1902, pp. 76–77.
"Insurance against damage suits." *Horseless Age*, July 9, 1902, pp. 27–28.
"An interesting automotive damage case." *Horseless Age*, Dec. 25, 1901, pp. 837–38.
"Investigating before legislating." *Horseless Age*, June 28, 1899, p. 14.
"A judgment reversed." *Horseless Age*, Apr. 25, 1900, p. 11.
"Jury wants auto speed cut down." *Evening World* (NY), June 3, 1902.
"Kansas City vehicle ordinance." *Horseless Age*, Oct. 22, 1902, p. 462.
"Killed by racing auto." *New York Tribune*, June 6, 1902.
"The law of the road for automobiles." *Horseless Age*, Apr. 24, 1901, pp. 73–74.
"The law puts on the brake in France." *Horseless Age*, Feb. 1899, p. 6.
"Laws and automobiles." *New York Tribune*, July 22, 1900.
"League being organized for protecting motorists." *Savannah Morning News* (GA), July 6, 1903.
"The legal idea of speed." *Horseless Age*, Sept. 5, 1900, p. 23.
"Legislation against petroleum boats." *Horseless Age*, Feb. 1896, p. 4.
"Legislative and legal." *Horseless Age*, July 16, 1902, p. 76.
"Legislative and legal." *Horseless Age*, Oct. 1, 1902, pp. 364–65.
"Legislative and legal." *Horseless Age*, Oct. 15, 1902, p. 403.
"Legislative and legal." *Horseless Age*, Oct. 22, 1902, p. 462.

"Legislative and legal." *Horseless Age*, Nov. 12, 1902, p. 541.
"Legislative and legal." *Horseless Age*, Nov. 19, 1902, pp. 568–69.
"Legislative and legal." *Horseless Age*, Nov. 26, 1902, p. 596.
"Legislative and legal." *Horseless Age*, Jan. 21, 1903, p. 150.
"Legislative and legal." *Horseless Age*, Jan. 28, 1903, p. 189.
"Legislative and legal." *Horseless Age*, Feb. 11, 1903, p. 248.
"Legislative and legal." *Horseless Age*, Apr. 29, 1903, pp. 540–41.
"Legislative and legal." *Horseless Age*, Mar. 11, 1903, p. 359.
"Legislation and legal." *Horseless Age*, May 6, 1903, p. 564.
"Legislative and legal." *Horseless Age*, May 20, 1903, p. 613.
"Legislative and legal." *Horseless Age*, July 8, 1903, pp. 49–50.
"Legislative and legal." *Horseless Age*, July 15, 1903, pp. 79–80.
"Legislative and legal." *Horseless Age*, Aug. 19, 1903, p. 206.
"Legislative and legal." *Horseless Age*, Aug. 26, 1903, pp. 230–31.
"The legislative era." *Horseless Age*, Feb. 27, 1901, p. 11.
"Liability of fire." *Horseless Age*, Oct. 11, 1899, p. 5.
"Liability of motor vehicle owners." *Horseless Age*, July 1898, p. 4.
"License numbers required in Boston parks, too." *Horseless Age*, Nov. 14, 1900, p. 38.
"License on automobile operators." *San Francisco Call*, Nov. 28, 1901.
"List of automobile clubs and organizations." *Horseless Age*, Oct. 1, 1902, p. 70.
"Look for it here." *Public Ledger* (Maysville, KY), Feb. 28, 1901.
"Made no case." *Akron Democrat* (OH), July 14, 1902.
"Major Sylvester's school for police to open this week." *Times* (Washington, D.C.), Aug. 22, 1903.
"Make the punishment fit the crime." *Horseless Age*, Sept. 19, 1900, p. 10.
"Make way for the automobile." *San Francisco Call*, July 14, 1899.
"Manchester denied automobile license." *St. Louis Republic*, Dec. 20, 1900.
"Manufacturer's Association endorses Boston show." *Horseless Age*, Feb. 13, 1901, p. 13.
"Manufacturers' Association to be heard on the speed question." *Horseless Age*, Feb. 27, 1901, p. 15.
"Massachusetts motor vehicle bill." *Horseless Age*, Mar. 1897, pp. 1–2.
"Massachusetts speed legislation." *Horseless Age*, Apr. 2 1902 p. 429.
"Mayor gets first licenses." *St. Louis Republic*, Dec. 25, 1901.
"Mayor vetoes automobile law." *New York Tribune*, Sept. 4, 1902.
McNaught, John. "Editorial variations." *San Francisco Call*, July 2, 1899.
"Meeting of the American Motor League." *Horseless Age*, Mar. 12, 1902, p. 341.
"Membership and constitution of the national association." *Horseless Age*, Jan. 16, 1901, p. 17.
"Memphis park board passes offensive measure." *Horseless Age*, June 24, 1903, p. 743.
"Millionaires in craze for speed." *Evening World* (NY), Aug. 29, 1902.
"Minor mention." *Horseless Age*, Apr. 9, 1902, p. 460.
"Missouri's drastic law." *Horseless Age*, June 24, 1903, p. 722.
"Mr. And Mrs. Charles Fair instantly killed." *Evening Bulletin* (Honolulu, HI), Aug. 23, 1902.
"Mr. And Mrs. Charles Fair killed by automobile." *St. Louis Republic*, Aug. 15, 1902.
"Mr. Vanderbilt's fast auto." *New York Tribune*, June 12, 1900.
"Mobiles must travel slowly." *San Francisco Call*, Aug. 21, 1901.
"More park permits." *Horseless Age*, Dec. 13, 1899, p. 8.
"More trouble for the poor." *Omaha Bee* (NE), Oct. 21, 1903.
"Motor carriages excluded from Boston parks." *Horseless Age*, Mar. 1899, p. 7.
"Motor vehicle accident insurance." *Horseless Age*, Jan. 10, 1900, p. 13.
"Motor vehicle laws endorsed." *Evening Times* (Washington, D.C.), Mar. 25, 1902.
"The motor vehicle wins in Chicago." *Horseless Age*, July 12, 1899, p. 17.
"Mounted policemen." *Minneapolis Journal* (MN), May 21, 1902.
"Movement for a joint show." *New York Tribune*, Nov. 22, 1901.
Muller, Julius W. "On the edge of the future." *Evening Star* (Washington, D.C.), Dec. 24, 1904.
"Must be registered." *Evening Star* (Washington, D.C.), Apr. 21, 1903.
"A national automobile association." *Indianapolis Journal*, Mar. 5, 1902.
"National drivers' license again." *Horseless Age*, Dec. 10, 1902, p. 629.
"National legislation." *Horseless Age*, Apr. 23, 1902, p. 493.
"A national protective association." *Horseless Age*, July 19, 1899, p. 6.
"New auto road." *Jersey City News* (NJ), Feb. 11, 1903.
"New automobile bill." *Sun* (NY), Mar. 12, 1903.
"The new glory of automobilism." *Horseless Age*, May 15, 1901, p. 141.
"New Jersey automobile law comprised." *Horseless Age*, Feb. 25, 1903, p. 309.
"New Jersey automobile legislation." *Horseless Age*, Mar. 12, 1902, p. 341.
"New ordinances presented." *Record-Union* (Sacramento, CA), Feb. 15, 1898.

"New regulations for automobilists." *Evening Times* (Washington, D.C.), Apr. 21, 1903.
"The New York automobile bills." *Horseless Age*, Feb. 5, 1902, p. 162.
"New York automobile show opens Saturday." *Rock Island Argus* (IL), Jan. 15, 1903.
"New York court will not spare reckless automobilists." *Horseless Age*, July 30, 1902, p. 113.
"New York courts to deal with speed offenders." *Horseless Age*, July 30, 1902, p. 110.
"The New York license." *Horseless Age*, Mar. 14, 1900, pp. 10–11.
"New York speed violation cases." *Horseless Age*, May 21, 1902, p. 620.
"New York State register." *Horseless Age*, June 17, 1903, p. 713.
"New York State speed bills." *Horseless Age*, Feb. 5, 1902, pp. 186–87.
"No discrimination." *Evening Star* (Washington, D.C.), Mar. 26, 1902.
"No disruption in the A.C.A." *Horseless Age*, May 6, 1903, pp. 545–46.
"No law to cover motor vehicles." *Horseless Age*, June 28, 1899, p. 14.
"No motor vehicles in this cemetery." *Horseless Age*, Feb. 14, 1900, p. 12.
"No municipal paternalism needed." *Horseless Age*, Oct. 30, 1901, pp. 631–32.
"No permit for motor carriages in Central Park." *Horseless Age*, July 5, 1899, p. 10.
No title. *Atlanta Journal* (GA), Aug. 25, 1902.
No title. *Daily Ardmoreite* (Ardmore, OK), July 24, 1899.
No title. *Minneapolis Journal* (MN), July 22, 1903.
No title. *Omaha Bee* (NE), June 21, 1901.
No title. *Rock Island Argus* (IL), Sept. 21, 1901.
No title. *Seattle Republican* (WA), Sept. 30, 1904.
No title. *Stark County Democrat* (Canton, OH), Sept. 23, 1902.
No title. *The Watchman and Southron* (Sumter, SC), Oct. 22, 1902.
"The noise question." *Horseless Age*, Dec. 19, 1900, pp. 11–12.
"Not worried by views of owners." *Evening Times* (Washington, D.C.), May 22, 1903.
"Notice too owners of vehicles and automobiles." *St. Louis Republic*, Feb. 4, 1902.
"Numbering autos." *St. Louis Republic*, Dec. 11, 1902.
"Numbering section of Bailey law declared unconstitutional" *Horseless Age*, Aug. 12, 1903, p. 161.
"Object to Automobiles in park." *San Francisco Call*, Dec. 10, 1901.
"Observations." *Courier* (Lincoln, NE), Sept. 14, 1901.
"Of interest to automobilists." *New York Tribune*, Dec. 5, 1902.
"Official blacklist for speedy chauffeurs." *Washington Evening Times* (Washington, D.C.), May 7, 1902.
"The old year and the new." *Horseless Age*, Jan. 7, 1903, p. 1.
"An open challenge." *Times Dispatch* (Richmond, VA), June 14, 1904.
"Opposed to auto races." *Sun* (NY), June 25, 1903.
"Oppressive regulations proposed in New Jersey." *Horseless Age*, Jan. 28, 1903, p. 154.
"Oppressive speed ordinances." *Horseless Age*, Aug. 27, 1902, p. 210.
"Orders speedy automobile." *St. Louis Republic*, Feb. 1, 1901.
"An outrageous automobile bill in Pennsylvania legislature." *Horseless Age*, Mar. 18, 1903, p. 365.
"Paid his fine." *Evening Star* (Washington, D.C.), Apr. 4, 1902.
"Park authorities wavering." *Horseless Age*, Nov. 15, 1899, p. 7.
"Park board acts on automobiles." *New York Tribune*, Nov. 3, 1899.
"Park exclusion case to be tested at Baltimore." *Horseless Age*, Jan. 9, 1901, p. 13.
"Park rules relaxed." *Horseless Age*, Nov. 22, 1899, p. 5.
"Philadelphia parks open." *Horseless Age*, Oct. 3, 1900, p. 16.
"A plea for good roads." *Horseless Age*, Mar. 14, 1900, pp. 26–28.
"Police are instructed to enforce ordinance." *Stark County Democrat* (Canton, OH), Aug. 14, 1903.
"Police block test case." *New York Tribune*, May 5, 1901.
"Police issue waring to racing association." *Horseless Age*, Aug. 28, 1901, p. 464.
"Police traps in Evanston, Ill." *Horseless Age*, Aug. 27, 1902, p. 215.
"Police traps on the Merrick Road, L. I." *Horseless Age*, July 9, 1902, p. 47.
"Police watch chauffeurs." *San Francisco Call*, Mar. 16, 1903.
"The policy of the Motor League." *Horseless Age*, Dec. 1895, p. 8.
"Prejudice at Washington." *Horseless Age*, July 1897, p. 1.
"Present automobile laws in New York State." *Horseless Age*, Feb. 27, 1901, pp. 19–20.
"Presents the case of automobilists." *Evening Times* (Washington, D.C.), June 5, 1903.
"The prevention of noise." *Horseless Age*, May 1897, p. 1.
"Prison shave for Raymond." *Evening World* (NY), Oct. 31, 1902.
"Probable expansion of the A.A.A." *Horseless Age*, Sept. 23, 1903, p. 322.
"A progressive governor." *Horseless Age*, Apr. 1897, p. 17.
"Propose to brand the horseless." *St. Paul Globe*, May 12, 1903.
"The proposed licensing of automobile drivers." *Horseless Age*, June 25, 1902, p. 747.
"Proposed motor vehicle regulations at Chicago." *Horseless Age*, July 12, 1899, p. 18.
"The proposed New York licensing ordinance." *Horseless Age*, Oct. 8, 1902, pp. 395–96.
"Protest against the automobile." *Horseless Age*, Feb. 19, 1902, p. 244.

"Provision for automobiles." *New York Tribune*, Mar. 3, 1900.
"The public hearing on the Doughty-Bailey bill." *Horseless Age*, May 13, 1903, pp. 585–87.
"Public road question." *Middlebury Register* (VT), Nov. 14, 1902.
"Public to be heard." *Evening Star* (Washington, D.C.), Apr. 8, 1903.
"Puts ban on devil wagons." *Omaha Bee* (NE), Aug. 1, 1902.
"The question of automobile organization." *Horseless Age*, Jan. 22, 1902, p. 98.
"The question of speed under the new law." *Horseless Age*, Apr. 9, 1902, p. 454.
"Race up the hill." *Minneapolis Journal*, Apr. 28, 1903.
"Races and furious driving on the highways." *Horseless Age*, June 3, 1903, p. 643.
"Racing in automobiles." *New York Tribune*, Oct. 14, 1900.
"Ran foul of the police board." Horseless Age, Apr. 1896, p. 24.
"Reckless automobiling." *Evening Star* (Washington, D.C.), Dec. 20, 1900.
"Reckless driving in France." *Horseless Age*, June 1898, p. 1.
"Red Flag law in Vermont." *Horseless Age*, Sept. 5, 1900, p. 21.
"Regulate automobiles." *St. Louis Republic*, Aug. 23, 1903.
"Regulating the automobile." *Minneapolis Journal*, Apr. 9, 1903.
"Regulation of autos." *Evening Star* (Washington, D.C.), Apr. 14, 1903.
"Regulations for automobiles." *San Francisco Call*, July 21, 1899.
"Regulations for automobiles." *San Francisco Call*, July 24, 1899.
"Regulations regarding the use of vehicles in New York City." *Horseless Age*, Mar. 1896, p. 22.
"Responsibility of the horse owner." *Horseless Age*, Mar. 14, 1900, p. 10.
"Restricted license in Massachusetts." *Horseless Age*, Oct. 28, 1903, p. 67.
"Resume." *Horseless Age*, Jan. 24, 1900, pp. 9–10.
"Review of the year." *Horseless Age*, Jan. 1, 1902, p. 1.
"Rhode Island automobile law." *Horseless Age*, Apr. 23, 1902, p. 511.
"Road racing forces attention at last." *Horseless Age*, Feb. 13, 1901, p. 30.
"The road vehicle and the track vehicle." *Horseless Age*, Apr. 1896, pp. 3–4.
"A Rothschild in jail." *Spokane Press* (WA), Sept. 24, 1903.
"Runaway in Fifth Ave." *New York Tribune*, Apr. 7, 1902.
"Runners for automobiles." *Evening Star* (Washington, D.C.), Feb. 9, 1901.
"S.W. Elston appointed." *Indianapolis Journal*, Apr. 3, 1902.
"Scared by Billings." *Chicago Eagle*, Oct. 28, 1899.
Scarritt, Winthrop E. "Invitation extended." *Horseless Age*, Apr. 23, 1902, p. 511.
"The Scovel automobile law." *Horseless Age*, Mar. 25, 1903, pp. 409–11.
Septhton, Edward. "Why there are so many auto accidents." *Deseret News* (Salt Lake City, UT), Sept. 20, 1902.
"Serious charge against automobile driver." *Horseless Age*, June 24, 1903, p. 744.
"Sharp debate on auto bill." *New York Tribune*, Feb. 21, 1902.
"Short stories of the day." *Omaha Bee* (NE), Aug. 13, 1899.
"Signed by the mayor." *Indianapolis Journal*, May 10, 1903.
"A simon pure automobile exhibition needed." *Horseless Age*, Jan. 24, 1900, p. 10.
"Some advantages of the automobile." *Horseless Age*, Oct. 8, 1902, p. 377.
"A sound legal opinion." *Horseless Age*, Sept. 6, 1899, p. 6.
"Sowing the wind, reaping the whirlwind." *Horseless Age*, May 14, 1902, p. 572.
"Speed excesses punished." *Horseless Age*, May 28, 1902, p. 626.
"Speed limit for autos." *Columbus Journal* (NC), Jan. 22, 1902.
"The speed limit in France." *Horseless Age*, Aug. 1898, p. 4.
"Speed madness." *New York Tribune*, Apr. 3, 1902.
"Speed of automobiles." *Evening Star* (Washington, D.C.), Apr. 25, 1902.
"Speed of automobiles." *Indianapolis Journal* (IN), Apr. 30, 1903.
"Speed of automobiles." *Sun* (NY), May 6, 1900.
"Speed of motor vehicles." *Horseless Age*, Jan. 22, 1902, p. 127.
"Speed on the streets." *New York Tribune*, Mar. 25, 1901.
"Speed restrictions and police traps in Massachusetts." *Horseless Age*, Dec. 10, 1902, p. 627.
"Speedometers required by law." *Horseless Age*, July 30, 1902, p. 111.
"Stand fast on the speed question." *Horseless Age*, Feb. 20, 1901, p. 13.
"The status of the race." *Horseless Age*, Dec. 1895, pp. 5–6.
"A steam automobile." *Times* (Washington, D.C.), Oct. 26, 1899.
"Steam vehicle licenses." *Horseless Age*, Dec. 13, 1899, pp. 7–8.
"Steam vehicle licenses." *Horseless Age*, Dec. 6, 1899, pp. 11–12.
"Steam vehicle licenses." *Horseless Age*, Nov. 8, 1899, p. 5.
"Stop that cough." *Minneapolis Journal* (MN), Nov. 22, 1902.
"Storage of gasoline." *Horseless Age*, Dec. 27, 1899, pp. 7–8.
"Storage of gasoline." *Horseless Age*, Jan. 24, 1900, pp. 14.
"Storage of gasoline in New York." *Horseless Age*, Dec. 27, 1899, p. 10.

"Suffolk wants no automobiles." *Times Dispatch* (Richmond, VA), May 3, 1903.
"Surprise sprung on District by autoists." *Evening Times* (Washington, D.C.), June 9, 1903.
"Taxes and licenses." *Horseless Age*, May 17, 1899, p. 3.
"Terminal transfer." *Horseless Age*, Apr. 1898, p. 1.
"Third annual banquet." *Horseless Age*, Mar. 12, 1902, pp. 334–36.
"To arrest steam drivers." *New York Tribune*, June 17, 1900.
"To begin auto speed crusade." *New York Tribune*, Apr. 13, 1902.
"To check speed in Chicago." *Horseless Age*, Feb. 20, 1901, p. 27.
"To conciliate the masses." *Horseless Age*, Sept. 10, 1902, p. 266.
"To control automobiles." *Omaha Bee*, Feb. 14, 1902.
"To curb speed of automobiles." *Evening World* (NY), Oct. 8, 1901.
"To drive out fear." *Telegraph-Courier* (Kenosha WI), June 12, 1902.
"To fight Bedell bill to-day." *New York Tribune*, May 6, 1903.
"To guard Queen Victoria." County Record (Kingstree, SC), Mar. 1, 1900.
"To increase the city's revenue." *St. Louis Republic*, June 26, 1901.
"To minimize the dangers." *Evening Times* (Washington, D.C.), Apr. 24, 1901.
"To regulate speed of automobiles." *St. Louis Republic*, Aug. 2, 1901.
"To restrict speed in Tarrytown." *New York Tribune*, June 19, 1900.
"To stop dangerous auto-speeding." *Wauwatosa News* (WI), June 27, 1903.
"To test the law." *Horseless Age*, June 21, 1899, p. 11.
"To test the New York State law." *Horseless Age*, May 14, 1902, p. 572.
"Topics of the times." *Evening Times-Republican* (Marshalltown, IA), Mar. 19, 1900.
"The tortured horse." *Orleans County Monitor* (Barton, VT), Oct. 25, 1897.
"Uniform federal license law." *Horseless Age*, July 2, 1901, p. 3.
"Unmanageable automobiles." *New York Tribune*, May 12, 1903.
"Vanderbilt is disgusted." *Wichita Eagle* (KS), Nov. 30, 1910.
"Victory for the automobile." *Horseless Age*, Nov. 8, 1899, p. 8.
"Violates law relating to speed." *Evening Star* (Washington, D.C.), Sept. 6, 1902.
"W. K. Vanderbilt is fined." *Omaha Bee* (NE), Aug. 31, 1901.
"Want all motor vehicles licensed." *Horseless Age*, June 21, 1899, p. 6.
"Westchester County anti-speed." *Horseless Age*, Jan. 15, 1902, p. 67.
"Whalen on automobile licenses." *New York Tribune*, May 21, 1901.
"Who are the enemies of the automobile industry?" *Horseless Age*, Jan. 1. 1902, pp. 4–5.
"Wife of United States senator." *San Francisco Call*, Sept. 13, 1902.
"Will test automobile ordinance." *San Francisco Call*, June 25, 1903.
"Willing to be convinced." *Horseless Age*, July 5, 1899, p. 6.
"Win the right to the road." *San Francisco Call*, July 6, 1899.
"Woman barely escapes death." *San Francisco Call*, Mar. 16, 1903.
"Work for the automobile club." *Horseless Age*, Oct. 11, 1899, p. 5.
"Would keep out the automobile." *San Francisco Call*, July 7, 1901.

Index

www.ingramcontent.com/pod-product-compliance
Ingram Content Group UK Ltd.
Pitfield, Milton Keynes, MK11 3LW, UK
UKHW051930100926
8556IPUK00022B/1473